JOHN COBB'S THEOLOGY IN PROCESS

Published by The Westminster Press

BOOKS BY DAVID RAY GRIFFIN

John Cobb's Theology in Process,
  ed. (in collaboration with Thomas J. J. Altizer)

God, Power, and Evil: A Process Theodicy

A Process Christology

Process Theology: An Introductory Exposition
  (in collaboration with John B. Cobb, Jr.)

BOOKS BY THOMAS J. J. ALTIZER

John Cobb's Theology in Process,
  ed. (in collaboration with David Ray Griffin)

Mircea Eliade and the Dialectic of the Sacred

Oriental Mysticism and Biblical Eschatology

The Gospel of Christian Atheism

JOHN COBB'S THEOLOGY IN PROCESS

Edited by
DAVID RAY GRIFFIN
and

THOMAS J. J. ALTIZER

THE WESTMINSTER PRESS
Philadelphia

Book Design by Dorothy Alden Smith

Published by The Westminster Press®
Philadelphia, Pennsylvania

PRINTED IN THE UNITED STATES OF AMERICA

Library of Congress Cataloging in Publication Data

Main entry under title:

John Cobb's theology in process.

"Bibliography of John B. Cobb's writings": p.
1. Cobb, John B.—Addresses, essays, lectures.
2. Cobb, John B.—Bibliography. I. Griffin, David,
1939–   II. Altizer, Thomas J. J. III. Title.
BX4827.C6J63   230'.092'4   77–23135
ISBN 0-664-21292-1

Contents

Contributors

THOMAS J. J. ALTIZER is Professor of English at the State University of New York at Stony Brook. He is the author of *Oriental Mysticism and Biblical Eschatology, Mircea Eliade and the Dialectic of the Sacred, The Gospel of Christian Atheism, The New Apocalypse: The Radical Christian Vision of William Blake, The Descent Into Hell,* and *The Self-Embodiment of God.*

JOHN B. COBB, JR., is Ingraham Memorial Professor of Theology at the School of Theology at Claremont, and Avery Professor of Religion at Claremont Graduate School.

MARY DALY is the author of *Beyond God the Father: Toward a Philosophy of Women's Liberation,* and *The Church and the Second Sex, With an Autobiographical Preface and Postchristian Introduction by the Author.* She teaches feminist ethics at Boston College and is currently writing a new book on feminist metaethics.

DAVID RAY GRIFFIN is Associate Professor of Philosophy of Religion at the School of Theology at Claremont. He is the author of *A Process Christology, God, Power, and Evil: A Process Theodicy,* and (with John B. Cobb, Jr.) *Process Theology: An Introductory Exposition.* He has coedited (with John B. Cobb, Jr.) *Mind in Nature: Essays on the Interface of Science and Philosophy.*

CHARLES HARTSHORNE is now Emeritus Ashbel Smith Professor of Philosophy at the University of Texas. His many publications include *Man's Vision of God and the Logic of Theism, The Divine Relativity: A Social Conception of God, Reality as Social Process, The Logic of Perfection and Other Essays in Neoclassical Metaphysics, Anselm's Discovery: A Re-Examination of the Ontological Proof for God's Existence, A Natural Theology for Our Time, Creative Synthesis and Philosophic Method, Born to Sing: An Interpretation and World Survey of Bird Song,* and *The Structure of Creativity.*

TRAUGOTT KOCH is Professor of Systematic Theology in the Department of Protestant Theology at Hamburg University in West Germany. Besides many articles in philosophical and theological journals, he has written *Differenz und Versöhnung. Eine Interpretation der Theologie G. W. F. Hegels nach seiner Wissenschaft der Logik* (1967).

ROBERT NEVILLE is Professor of Philosophy at the State University of New York College at Purchase. He is the author of *God the Creator: On the Transcendence and Presence of God, The Cosmology of Freedom,* and *Spiritual Liberation.*

WOLFHART PANNENBERG is Professor of Systematic Theology at the University of Munich in West Germany. His many publications include *Revelation as History, What Is Man?, Jesus—God and Man, The Apostles' Creed: In the Light of Today's Questions, Theology and the Kingdom of God, The Idea of God and Human Freedom, Basic Questions in Theology* (2 vols.), and *Theology and the Philosophy of Science.*

DAVID P. POLK is minister of the First Christian Church in Cedar Rapids, Iowa, and teaches courses in religion at Coe College.

CHARLES H. REYNOLDS teaches Christian ethics in the Department of Religion at the University of Tennessee in Knoxville. He is editor of the *Journal of Religious Ethics.*

TAKAO TANAKA, a graduate of philosophy from Kyoto University, is in charge of logic and philosophy in the Department of General Arts and Sciences of Osaka-Furitsu University in Japan.

DAVID TRACY is Professor of Theology at the Divinity School of the University of Chicago. His publications include *The Achievement of Bernard Lonergan* and *Blessed Rage for Order: The New Pluralism in Theology.*

CLARK M. WILLIAMSON is Professor of Theology at Christian Theological Seminary in Indianapolis. He is the editor of the quarterly journal *Encounter* and the author of *God Is Never Absent.*

Preface

THIS BOOK of critiques and responses focuses upon the theological work of a man who has only recently turned fifty years of age and hence is only at mid-career. Such a book was conceived by the editors on the basis of two convictions: First, John Cobb's theological output thus far has not only made him already one of the world's most important and respected theologians but also has given promise of even more significant fruit in the future. Second, a book of critiques by a theologian's colleagues will be much more likely to make a valuable contribution to the ongoing theological enterprise if it appears before the theologian is near the end of his or her career.

All the essays except one are entirely original, written specifically for this volume. Traugott Koch's is a slightly revised version of a review article that appeared in German; this is its first appearance in English translation.

The title of this volume points not only to the fact that Cobb is a representative of the movement known as 'process theology,' but more decisively to the fact that his is a theology in the process of development. In fact, the most fundamental change in his position thus far has occurred during the period between the planning and the completion of this manuscript. (The nature of this change is pointed to in the latter part of Griffin's Introduction, and is also reflected in many of Cobb's responses.) Since some of the essays are based on writings in which Cobb's new position and emphases had not yet emerged, they may contain statements and language (e.g., language about deity and/or humanity that could be considered sexist) that do not adequately reflect their authors' present positions and/or sensitivities.

All citations in the text are to Cobb's writings. Books are indicated by abbreviations, and articles are designated by number; the abbreviations and the numbers are given in the bibliography at the end of the book. For example, *LO* 274 refers to page 274 of *Living Options in Protestant Theology,* and 9:532 refers to page 532 of the ninth article listed. Of Cobb's unpublished writings, the bibliography contains only those which are cited in the text; these are symbolized by a letter of the alphabet.

Single quotation marks are used for highlighting a phrase or a term and for technical terms; double quotation marks are used only for direct quotations.

A HOLISTIC, NON-ALIENATED THEOLOGIAN

ALTHOUGH OUR WORLD is scientifically and technologically one world, it is humanly divided as never before, most deeply so in the domain of ultimate values and convictions. This is due both to the triumph of science and technology and to the corresponding diminution of the power of religion, which, since the Enlightenment, has been forced to retreat into a wholly interior realm, having lost all integral power in the real worlds of culture and history.

In this situation it is not surprising that what we once knew as theology is threatening to come to an end. At most it seems able to survive only as the voice of an isolated community. An integral theology, or a theology deeply engaged with culture and society, now seems to be wholly in our past. In the Protestant theological world, this fundamental transformation occurred when Karl Barth moved from a dialectical to a church theology. Now, a church theology, whether Catholic or Protestant, is by necessity an isolated and sectarian theology, and is so because the churches, and with them all religious institutions throughout the world, are so isolated from modern culture and society. In America today, the theologies of our churches and seminaries are almost wholly sectarian, and it is theologians themselves who are virtually banishing theology from our colleges and universities. Nor is this occurring for accidental or insignificant reasons. Neither our religious nor our academic institutions can now be homes for theology, and this because religion and culture now exist in a polarized relationship to each other.

The contemporary theologian is an alienated theologian, more deeply alienated than ever before. This alienation is so deep that the very possibility of a theological vocation has now been placed in question. And the human costs for today's theologian, or for any critically thinking religious person, are shattering. For in our world simply to think critically and yet religiously is to live in a schizophrenic consciousness. But this is not

1

wholly true. For the theological work of John Cobb is critical but never-theless non-alienated. This is not to say that Cobb has not been deeply affected by the society, the consciousness, and the sensibility of the modern world. Yet it is to say that he has survived as a whole and integral theologian in that world, and at this point he has no peers among his fellow theologians, at least in the United States.

Not only is Cobb a non-alienated theologian, but his is a holistic theology, a theology comprehending the apparently estranged worlds of Bible, tradition, modernity, metaphysics, epistemology, ethics, world religions, and nature. Above all, his theology is a revolt against dualism, against dualism of any kind, and yet it proceeds with a spontaneity showing little sign of the strains and tensions imposed by the dualisms against which he is in revolt. Cobb may well be the most revolutionary theologian among us, just as he equally could be the most reactionary, even though his work bears no signs of either a revolutionary temper or stance. Here, it would appear, right and left or revolutionary and reactionary or for-ward-moving and backward-moving poles are non-polarized. This is surely one meaning of 'polar theology' today, and thus far John Cobb is the only theologian who has constructed a systematic and comprehensive polar theology. In this perspective, polar theology fits into none of our established theological classifications. It is neither theistic, atheistic, nor pantheistic. Nor is it Biblical, historical, philosophical, or ethical. For it intends both to transcend and to unify these seemingly incompatible forms of theology, and to do so by way of seeking a human, a cosmic, and a universal theology.

What we should take most seriously in Cobb is his theological project, a project promising not only a new theology but a whole theology, a theology embodying the promise of a universal humanity. Of course, one cannot speak of humanity in this context, nor of what we know and experience as humanity. For the humanity that Cobb envisions is not only a universal humanity, and one universal in both time and space, but also a humanity that is not only integrally but also holistically related to both nature and deity.

At this point it would be useful to remark upon Cobb's relation to Whitehead. There is no doubt that Cobb is a Whiteheadian in a funda-mental sense, and that his theological categories as well as his theological project have been deeply affected if not inspired by Whitehead. Yet it is also noteworthy that, despite his great influence, Cobb largely stands alone as a Whiteheadian or process theologian. In large measure this is due to Cobb's holistic project, a project that is alien both to ecclesiastical and to academic theology. But it is also true that, despite its long history,

Christian theology has truly known only one philosopher, and that is Aristotle. Only Aristotelian philosophy has entered into the very center of Christian theological thinking, and done so in such a way as thereby to extend itself throughout the whole range of Christian understanding. While this may also be true of Judaism and Islam, theology has never played the central role in these traditions that it has played in Christianity. Only in Christian theology has a sustained attempt been made to reach a comprehensive or universal understanding that is grounded in faith. And the only full expressions of that attempt are Aristotelian. Even today the great body of Christian philosophical theology is Aristotelian.

Thus it is not accidental that Cobb is the only process theologian today who has evolved a systematic or comprehensive theology. Christian theology, just as the Christian church, has only begun to enter the modern world. And the greatest challenge to Christian theology remains the Enlightenment. Pietism was the real source of post-Enlightenment Christian theology, but even pietistic theology has become impossible in the second half of the twentieth century. Most theologians today are attempting to reach a post-modern theology. While this may well be a laudable goal, it is obviously premature if theology has not yet passed through modernism, and this means if it has not yet come to a positive as well as a negative response to the Enlightenment. Thus far the sustained attempts in this direction have been dualistic, and dualistic because they never allow scientific or historical or modern philosophical understanding to enter the center of faith. Thereby Christian theology has become hopelessly isolated from the modern world, and consequently isolated from the world itself.

Cobb is drawn to Whitehead not only because Whitehead is a great modern philosopher but also because Whitehead created both the most comprehensive and the most profound revolt against modern dualism. Whitehead's real opponent was the Enlightenment itself, and it is noteworthy that he did not simply transcend or move beyond it but that he incorporated many, if not most, of its greatest achievements. Accordingly, Whitehead is both a modern and a post-modern philosopher, and therein, too, he is a model for Cobb. Cobb is a theological son of the Enlightenment, and he is engaged in an Oedipal revolt against his father. But an Oedipal revolt never actually kills; it always remains bound to the distant father. So likewise Cobb is bound to the Enlightenment; this is the real meaning of his theological liberalism, and if only for this reason he refuses all theologies that are bound to a pre-modern world. This means that he refuses virtually all modern theology, and this despite his irenic spirit. Thus the Cobb who is seemingly most open to the modern theological world is also the Cobb who is most isolated from it, and isolated from modern theology because he has decisively chosen the modern world.

Ours is a time for radical theological experiment, and for a new and more universal theological community. Cobb's project is not only daring but also one that can scarcely be borne by a single theologian. At the very least it demands response, and critical response, even if that response should disrupt his project. For even if Cobb's project fails, its very failure could deepen and enlighten our theological work. This could be said of the work of few theologians today, and perhaps it is the very failure of a theological project which is its greatest achievement. We are coming to sense that this is true of the projects of Barth and Tillich, and perhaps it is likewise so even now with those of Bultmann and Rahner. If we must die to live, then theologies must die so that theology may live. Surely we cannot become open to Cobb's project if we cannot die to the great body of modern theology. And if nothing else, this is the kind of theological project that can teach us to die as theologians. Perhaps only thereby can theology continue to exist.

POST-MODERN THEOLOGY
FOR A NEW CHRISTIAN EXISTENCE

JOHN COBB is increasingly being recognized as one of the leading theologians of our time. He has shown himself to be not only a careful and fair critic of the work of others but also a highly creative thinker, writing with originality and depth on a wide range of topics. He has combined a grasp of the central presuppositions and implications of Christian faith with an equal sensitivity to the contemporary currents of thought and sensibility. He is perhaps most often thought of as a philosophical theologian who is at his best exploring subtle epistemological and ontological issues. Yet his work can also be seen as an attempt to clarify the central mission of the church, to justify this mission as important and appropriate, and to help create a context in which it can be carried out.

It has well been said that any thinker is easy to understand once you grasp the central vision behind the thought. Because of the breadth of issues that Cobb covers, and his concern to take into account all the factors relevant to those issues, his central vision may not be readily apparent to those who have not explored his writings systematically. An understanding of Cobb's position and program is complicated by the fact that he, like all thinkers who desire adequacy more than attention, escapes easy classification. He has with justification been called a radical theologian, and yet he affirms positions that many radicals would consider hopelessly conservative (e.g., not only is he a theist and an ontological realist, but he affirms a unique presence of God in Jesus, and does not even rule out an objective view of Jesus' resurrection). Along with many Protestant theologians he rejects 'natural' theology, yet he has affirmed the possibility and the necessity of a *Christian* natural theology. He confesses to an empirical over a rationalistic temper, yet he affirms the traditional rationalistic criteria. And he calls us neither to embrace nor to shut out the modern world.

5

The critical essays following this introductory essay deal with particular aspects of Cobb's thought. The purpose of this introduction is to bring out the central purposes and convictions behind his various writings. This will be attempted in a primarily thematic rather than chronological manner, since most of Cobb's productive career has been characterized by an overall consistency of outlook in basic purposes and convictions. However, in recent years there have been some important changes in emphasis and even in basic convictions. These are indicated in sections V and VII of this Introduction.[1]

I. TWO MAJOR FOCI

Two of the central ideas in Cobb's program are suggested by the title of this essay, i.e., 'post-modern theology' and 'Christian existence.' And the title indicates that the former is to be carried out for the sake of the latter. (The title also points to the fact that Cobb is interested in a *new* form of Christian existence; this will be discussed later.) It was mentioned above that Cobb's writings are intended to serve the needs of the church. This does not mean that he is a 'church theologian' in the conventional sense of the term (even though he does participate actively in the life and thought of the church). For the theologian's *central* task today is understood by Cobb not to be primarily that of speaking to those who are certain of their faith and firmly committed to the church, but rather that of speaking to those "citizens of the modern world inside and outside the church questioning whether there is some reason to support an institution or further a tradition that calls itself Christian," and whether there is even any reason to continue speaking of 'God'—and Cobb numbers himself among those who thus question (27:343; D:7, 9). In short, Cobb does not characterize his task as speaking "from faith to faith," but finds more apt Tillich's image of standing "on the boundary" (27:342).

From this standpoint, "the theological task today is that of determining what Christianity is all about and whether it is worthy of our support and participation" (E:13). To be thus worthy, there must be something *distinctive* about Christianity. Also, insofar as Christianity involves cognitive beliefs, they must be ones that can be *held with integrity*. It is these two requirements that lie behind his concern with the two major foci of his thought, 'Christian existence' and 'Christian natural theology.'

A. STRUCTURES OF EXISTENCE

What is Christianity all about? As a first step toward answering this question, Cobb agrees with those who focus on Christian *faith*. And he further agrees with the existentialist theologians that this faith is primarily a mode of existence rather than a matter of believing certain doctrines (E:4f). But he disagrees strongly with the existentialists' tendency simply to equate Christian existence with authentic human existence. That approach is inadequate for several reasons. First, it implies that the complex structure of modern Western human beings, as illuminated, for example, by Heidegger's *Being and Time*, emerged full-blown with the first appearance of beings worthy of the name 'human.' But this is incredible: there must have been many stages of development between modern human beings and their apelike ancestors. Second, the existentialist tendency implies that everything other than the Christian mode of existence is simply to be labeled 'inauthentic.' But to combine in this category modes of being as diverse as those of an Eastern mystic and a Western 'other-directed' individual is crude and unilluminating (E:10; 26:328; 27:344).

Third, this tendency implies that considerable content can be given to the idea of 'human nature,' where this term refers to that which is both (1) distinctive to human beings over against other creatures, and (2) common to all human beings. But virtually the only thing fitting this category is the capacity for language, i.e., for symbols as opposed to mere signals. Another way of saying the same thing is that human nature is its historicality, i.e., a person's capacity to be formed by history, by the particular cultural tradition in which one stands. In short, virtually the only distinctive thing that all human beings have in common is their capacity to be so different from each other (*CNT* 62f; 22:125; 52:44ff; C:5).

Fourth, to assume that Christian existence is an ideal possibility given to humanity as such, and thereby not to see it as being essentially historically conditioned, undercuts the possibility of any intelligible formulation of the necessary dependence of Christian existence on the Biblical tradition in general and on Jesus in particular. Hence the continued appeal to the Bible and Jesus becomes arbitrary.

In contrast to this tendency to divide all human beings into the two categories of authentic and inauthentic, Cobb insists that we must recognize a plurality of 'structures of existence.' People differ not simply in having different ideas about themselves, but in *being* different. They actually structure the dimensions of their psyches differently, and in some cases even exemplify different dimensions. For example, axial existence differs from primitive in that the organizing center of axial existence is in the conscious rather than the unconscious part of experience (*SCE* 54; 22:127). Also there are many different structures within axial existence, some of them representing successive stages within a tradition; Buddhist existence emerged out of Hindu, Socratic out of Homeric, and Christian out of prophetic (*SCE* 22, 108).

Furthermore, besides this plurality of structures, there are various *modes* in which each structure can be actualized. Each structure has an ideal mode, and one or more ways in which this ideal can fail to be attained. For example, 'prophetic' and 'Christian' were used above to refer to structures of existence. More precisely understood, they are modes within more general structures. 'Personal' existence is the structure of existence in which one combines a sense of one's inwardness with responsibility for one's action. 'Prophetic' existence is the mode in which this responsibility is carried out in trust and obedience. 'Spiritual' existence is the structure of self-transcending selfhood, in which one knows oneself to transcend all the dimensions of one's psyche, and hence to be responsible for them, even one's motives and emotions. 'Self-preoccupation' is unhealthy spiritual existence, wherein one is preoccupied with one's own inner life, especially the purity of one's motives. 'Christian' existence is healthy spiritual existence, wherein one is motivated by genuine concern for the other, having been freed from self-concern by faith in God's love, forgiveness, and acceptance (26:334–337; *SCE* 119–124, 133–136).

B. Vision of Reality

Closely related to the above is another way in which Cobb disagrees with the existentialist theologians. Defining Christian faith as a mode of existence, they tend to disparage the importance of cognitive beliefs. Cobb agrees that the church has often insisted upon all kinds of propositions that are unnecessary and even false. Nevertheless, he maintains (1) that the Christian mode of existence cannot long endure without a vision of reality that supports it, and (2) that a vision of reality, which is a preconscious, precognitive way or ordering and interpreting the data of experience, cannot long survive apart from conscious, cognitive beliefs that articulate and support it. These two propositions will be examined in order.

'Vision of reality' is one of Cobb's central technical terms. It can be compared with the British 'blik' and the existentialist 'understanding of existence,' both of which refer to a non-cognitive ordering of the data of experience. Cobb holds that, prior to any conscious judgments about reality, there is a "perception of the locus and the character of the real that is taken for granted in all of our ordinary judgments." Rather than reflecting on it, we generally presuppose it in reflecting upon other matters (58:81).

In the light of this notion, the plurality and the historical conditionedness of the structures of existence can be understood. Christian existence emerged under determinate conditions, and could not have emerged where those conditions did not obtain. Of decisive importance was the vision of reality underlying the Hebrew tradition. Just as the emergence of the Greek and Indian structures of existence were correlated with particular visions of reality, so is the rise of spiritual existence, as well as the Hebrew personal existence from which it emerged, unthinkable apart from the Biblical vision of reality (*GW* 122; E:10; 18:42f). In this vision of reality, the world is seen as the creation of a personal, righteous, knowing God. As creation the world is both finite and purposed, and as such neither sacred, on the one hand, nor devoid of meaning, on the other (*LO* 315; *GW* 121; *TA* 25f). In this context, Hebrews came to see themselves as personal, historical, and responsible, and to equate their true selves with their wills, by which they partially transcended their bodily, emotional, and rational dimensions. Of increasing influence was the notion that God looked upon the heart, so that not only one's actions but also one's intentions and motives were important (22:130; *GW* 120, 136; 26:339). Under the impact of Jesus emerged spiritual existence, a further development of personal existence in the direction of greater transcendence and a corresponding greater responsibility. It presupposed the same vision of reality, except that the relations between the elements were altered. Essential to the rise of the Christian vision of reality was the radical obedience demanded, and the radical forgiveness offered, by the righteous and loving God (26:339; 6:217f; *SCE* 109–116, 124, 135).

Besides not being able to *emerge* without a Christian vision of reality, Christian existence also cannot long *endure* without a Christian vision (50:190; E:12f). And the endurance of this vision in turn requires a continued attention to Christian *doctrines*. To make this connection intelligible, a further facet of the notion of a vision of reality must be brought out.

Although Cobb describes a vision of reality as precognitive, its status in regard to cognitive beliefs differs from Bultmann's 'understanding of existence.' A vision of reality has cognitive implications in that it is compatible with certain objective assertions (i.e., assertions intended to speak about realities in themselves), and incompatible with certain other ones, whereas an understanding of existence is generally understood to be non-cognitive in the sense that all attempts to express it in objective statements are *ipso facto* distorting. Accordingly, whereas Cobb agrees that the New Testament needs demythologizing, he does not agree that this entails completely de-objectifying it. That is, the objective assertions about God and the world should not be translated exhaustively into statements about human beings, and certainly not into conative statements. Rather, they need to be translated into analogous statements about God and the world, ones that support Christian existence and can be held with integrity. Without such Christian doctrines, Christian faith cannot long survive (E:13, 16; 26:339).

This discussion of Cobb's answer to the question as to the essence of Christian faith has revolved around the terms 'structure of existence' and 'vision of reality.' These correspond, of course, to the subjective and objective sides of faith, respectively—in traditional terms, *fides qua creditur* and *fides quae creditur*. There has been much controversy in the past few centuries as to which side of faith has priority. At one time Cobb tended to identify faith with a vision of reality (9:524; *GW* 117–119). More recently, as seen above, he tends to identify faith with a mode of existence, and to see the vision of reality as a necessary condition. But, in either case, he has avoided the tendency to see one of the sides as a mere shadow of the other. If forced to choose, he would give a certain logical priority to the vision of reality (*SCE* 98f). However, he would rather stress the dialectical relation obtaining between them, i.e., each finally presupposes and supports the other.

In the light of this close connection, some of Cobb's seemingly contradictory statements about the fundamental purpose of the church can be understood. On the one hand, Cobb says that this purpose is to promote Christian existence; on the other hand, he says that its basic mission is to worship. The reconciliation between these two statements is found in Cobb's conviction that it is in worship that attention is "focused on those features of experience which for Christians have been the organizing clues for the whole," and in which this "vision of reality has become sufficiently real to become also the shaper of existence" (50:191; cf. 26:339).

II. THE DOMINANT MODERN VISION OF REALITY

Having discussed Cobb's understanding of the nature of Christian faith, we must now consider his analysis of our current situation. The term 'modern' takes on the status of a technical term in his thought to point to this situation, as does the term 'dominant.' The modern world, or the modern mind, is one that is primarily formed by the dominant thought of the recent past (*GW* 123; D:8). This dominant thought has been based primarily on admiration for the achievements of natural science (*CNT* 270f; D:9). Although this modern mentality achieves clearest expression in the writings of the dominant academic philosophies, what is pointed to is also becoming a widespread sensibility among Westerners generally (*LO* 82; D:8f). In essence, this sensibility is one that tends to equate the real with the objects of sense experience, especially vision and touch. This results in taking the world of sense data, or confusedly some blurring of it and the world of material things, as the real (24:7; D:10). Cobb sometimes refers to this modern mentality as phenomenalistic or positivistic, sometimes as the materialistic-positivistic conception of the world (*GW* 133; D:10). In the former case he is thinking primarily of the attitude that does not ask the ontological question about the nature of being, that rejects the concept of causality, and simply rests content with the phenomena as they appear in sense experience. In the latter case he is thinking of the more general tendency not to attribute any significant reality to any objects of experience in themselves (9:523; 41:51; *TE* 98). That is, positivism attributes no independent reality to the objects; materialism attributes reality to them, but no *significant* reality.

We are now in a period of transition that began with the modern scientific world view and, in regard to the phenomenalistic side of the modern vision, with David Hume (*GW* 131f; 9:521). Prior to this time, the Biblical vision of reality had become ingrained in the West, determining to a large extent what was considered 'common sense.' But now the Biblical vision is increasingly being replaced by the modern vision. And the two are definitely antithetical. The modern vision leads to a complete relativism, whereas the Christian vision necessarily involves presuppositions about truth and reality (15:195f, 202f). The modern vision tends toward complete nihilism, whereas Christianity sees the world as meaningful because grounded in a purposive sacred reality (9:523, 525). Furthermore, the positivistic vision with its theory of meaning tends to exclude all religious questions, questions to which a theistic world view could provide the best answer (*GW* 134; 28:106; *LO* 22). The modern mentality leads to the 'death of God.' This death follows not primarily from rational argumentation, but from the materialistic-positivistic vision that simply has no 'place' for God and God's relations to the world. The 'modern' notion of what is real excludes the type of reality that God would have. And the correlative notion of causality, if causality be accepted at all, excludes God's possible interaction with the world (D:18; *LO* 24; 41:62; *GW* 68).

In sum, to the degree to which the dominant currents of thought have permeated the conscious and the unconscious dimensions of the human psyche, the Christian vision of the world is rendered, at best, radically problematic. Belief in God is less and less seen to be supported by 'common sense.' Although the modern person may for some time be able to *believe* some Christian doctrines, he or she can no longer simply *see* the world as God's (D:10f). And this means that the Christian belief will become increasingly less vital and finally non-existent.

This contradiction between the modern vision of reality, on the one hand, and the vision implicit in Christian faith, on the other, sets the stage for the question as to the task and procedure of the contemporary theologian. One possibility would be to continue assuming aspects of the Christian vision of things, as do Thomism and Personalism for the most part. But this means that theology will become increasingly irrelevant to sensitive moderns, both within and without the church. Another alternative would be to give up the Christian vision of the world in order to share fully the modern perspective. But then the Christian character of theology would be lost; Christian existence would not be supported; and of course no answer could be given to the question of the distinctive mission of the church (*GW* 137; 28:109, 15:193f). Accordingly, one simply must conclude that, in the 'modern world' as such, Christian theology is not possible, for it is impossible apart from a Christian vision of reality (*GW* 124, 129).

III. CHRISTIAN NATURAL THEOLOGY

It is this analysis which lies behind the second distinctive motif of Cobb's theology: the theologian must *challenge* the dominant modern mentality (15:197; *GW* 138). "Unless the now dominant vision is challenged it will continue to relegate theistic beliefs increasingly to the periphery" (D:18). And not only that. As the logic of this modern vision is further worked out in the common sensibility, as it will be if not challenged, those who have had their concern for love and ethics nourished by Christian faith and its effects will lose this concern. Humanism provides no stable halfway house between Christianity and nihilism or some new paganism, for the idea of the human being as a responsible being is as incompatible with the modern vision as is the idea of God (D:10; *CNT* 14; 15:197; 21:316; *TE* 119f). And few of those who have been affected by Christianity will be able to find satisfaction in some alternative vision that might in principle support a concern for love and ethics (58:80).

Cobb also believes that it is in philosophy that the doctrines that finally come to typify an age are first stated. It is this estimation of philosophy's importance which lies behind the great difference in approach that separates Cobb from those who, concentrating on art, literature, or the social sciences, are more readily characterized as 'theologians of culture.'

The congruence between Cobb's stress on philosophical theology, on the one hand, and his focus on Christian existence and his concern for the church, on the other, can now be made clearer. In order for the sensitive person of today to see the church as important, that person needs to see that it has something distinctive and important to offer. Cobb's answer is that this something is a mode of existence which is distinctive and intimately connected with those values which Christians and Western humanists alike prize most highly. This type of reflection, however, leads one to see that this mode of existence is dependent upon a vision of reality that is merely one among many, and that must be expressed in beliefs that are radically questionable in our time, being recognized not only as different from the beliefs of most of humanity but also as alien to the dominant mentality of the modern West. In this context, one needs some assurance that the Christian vision is somehow warranted, that the Christian mode of existence is somehow *appropriate* as well as distinctive (*LO* 317).

Furthermore, the problem of faith and reason is today even more critical than the above paragraph suggests. The dominant mentality renders Christian beliefs about God and the human spirit not only questionable but even meaningless. Accordingly we need a context in which such notions can be seen as meaningful, and this context is metaphysics in general, or natural theology in particular. Natural theology is absolutely essential if the church is to regain confidence in its mission and message, for the doors of the church do not keep out the debilitating vision that destroys the sense of the reality of God (*CNT* 12–15).

However, natural theology in its traditional sense is no longer possible. The traditional thought was that pure reason, unaffected by faith, could develop notions of God, humanity, and the world that were compatible with the specifically Christian doctrines based on faith in special revelation. This compatibility would show that it was not unreasonable to accept on faith the items that went beyond what reason alone could know. That these assumptions can no longer be accepted is one of the central points of Cobb's *Living Options in Protestant Theology*. There is no such thing as pure, i.e., unhistorical, reason. All philosophical thought is based on some historically conditioned vision of reality, a preconceptual way of ordering and interpreting the data of experience. If this vision is non-Christian, the results of reason will be incompatible with Christian presuppositions. That this has been the case to a large extent is one of the major reasons for the widespread explicit rejection of natural theology among Protestant theologians. However, if the results that are reached are compatible with Christian faith, one must recognize that this so-called natural theology is as foreign to people of other perspectives as is Christian theology proper (*LO* 316; *CNT* 259–263). That is, the result is really a *Christian* natural theology, since it is based on a fundamentally *Christian* vision of reality. Hence, the claim to establish an objective basis for belief in revelation is vitiated by circularity.

Making the prospects for natural theology even more difficult in our time is the recognition that "reason supports faith only when it begins with a self-understanding or vision of reality that is not shared by the intellectual leadership of our time" (*LO* 88f; cf. 316f). Hence the theologian cannot appeal to any philosophical consensus today even within his or her own culture to support Christian faith.

The above considerations mean that the theologian who cannot rest content with a purely fideistic or confessional approach must recognize that any philosophy from which support can be derived will be to some degree a *Christian* natural theology. They also mean that he or she must be prepared to defend it philosophically. This is another way of saying that the theologian must be prepared to challenge the dominant philosophy on its own grounds (*CNT* 263; *LO* 81f, n. 83; 18:40).

There is a possibility for Christian theology, and a hope for the Christian community to regain confidence in its perspective, if two conditions obtain. First, a review of the reasons for the dominance of the dominant philosophy must show that it is not rooted inescapably in the modern situation, especially that it is not necessitated by our scientific knowledge (*CNT* 15; *GW* 130–134; E: 14f; D:9; 28:109). Second, it must be possible to find or develop a minority viewpoint that one can honestly consider to be unrefuted, and that expresses the essentials of the Christian vision (*CNT* 15; E:15).

It is in the light of this analysis that Cobb is enthusiastic about the possibilities of the philosophy of Alfred North Whitehead. On the one hand, Whitehead provides a critique of the presuppositions of the dominant schools of philosophy. He shows that, far from being demanded by science, they are in serious tension with the assumptions and operations of the scientific enterprise (30:90; *GW* 135; 28:110; *CNT* 15, 271; 9:529). Especially important is Whitehead's epistemological critique, for the materialisms and phenomenalisms of the dominant philosophies are rooted primarily in the assumption that it is through sense experience that we are most fundamentally related to the real (41:55, 58f; D:12; 9:528f; 24:8). The importance that Cobb attaches to this point is shown by his returning time and time again to a critique of sensationalism in the light of Whitehead's alternative (9:528f; D:12–17; 41:55–62; 22:140–142; *GW* 73–76). In this alternative view, subjects of experience and non-sensuous relations are seen as fundamental in reality.

On the other hand, Whitehead's philosophy can be regarded as a fundamentally Christian philosophy, as articulating conceptually the essentials of the Christian vision of things (*CNT* 268). Hence those aspects of it which are especially relevant to theology can be regarded as constituting a Christian natural theology. However, Cobb does not simply take over those aspects from Whitehead. For one thing, there are several questions especially important to theology to which Whitehead gave little or no attention. Also, Cobb finds certain doctrines in Whitehead's philosophy which he thinks need modification in order to make the position more fully rational. The results of Cobb's development and modification of Whitehead must even more definitely be called a *Christian* natural theology. This is partly because it is Cobb's Christian perspective that leads him to raise the particular questions he does (*CNT* 17, 264, 268f). But also, even though the modifications are intended to make Whitehead's philosophy more consistent with his own criteria of excellence, and hence to be warranted only by purely philosophical considerations (*CNT* 17, 264, 267, 269), the resulting Whiteheadian position has even more affinities with Christian thought than Whitehead himself made explicit (15:200f; 9:531–533; 21:319).

IV. POST-MODERN PHILOSOPHY

The connection between the two major foci of Cobb's theological program, Christian existence and Christian natural theology, has now, it is hoped, been made clear. However, the term 'post-modern' has not been explained. In opposing the dominant currents of the modern world, Cobb does not call us back to a pre-modern outlook. There is no possibility of making such a return with integrity. For there is much in the modern world that must be affirmed, and much of this undercuts the traditional metaphysical outlooks and the theologies based upon them. If the dominant vision is to be challenged, it will have to be in the name of a post-modern vision (*GW* 135, 138; 28:105; 15:197). And Cobb finds Whitehead's philosophy to be post-modern in the requisite sense.

In general, he considers this philosophy post-modern in the sense that, while rejecting many of the doctrines of 'modernity,' it takes seriously and incorporates the scientific world view and arises out of a sustained reflection upon the fundamental presuppositions of the dominant modern view. Again, epistemology is of utmost importance. Cobb believes that Whitehead takes the principles of empiricism more seriously than do most of those who claim this name. It is precisely Whitehead's 'radical empiricism,' which rejects the primacy of sense data, that allows him to move beyond the conclusion that there is no basis in experience for affirming any significant or valuable reality. Accordingly, Whitehead's philosophy is post-sensationalistic and hence post-nihilistic.

To make the essential outline of Cobb's program clear, one of his central ideas about human nature needs to be mentioned. This involves the relation between a person's preconceptual vision of reality, on the one hand, and that person's consciously affirmed beliefs, on the other. Cobb does not subscribe to the intellectualist view that one's conscious beliefs determine one's whole psychic constitution. But neither does he hold the anti-intellectualist view that one's conscious beliefs are totally determined by subrational factors. Against those who hold the influence to be all in one direction or the other, he takes a both-and position. On the one hand, the preconscious vision of reality is the most important factor in determining one's total outlook and attitudes. One's conscious beliefs will be, to a large extent, an explication of this preconscious vision. But, on the other hand, one *can* hold beliefs consciously that are in some tension with one's underlying vision (*GW* 136). Hume, in whom the modern vision first broke through decisively, provides an example. To some extent the traditional vision retained its power in him. To resolve the tension, he distinguished sharply between his 'philosophy' and his 'practice' (*GW* 132). However, the important point is that, in time, the conscious beliefs can alter the vision itself (*GW* 136). Hence those doctrines which had to be held with some effort by the early moderns have increasingly come to constitute common sense.

It is precisely this phenomenon, however, that provides a ground for hope. To a large extent the Christian vision of reality has been rendered questionable for us, so we no longer simply *see* the world as God's creation. But we nevertheless have the capacity to accept an understanding of the world that is essentially Christian, if it can present itself as valuable and rationally convincing. This understanding will, at first, be in tension with our fundamental sensibilities, insofar as we are part of modern culture. But in time "such an *understanding* of the world may be able to reform and revitalize remnants of the still effective *vision* of the world as creation. It might even bring into being a new Christian vision for those among whom the old one has evaporated" (*GW* 138).

It is perhaps worthy of note that this position is fully in accord with Cobb's own self-description in terms of the issue between empiricism and rationalism. He says he is more empiricist in temper than rationalistic, meaning that he is more impressed by experiential evidence than by formal arguments. This coheres with his opinion, for example, that the death of God is due more to a loss of the sense of God's reality than to atheistic arguments (D:8f). But he does not thereby reject the criteria of the rationalist:

If a rational system that seems not to do full justice to my spontaneous interpretation of experience commends itself to my reason, if I can find no fallacy in it and can provide no better explanation, then I must finally also recognize that my primary understanding of my own experience is also fallible, subject to correction by reason as well as to explanation and clarification. (30:97)

V. SUBTLE SHIFTS IN BASIC CONVICTIONS

At this stage several subtle but important shifts that have recently occurred in Cobb's basic convictions should be mentioned. Until a few years ago, he tended to speak of *the* Christian vision of reality, and of the need for its *renewal.* For example, in 1969, with reference to an article written ten years earlier, he said: "I remain convinced that the possibility of Christian theology depends upon renewal of the vision of the world as creation and that the philosophy of Whitehead offers the best channel for this renewal" (*GW* 137f). However, recently he has begun to speak more of *reform* than simply of renewal. He has called not only for a new conceptuality in which to explicate the (unchanging) Christian vision of reality but also for a new Christian vision. And, since the two are so interrelated, he is also calling for a new mode of Christian existence.

To some extent, the need for a new mode of Christian existence is something to which he has been pointing for some time. In *The Structure of Christian Existence* he said, in discussing the question of the finality of Christian existence: "Certainly, we do not wish to say that nothing better is possible than the existence we now know!" (*SCE* 142). He distinguished there between two modes of analyzing structures of existence, the intrapsychic and the relational. The former deals with the various dimensions and elements within an occasion of the psyche's experience, while the latter deals with the relations between an occasion of experience and other realities, i.e., one's own past, one's body, the wider realm of nature, other persons, and God. It is in regard to this relational mode that "we can hope for something quite different from anything we now know" (*SCE* 143).

However, more recently the newness he seeks has become more radical. A little background is needed in order to understand the direction in which his recent thinking has been moving. According to his analysis, the rise of axial existence in India, Persia, China, Greece, and Israel involved the transference of the 'seat of existence' (the organizing center of the psyche) from the unconscious to the conscious portion of one's experience. This made possible the realization of new kinds of values, but it also involved alienation. Since a person's direct experience of other human psyches and of God is generally at the unconscious level, the transference of the seat of existence out of this level fostered a sense of estrangement from deity and from other persons, as well as from the relatively autonomous unconscious world of meanings. The reverse side of this estrangement was a rise of individuality. Rather than being primarily a member of an organic unity of psychic life, one came to identify oneself with a thread of consciousness remembered from the past and anticipated in the future. And since in axial existence one tends to identify oneself with one's conscious experience, in which the experience of other psyches and God is largely absent, the distinction from other individuals amounts to a real separation (*SCE* 54–57, 111).

It is on this basis that Cobb recognizes as a real temptation the call by many contemporaries to return to a primitive mode of existence. They witness to the lack of wholeness, spontaneity, and communion that has often accompanied axial individuality. But Cobb urges us not to go back, but to go forward to what he has tentatively labeled a 'post-personal' mode of existence (53:11). Here 'personal' is used to refer to the type of individuality described above, wherein one's appropriation of one's own past and one's anticipation of one's own future is exclusivistic, i.e., it is at the expense of any significant identification with the feelings and concerns of others. In this sense Cobb wants us to regain the sense of unity that characterized primitive existence. But the language *post*-personal indicates that he is not advocating a simple return, but something more like a Hegelian synthesis. If tribalism was the thesis, and individuality the antithesis, then post-personal existence is the synthesis, transcending and yet preserving the best aspects of both. He evidently believes that individuality at first had to negate tribalism in order to emerge, but now that it has emerged and developed it is strong enough to absorb aspects of the former without losing itself. That is, people could enter a new mode of existence, in which they not only would have a genuine concern for others but would much more fully appropriate and identify with the feelings of others, yet without losing the conscious, responsible reflectiveness that is necessary if life on this crowded planet is to survive.

Thus far I have spoken mainly of one aspect of the new relational mode of existence sketched by Cobb, the relation to other human psyches. He also points to a new relation to God. It is primarily in this regard that Jesus' structure of existence differed from the Christian structure of existence to which it gave rise. Jesus' uniqueness in this respect, Cobb suggests, was that his prehensions of God constituted his seat of existence, his 'I' (44:393). Hence there is a finality that can be claimed for Jesus that cannot be claimed for Christian existence, at least as it has developed thus far. And Jesus thereby points us toward an ideal actualization, in which the tension between desire and duty would be overcome (*SCE* 143f; 44:393, 395f).

The concerns for new modes of relatedness with God and other persons are ones that Cobb has expressed for some years. More recently he has been stressing also the need for new relationships with one's body (especially one's sexuality) and the rest of nature (58:87–94; 51:10–13; 41:47–49, 58f; 53:11; *TE,* chs. 8, 10, 13).

This new mode of Christian existence requires a correspondingly new vision of reality. The traditional Christian vision saw persons (divine and human) as the locus of reality. The new vision that we need would give priority to relations. The old vision saw humanity over against nature, and therefore contrasted nature and history. The new vision would see all of reality as historical, and would see all things in terms of mutual interpenetration. The old vision stressed the transcendence of God over the world; the new vision would see the world as in God, and God as in the world (50:192; 40:38–41; 58:91).

Cobb's shift in this direction has led him to think of Whitehead's philosophy as post-modern in another major sense, that of being post-individualistic. In Whitehead's conceptuality, enduring individuals with merely accidental relationships to others are not the basic ontological unities. Rather, the basic units are moments of experience ('actual occasions') which arise out of a multitude of relationships to ('prehensions' of) other units. Modern humanity's drastically autonomous individualism is hence merely a contingent fact, and one that excludes many positive values. Therefore Whitehead provides a way of *conceptualizing* a *vision* of reality in which relationships have priority over enduring individuals, a vision that could lead to the new mode of existence that Cobb envisages.

VI. A QUESTION ABOUT RELATIVISM

One issue that seems somewhat unclear in Cobb's thought is his attitude toward philosophical relativism. He confesses his acquiescence "to a considerable degree" (*CNT* 271, 275–277), but he also insists that relativism must be transcended to some degree (*LO* 32, 119). And he has offered suggestions as to how this might be done (*CNT* 271–274, 283f; 15:196, 198, 202–204). Yet Schubert Ogden has concluded that Cobb can be quoted on both sides of the issue, leaving "little doubt that his whole discussion of relativism is unsatisfactory."[2] Ogden is unhappy with Cobb's idea that there is some criterion by which to choose a philosophy for one's natural theology other than intrinsic philosophical excellence.[3] Cobb has argued that it is most likely that there is a plurality of philosophical positions of about equal excellence if judged in terms of criteria upon which they all agree. The basic source of their differences lies in their differing visions of reality, which lead to different perceptions of the data to be treated; hence there is a circularity in their criticisms of each other. In this situation the Christian is justified in choosing a philosophy that shares his or her vision of reality, as long as the philosophy is *at least equal* to others in consistency and coherence (*CNT* 264–266, 282; 1:221f).

Ogden thinks Cobb makes too much of the observation that the philosopher too always stands in a tradition that shapes his or her basic vision.[4] The real question at issue here seems to be the *extent* to which the data of experience are themselves determined by the perspective one brings to the experience. For example, Reinhold Niebuhr (whom Cobb has criticized for not being sufficiently sensitive to this problem in his otherwise excellent apologetic [*LO* 311; E:8]) has said that "guiding presuppositions do indeed color the evidence accumulated by experience; but they do not fully control evidence."[5] Sometimes Cobb does seem to allow the data some objectivity over against the person's perspective (28:103, 118f). In a statement that seems to be based on Whitehead's category of 'perception in the mode of causal efficacy,' Cobb says: "There are aspects of our experience of the world that I do not believe are determined by our conceptuality or imaginative vision at all," awareness of which remains at least "at the borders of consciousness" (F:3). At other times he seems to think of *all* the data of experience as colored by one's perspective (*GW* 118; *CNT* 265; *LO* 48–50, 311; 28:101), which would imply a complete relativism.

In my opinion, the other crucial question in this regard is whether the formal criteria by which philosophical positions are to be judged are themselves relative. Granted that the data of experience are determined or at least heavily conditioned by one's perspective, is not the ideal of adequacy to the facts (i.e., whatever 'facts' there seem to be) a universally valid criterion? Cobb himself has said that the criteria of coherence and consistency have "almost universal practical assent," and he often appeals to the criteria of adequacy as well as coherence (*CNT* 264; 28:117; 22:124). Yet at other times he suggests that these criteria are themselves relative (*CNT* 275; E:11; 15:194, 202).

VII. MORE FUNDAMENTAL SHIFTS

A pair of more fundamental shifts, with potentially much greater implications for the nature of Cobb's future theological work, is manifest in his 1975 book, *Christ in a Pluralistic Age*. Each of the shifts is due in part to the influence of Thomas Altizer. Prior to the 1975 book, Cobb had been concerned as a theologian primarily to achieve conceptual clarity, and this in regard to actual events. Thus, in Christology he had been primarily concerned to conceptualize how God had been related to Jesus of Nazareth, i.e., what the distinctive structure of Jesus' existence had been. This was in accord with Cobb's philosophical realism, based on Whitehead, and his belief that Christian notions could be wholeheartedly affirmed only if Christians could attain clarity about their meaning and insight into their credibility.

However, he had felt for some time that Altizer's approach to theology, while lacking somewhat in clarity, nevertheless possessed a power to evoke response that his own did not. Altizer's approach is idealistic rather than realistic, in the philosophical sense, and deals more with what the realist would call images as opposed to actualities. Hence, in Christology, Altizer deals with 'Christ,' and the reality thus named is related more to images in modern consciousness, particularly in literature, than to Jesus of Nazareth. Cobb, while feeling the power of Altizer's imaginative approach, could not adopt it, because of his belief in the necessity of conceptual clarity and his belief that the Christian theologian should deal with actual, historical events.

But in writing the 1975 book, Cobb found a way to combine his previous concerns with the growing belief that the theologian, if he or she is to be both responsible and widely effective, must help shape Christian images, since these, much more than concepts, provide motivation and direction for the Christian life. (How much effect this shift will have on Cobb's previous focus upon philosophy, as the crucial aspect of culture with which the theologian should be concerned, remains to be seen.) Cobb was aided in this regard by William Beardslee, who in *A House for Hope* treated 'Christ' as a proposition.[6] A 'proposition' in Whitehead's philosophy is a combination of possibility and actuality. Cobb, who had previously tended to avoid the term 'Christ' as confusing, came to employ the term in this way (without using the technical Whiteheadian term 'proposition'). Christ is Jesus as the full incarnation of the Logos. The Logos is what Whitehead had called, among other things, the Primordial Nature of God. It is the source of change or novelty in the world, and as such is the source of order. It confronts the actual with that which is possible for it. As the source of order, it is similar to traditional descriptions of the Logos. But Cobb stresses that a Christian understanding of the Logos, built on Jesus' call forward to the Kingdom of God, must be dynamic. Cobb calls the Logos the 'principle of creative transformation.' As such, it does not sanction any one form of life. Rather, it calls everyone in his or her own time and place to transform creatively the tradition in which he or she stands.

On this basis Cobb calls us to recognize Christ in all the creative movements of our time—for example, in the movement of Western art to become universalistic by understanding itself not in terms of particular forms but in terms of the basic process of creative transformation itself. Likewise he believes that theology is manifesting Christ in this sense as it begins to incorporate the truth in the Asian traditions and thus to become genuinely universal. For this incorporation will mean giving up all particularities that prevent this incorporation, and serving only the call for creative transformation.

This brings us to the second fundamental shift in Cobb's recent thinking. He now views all efforts to find an essence of Christianity as misplaced. This includes his own previous attempt to locate it in a vision of reality and/or a structure of existence. In Whiteheadian terms, this means that the 'society' designated by the adjective 'Christian' has no 'defining essence,' in the usual sense of that term. The only (normative) characteristic of Christianity is a mode of relating to its own past—this is the mode of 'creative transformation.' Cobb likens the Christian tradition to a 'living person.' Whitehead defined a living person as a personally ordered society characterized by 'hybrid' prehensions. That is, each member of the society prehends its predecessor in terms of the novel elements in the predecessor's experience. This differentiates a living person from an ordinary tradition or temporal society, in which each member repeats a complex form which the preceding member itself had received from its predecessor. Whitehead himself did say that a living person has a defining essence which characterizes that person from beginning to end. But Cobb believes that, had Whitehead sufficiently reflected upon his own account of a society characterized by hybrid prehensions, he would have seen that it was inappropriate to speak as if such a society necessarily had a defining essence in the ordinary sense. As a result of a series of creative transformations, a person may have no formal characteristics in common with his or her previous self of many years ago, and yet still be the same person. Likewise, Christianity could go through a series of creative transformations, at the end of which it would have no formal properties in common with Christianity in an earlier age. Yet it would still be Christianity, as long as it still embodied the principle of creative transformation, which is not a formal property in the ordinary sense but a mode of relatedness to the past.

VIII. A FURTHER QUESTION ABOUT RELATIVISM

At first glance, this line of thought seems to suggest a completely relativistic notion of Christianity. However, when Cobb says that Christianity could be transformed into something quite different and still be worthy of the name 'Christianity,' he does not imply a total relativism. For he does not mean simply that *any* type of transformation would qualify, so that any resulting reality (e.g., Nazism) could be called Christianity, simply by virtue of standing in historical continuity with what was previously called by that name. Rather, there is a normative requirement—the transformation must be a 'creative' one.

Now, there must be some criterion or criteria for differentiating creative from non-creative transformations. It would seem that the criterion (or criteria) would have to be non-relativistic. And would not the criterion (or criteria) be rooted in some fundamental, perhaps preconceptual, view of reality—for example, in what Cobb has called a 'vision of reality'? In other words, does not the idea that a mode of Christianity is characterized by a mode of relatedness to its past, and that this is the mode of creative transformation—does not this idea presuppose a defining essence in the more ordinary sense (although, as Cobb has always seen, this essence cannot consist of explicit doctrines)? If this rhetorical question is correct, then it would seem that Cobb must either drop the word 'creative,' and accept a completely relativistic notion of the Christian tradition, or else recognize that his own previous attempts to point to an essence of Christian faith are not rendered invalid by his recent stress on creative transformation.

NOTES

1. Sections I-VI of this introductory essay were written in 1972 and sent to the persons who were invited to write essays for this volume. Sections VII and VIII were written in 1975 and deal with Cobb's recent changes. Although some of these changes involve rejections of earlier positions, I decided to leave the earlier sections virtually unchanged, since they serve as an introduction to those writings which still constitute the bulk of the Cobbian corpus, and those upon which all the essays except Pannenberg's are based. Clarification as to which aspects of Cobb's previous positions are now rejected by him can be gained from his "Responses" as well as from sections VII and VIII of this Introduction.

2. Schubert M. Ogden, "A *Christian* Natural Theology?" in Delwin Brown, Ralph E. James, Jr., and Gene Reeves (eds.), *Process Philosophy and Christian Thought* (The Bobbs-Merrill Company, Inc., 1971), 111–115, esp. 114.

3. *Ibid.*, 115.

4. *Ibid.*, 114.

5. C. W. Kegley and R. W. Bretall (eds.), *Reinhold Niebuhr: His Religious, Social, and Political Thought* (The Macmillan Company, 1961), 16.

6. William A. Beardslee, *A House for Hope* (The Westminster Press, 1972).

JOHN COBB'S THEOLOGICAL METHOD: INTERPRETATION AND REFLECTIONS

By David Tracy

I. INTRODUCTION: COBB'S METHOD

It is a pleasure to be invited to comment on the theology of John Cobb. The critical side of that invitation is not entirely easy to fulfill for the most basic of reasons: in a fundamental sense, I find my own position on the nature of theological method in basic accord with the distinctive position of John Cobb. To be sure, both of us realize that this shared position is a minority one in the contemporary theological spectrum of 'living options.'[1] However, I continue to find that shared position fundamentally sound. Indeed, a rereading of Cobb's work over the past few months has convinced me anew of the basic soundness of the approach which, from his earliest to his present work, Cobb, with typical care and consistency, has articulated. Hence I shall spend the main body of this essay articulating my relatively minor differences from and questions to the position on theological method articulated by Cobb. It would prove helpful to state first and as clearly as possible that I understand these differences to be ones emerging from a shared basic position on this central question of method. This is not to argue that such differences are of lesser seriousness. But it may remind the reader (and myself) that such differences can be articulated as real differences only from within the context of contemporary reflection which Cobb, as much as any other contemporary theologian, has done so much to make possible.

I understand Cobb's position on theological method to include the following basic components.[2] First, Cobb insists that an integral contemporary Christian theology must assume responsibility for a critical investigation of both the Christian tradition and the modern world vision. Second, Cobb further argues that historical consciousness must inform our understanding of the *distinctive* character of both the central Christian vision and the central visions of the modern and post-modern traditions. There, is, then, no substitute via any 'authorities' for careful historical investigation of either the 'vision of reality,' 'structure of existence,' or 'cognitive beliefs' of Christianity.[3] Correspondingly, there is no substitute via any highly personal and presumably authoritative vision for careful cultural analysis of the 'vision,' 'structure of existence,' or 'cognitive beliefs' of the modern and post-modern periods. Third, Cobb continues to insist that philosophy remain the principal conversation partner for theology for a critical investigation of the cognitive claims of both Christianity and modernity. This latter insistence leads to the argument that the specific philosophical position initiated by Alfred North Whitehead has developed an adequate philosophy (*CNT;* 16; 48; A) by means of its understanding of modern science and its anti-sensationalistic understanding of experience. This latter claim holds insofar as the Whiteheadian position not only is faithful to such classical philosophical criteria as coherence and adequacy to experience but also develops classical philosophy in authentically 'post-modern' and 'post-classical-theistic' directions (15:195–199). Indeed this latter doctrine, a constant motif in Cobb's work, represents the most widely recognized aspect of Cobb's constructive position. In my judgment, Cobb's formulation of the significance of Whitehead for the contemporary theological context is a sound one—and for exactly the post-modern philosophical reasons he advances. In the next section, I shall take issue with his formulation of this task as best described as a 'Christian natural theology.' For the moment, however, it may prove sufficient to note that at least one reader continues to be convinced by the arguments for the relative adequacy of Whitehead's philosophy which Cobb has consistently advanced.

As a summary statement on the meaning of theological method for Cobb, the following formulation may suffice: A contemporary Christian theology must employ methods of historical and cultural analysis to show the distinctive 'visions of reality,' 'structures of existence,' and 'cognitive beliefs' of both Christianity and modernity. That same theology, by the intrinsic logic of those commitments to meaningfulness, meaning, and truth operative in both the Christian and the modern position, must also employ philosophical criteria of coherence and adequacy. These latter criteria may be employed to adjudicate the clash between the basic Christian vision and cognitive beliefs and those of modernity. What strikes one above all else in Cobb's many-sided writing is his consistent fidelity to this multidimensional and demanding method for Christian theology. When the evidence so suggests, Cobb does not hesitate to demand a new formulation of the central theistic belief of classical Christianity.[4] Nor does he even hesitate to suggest, when new existential evidence on the post-modern visions of the body, on sexuality, and on nature come to view, that we may need a new Christianity (58; B; 43; *TE*). In short, we may need a reformulation not merely of Christian beliefs but even of the central Christian vision of reality and its correlative classical structure of existence which Cobb describes as a 'spiritual,' self-transcending existence fulfilled in love.[5] Correlatively, when the evidence so suggests, Cobb does not hesitate to challenge the cognitive beliefs of the 'modern' reigning conventional philosophical wisdom of 'positivism, materialism, existentialism, and nihilism' (9; 20; 40; *LO* 312ff; *CNT* 270–277; *SCE* 137–151) in favor of the philosophically more adequate and more coherent post-sensationalistic (and thereby post-modern) positions of Whitehead and Hartshorne. Similarly, when the evidence so suggests, Cobb does not hesitate to insist that the basic vision and structure of existence of planetary man cannot naively return to a pre-axial position nor even simply bypass Christian 'personal' and 'spiritual' existence in favor of either Buddhist or purely secularist visions. Rather, we must discover a 'post-personal' structure of existence which does not simply negate but transforms the traditional Western Christian structure of existence (58: 92–94). More exactly, Cobb's arguments for new Christian cognitive beliefs, a new Christian theology, a new philosophy, and a new Christianity are neither clarion calls for us to accept a personal vision nor surreptitious exercises in 'baptizing' modernity. Rather, these arguments are calls prompted by the empirical and rational evidence which Cobb advances for the reflection of anyone. By that demand for evidence and by that reformulation of the task of theological method, Cobb has, I believe, articulated a position that is both fundamentally sound and authentically promising. In the following sections, I shall advance some criticisms of Cobb's specific formulations for that task which I hope may serve to advance his important enterprise.

II. A CHRISTIAN NATURAL THEOLOGY: AN AMBIGUOUS CONCEPT?

With Cobb's insistence that theology must employ an explicitly philosophical method in order to fulfill its properly critical role, I, at least, have no quarrel. With his further insistence that such a philosophy must be post-modern at least in the senses of 'post-sensationalistic' and post–'pure reason' (and thereby conscious of the historicity of reality) there also seems good reason to agree. That the Anglo-American empirical tradition in philosophy as summarized and transformed in the direction of a metaphysics by the positions of Whitehead and Hartshorne can fulfill this role Cobb (especially in *A Christian Natural Theology* and *God and the*

World) has advanced evidence which, I continue to believe, can be considered convincing. But that such a critical role for the use of philosophy can best be described by means of the model 'Christian natural theology' I find at best an ambiguous position, at worst an incoherent one.[6] The systematic questions which must here be answered by Cobb to remove that ambiguity can be formulated as follows: First, what are the proper uses by the theologian of a critical philosophical method? Second, does a 'post-modern' philosophical position transcend its given historical situation in any philosophically meaningful sense? Since the latter consideration seems to be the principal reason for Cobb's articulation of the model 'Christian natural theology' (*CNT* 252–277), that philosophical problematic remains the principal systematic question at issue. But since that question probably is best raised in the context of the various uses of philosophy by the theologian, I will raise that 'use' question first in an attempt to clarify just where the ambiguity problem may lie.

A. THEOLOGY AND THE USES OF PHILOSOPHY

A fair generalization would seem to be the following. Where a positive role is assigned to the use of philosophy in theology, one of three roles is assigned it: first, the use of philosophical categories to articulate the Christian cognitive beliefs; second, the use of philosophical world view analysis to explicate the basic Christian vision of reality; third, the use of philosophical analysis as a critical resource to reflect upon any and all 'visions of reality.' I shall now try to summarize the meaning and possibility of each of these uses as applicable to Cobb's own position.

First, a specific philosophy is employed to provide the principal systematic concepts for theological reflection upon an originating religious language of a specific tradition. This role for the use of philosophy is time-honored in Christian theology. From the earliest apologists through Augustine, Aquinas, Calvin, and others, to several of the specific constructive positions of John Cobb (especially, for this use, his Christological positions [see esp. 22:138–151; 44: 382–394; C: 8–13]), this limited but legitimate use of philosophy is widely recognized. However, both the critical relationship which the modern Christian bears toward the Christian tradition and the critical relationship which the modern historically conscious philosopher bears toward the classical philosophical tradition would seem to disallow the claim that such a legitimate use of philosophy by the theologian, of and by itself, resolves the contemporary theological problematic. Indeed, save for such essentially conservative positions as the kind of neo-Thomism represented by E. L. Mascall[7] or even of the kind of process thought ordinarily represented by Norman Pittenger, this limited use of philosophy is widely recognized as legitimate but inadequate. Such a judgment seems clearly to be the position of Cobb himself. Hence the need to consider what further uses philosophical method may have for the theologian. At least two such further uses seem operative in Cobb's own position.

The second use of philosophy can, I believe, be legitimately labeled philosophy as world view analysis. In such reflection, philosophy is basically understood as the profoundest articulation of the dominant world view (or basic vision) of a given cultural movement and/or historical period. As such, a philosophy develops concepts that can explicate that vision (and its correlative cognitive beliefs) in a manner that is both systematically coherent in itself and appropriate to the vision. This philosophical task is also a legitimate one, and one that Cobb's notion of 'vision' would seem to imply.[8] Although ordinarily informed by historical consciousness in the modern period, such analysis is also ordinarily unable to make convincing claims that the position advanced is other than the most basic articulation of a given cultural movement. In short, this second use of philosophy cannot ordinarily make a convincing case that, besides providing a fundamental explication of the basic preconceptual vision of a given period, the analysis also philosophically transcends its origins in that period. For example, the philosophies of Samuel Alexander, Lloyd Morgan, and, later, Teilhard de Chardin seem to be adequately described as 'philosophies of world view,' i.e., as philosophies that admirably explicate the basic vision (here, evolutionary optimism) of a given historical and cultural movement. Aspects of Cobb's own enterprise (especially his frequent references to 'preconceptual visions of reality' and 'common sense') also seem to employ this use of philosophy for theology (e.g., in comparing the Christian 'vision of reality' and alternative 'visions' [*SCE* 137–151]). Such an understanding of philosophy, however, renders any philosophical claim to transcendence of a relative cultural condition extremely dubious.

If only this and the first use of philosophy are employed by a theologian, only some such model as '*Christian* natural theology' can emerge— a model which, although it employs philosophical criteria and concepts, clearly understands itself as not transcending the given cultural visions (here the Christian vision and the modern) which it articulates. I see no reason to deny that this second use of philosophy, like the more limited first use, is a legitimate one. I see no reason to deny that if these two uses are the exhaustive understandings of philosophy, then a 'Christian natural theology' is an acceptable model. However, there are, I believe, good reasons to deny that these first two uses of philosophy are exhaustive of (or even definitive of) philosophy's central critical task. The burden of the next section will be to advance that systematic claim—and to advance as well the interpretative claim that Cobb's own position on philosophy includes not only these first two uses but also what I shall call a third, critical use of philosophy. If that latter claim holds, then there emerges good reason to deny that Cobb's own enterprise can be designated 'a Christian natural theology' without serious ambiguity.

The crucial systematic issue, then, becomes an examination of the claim that the central critical task of philosophy (the third use) in some way transcends a given cultural situation.[9] Since the emergence of historical consciousness in philosophy itself, this question has, for many contemporary philosophers, become the principal philosophical question. The move to either the concept 'historicity' or the concept 'process' as the central philosophical category in Heidegger and Whitehead respectively amply indicates that for at least these two representative contemporary philosophers this is the case. For there is no authentic contemporary philosophical thought which does not take this historical consciousness of its own condition as the starting point of all reflection. Correlatively, there is no authentically critical philosophy which does not somehow advance the claim that *even* with this starting point philosophical thought transcends its given historical situation. This crucial point is worth dwelling upon. For even if one agrees (as I do) with Cobb's argument that the early Heideggerian dichotomy between 'authentic' and 'inauthentic' existence is too narrowly Western (*SCE* 17; 26:328; E:10); even if one agrees (as I do) with the analysis of Otto Pöggeler to the effect that Heidegger's own position is deeply informed by the Christian tradition,[10] still it remains the case that Heidegger's philosophical positions on the 'ontological difference' or for that matter on the basic components of *an* authentic human existence, if sound, transcend their historical condition. The authentic universality of critical philosophical concepts is not exhausted by the ahistorical pretensions of the age of 'universal reason.' Just as the classics of literature are both rooted in a given period and still 'universal,' so too are the conceptual categories of an authentically critical and self-transcending philosophy. From a specifically Christian viewpoint, moreover, the search for an adequate philosophy would seem to involve a search for a position that can make some such self-transcending claims. This remains true insofar as Christian theologians attempt to render meaningful and true the Christian claim not to exclusivity of truth about the human situation but to the genuine *truth* of the Christian claim for *all* human beings.[11]

Thus far I have employed an example from Heidegger. The important point, however, is that the same claim to philosophical transcendence can be found in Cobb's own work—especially in his interpretation of White-head. The clearest example of this would seem to be Cobb's frequent citation of the Whiteheadian doctrine of experience and its correlative critique of sensationalism (*CNT* 23–46, *inter alia*). I understand Cobb to argue not merely that Whitehead's doctrine of experience is a useful one for Christian theologians to develop more adequate concepts for Christian cognitive beliefs (use 1); nor that this doctrine is merely a profound articulation of our contemporary Western vision of reality (use 2); but rather that Whitehead's critique of sensationalism and his alternative doctrine of experience are adequately and coherently described *as true*. If this is correct, then the implications of that position must be faced without ambiguity: we should employ Whitehead's philosophical doc-trine not solely because it is useful for articulating the Christian vision and for criticizing classical formulations of Christian cognitive beliefs but because it is coherent, adequate, appropriate: in a word, true. Yes, White-head's position, like Heidegger's, is informed by such specific visions of reality as that of Western Christianity. But it is not the case that such cognitive claims are adequately interpreted as expressions of a particular world view. Rather, Whitehead's doctrine of experience can only stand *if* it claims, as it does, to transcend a vision that is *exhaustively* determined by specific cultural contexts.[12] It would seem to follow that insofar as the claims of this third use of philosophy are legitimate, then the theological use of philosophy for a natural theology should find itself committed to only and solely philosophical evidence. In short, the phrase 'a *Christian* natural theology' is a misnomer. To be sure, practically no one remains to defend the indefensible, viz., 'natural theology' in the refuted eight-eenth- and early-nineteenth-century sense of an ahistorical and thereby universal reason. To be sure, most contemporary philosophers are com-mitted to recognizing the intrinsic historicity of all human thought. But that latter claim—as Heidegger and Whitehead among others witness—does not involve the concession that authentic philosophical thought is explained without remainder in terms of its particular cultural world view (or world views). Alternatively, Christian theologians can be more faithful to the critical task which Cobb's own sophisticated position demands, I believe, if they and he refuse to allow the model 'a Christian natural theology' to render the systematic issue of the role of philosophy in theology ambiguous.

B. NATURAL THEOLOGY

Insofar as my preceding analysis is accurate on Cobb's own use of philosophy in the third sense, this properly philosophical moment of his theology can be better described as a 'natural theology.' Indeed, this latter concept is coherent with both the critical task of philosophy (use 3) and the critical task of theology vis-à-vis both the Christian tradition and modernity as outlined by Cobb himself. Methodologically, one has a clear (i.e., nonambiguous) sense of the kind of evidence appealed to in natural theology when one simply states that philosophical evidence alone is applicable here. The historical reasons for adopting the phrase 'natural theology' are also solid. For especially since the unmourned demise of the concept 'Christian philosophy' among Catholic thinkers and the welcome resurrection of the legitimate use of the term 'natural theology' by John Cobb and others, I believe that there is every good historical reason to abandon the ambiguous term 'Christian natural theology' in favor of 'natural theology' as best fitting this crucial aspect of Cobb's own task.

My suggestion has been that each one of the three uses of philosophy in theology can be found in the work of John Cobb. However, a seeming failure on Cobb's part to distinguish clearly and systematically between the second use (world view explication) and the third use (critical, self-transcending argumentation) of philosophy may have led him into what seems to be the ambiguous position implied by the model 'Christian natural theology.' A further formulation of this problem can be made by distinguishing the logical differences between the philosophical questions of religion and theism, on the one hand, and the philosophical questions of a Christology, on the other. In strict logical terms, I believe that the position articulated by Charles Hartshorne (and sometimes by John Cobb) on theism is sound (e.g., 28; D). That position can be rather summarily stated as follows: The questions of religious language (as re-presentative of a dimension of ultimate meaning in common human experience) and of theistic language (i.e., of 'God' as the only adequate and coherent referent of such a dimension) fall under the categories of strict necessity or impossibility. As such, these questions are not properly analyzed by means of the ordinary principles of verification or falsification by particular sense experiences. Rather, theism and religion are strictly metaphysical questions whose logic is one of necessity or impossibility and whose criterion of adequacy must be one applicable to all possible experience (or, alternatively, to the conditions of the possibility of experience). I mention this argument in such summary fashion since it is one with which Cobb is fully familiar.[13] The logical implication of such a position, I believe, is clear: a 'natural theology,' as that discipline committed to reflection upon the cognitive claims of religion and theism, must be a strictly philosophical discipline which investigates all religious and theistic claims and counterclaims.

The questions peculiar to Christology, however, do not entirely fit this rubric. On the one hand, insofar as Christological understanding re-presents the basic religious and theistic meanings of human existence present in those re-presentative events, symbols, concepts, and myths of the Christian tradition, that central aspect of Christology's task falls under the same analysis as explicated above. On the other hand, insofar as Christological understanding also includes an appeal to 'special occasions,' particular events, symbols, concepts, and myths, this aspect of its analytic task falls under the rubric, first, of historical-hermeneutical analysis and, second, of the logic not of necessity but of particularity and contingency. The distinction advanced here is, I believe, an important one. For Christological investigation ordinarily involves both kinds of analysis: first, a strictly philosophical analysis of the necessary or impossible cognitive claims of the religious and theistic meanings represented in Christological language; second, an analysis of the relative existential adequacy of the particular set of Christological events, symbols, concepts, and myths. This latter task, to be sure, cannot appeal to the strict logic of necessity or impossibility. It can, however, develop criteria of relative existential adequacy to analyze the claims of competing symbol systems to re-presenting the necessary religious and theistic meanings of our common experience. Examples of this latter kind of analysis can be found in contemporary theology in such familiar instances as the following: Reinhold Niebuhr's argument for the relative adequacy of the Christian interpretation of our historical existence over alternative interpretations; Paul Ricoeur's analysis of the relative adequacy of the Genesis myth for transforming the human experience of evil over such alternative myths as the Orphic; John Cobb's analysis of the relative adequacy of his proposed post-personal *new* Christian 'structure of existence' over such alternative structures as the Buddhist or the classical Christian.

My point in raising this issue of the different types of evidence and analysis present in the Christological task as distinct from the task of religious and theistic analysis is to suggest that a 'natural theology' can adequately encompass both tasks. Certainly the latter task (the search for the relative existential adequacy of a particular symbol system) is, as Cobb observes, much more likely to be unable to transcend a specific historical vision (e.g., Christian or Buddhist). Still, as Cobb shows by his own proposal of the relative adequacy of 'post-personal' Christian existence, arguments appealing to commonly available existential evidence can in fact be advanced. If this is in fact the case, there seems renewed reason to abandon the residual ambiguity of the phrase 'a Christian natural theology.' The alternative model also seems clear: a 'natural theology' which appeals solely to (1) metaphysical criteria and evidence for analyzing the cognitive claims of all religious and theistic meanings; (2) criteria of 'relative existential adequacy' for analyzing the relative strengths and weaknesses of competing particular symbol systems.

Both tasks are notoriously difficult to execute successfully. Yet precisely my appreciation for Cobb's contributions to both tasks impels me to urge him to drop the ambiguity latent in his 'Christian' model and opt systematically for a model that is well described as a reformulated 'natural theology.'

III. THE HISTORICAL COMPONENT:
ANALYSIS OF STRUCTURES OF EXISTENCE

John Cobb's consistent attention to the problem of relativism for Christian theology has impelled him to develop a positive solution to that central problematic by means of his analysis of various structures of existence. Here a careful scholarly study of various 'structures of existence' and basic 'visions of reality' is combined with Cobb's own original psychological and philosophical development of his basic concepts 'vision of reality,' 'structure of existence,' and 'cognitive beliefs.' Furthermore, since Cobb's most systematic statement of his proposal in the important work, *The Structure of Christian Existence*, it seems clear that he has quietly introduced still more radical concerns (especially concerns for the body, sexuality, and nature) into his own proposal for a *new* postpersonal structure for Christian existence. Like many other readers, I remain indebted to this dimension of Cobb's enterprise and hopeful that it shall soon find its complete systematic expression from Cobb himself. Given my positive assessment of the enterprise as a whole, I shall spend the brief space remaining to articulate certain concerns and questions which if incorporated may strengthen that enterprise.

The first concern can be formulated as follows: if one grants the basic need for and meaning of the central systematic categories 'structure of existence,' 'vision of reality,' and 'cognitive beliefs,' may one not also suggest that such categories can receive some further clarification? At least three explicit clarifications would seem helpful here. First, can we have an explicit philosophical treatment of the exact logical and psychological *relationships* that obtain for Cobb between a 'vision of reality' and a 'structure of existence'? Such an explication would surely aid the drive to systematic coherence to which Cobb has committed himself. Second, do not such secondary systematic categories as 'preconceptual' and 'common sense' also need some sorting out? At times these realities seem almost synonymous. At other times there seems to be some not very clear distinction between them. Since my own position would maintain that the 'common sense' of a particular culture influences but does not exhaustively determine the more basic preconceptual vision of reality operative in that culture, I would be pleased to be informed as to Cobb's final systematic judgment on this question of some importance.

The final question of this first 'internal' concern is a more explicitly methodological one. It seems clear that Cobb is employing both psychological and philosophical methods and categories to develop his central concepts for structural analysis. Granted the general encouragement that Cobb's philosophical commitment to the 'reformed subjectivist principle' gives to such an enterprise, the following question still remains: Is the reader to understand the explicit models for given 'structures of existence' as psychological models, philosophical models, or, as seems more likely, somehow both? If the latter, then what exactly is the relationship between psychological consideration of 'unconscious' and 'conscious' centers of existence and properly philosophical consideration of them? This question can become one of central importance whenever the reader wishes to understand what kind of evidence is proper for judging the models advanced for critical consideration. It may bear repetition, however, to note that I do not understand any of these 'internal' questions as suggestive of some 'fatal flaw' in Cobb's ambitious and impressive structural-analysis method. Rather, these questions are intended to suggest certain moments in the analysis which may need some explicit clarification, not radical revision.

A final, more general and more 'external' hermeneutical concern may also prove helpful for clarifying the exact role that Cobb's analysis may play in the wider discussion of interpretation theory. The basic question informing all these final questions may be formulated as follows: Exactly what method of textual interpretation informs Cobb's analysis? This question is of some methodological importance when one considers the following situation: From the viewpoint of a general interpretation theory, Cobb seems fundamentally interested in the 'referent' as distinct from the 'sense' of Homeric, Socratic, Hindu, prophetic, Jewish, Christian, modern, and post-modern texts. This seems clear precisely since Cobb in fact is concerned to articulate categories ('structure of existence,' 'vision of reality,' 'cognitive beliefs') which serve the function of clarifying the modes of existence and the cognitive claims to which such texts refer.

There is, I believe, every good reason to agree with Cobb that precisely such referential meanings are the principal meanings which the theologian *qua* theologian must find.

However, there remain good reasons for not skirting the issue of the exact relationship of the existential and cognitive referents of texts to the linguistic sense of the texts themselves. Summarily stated, those reasons are the following: From a linguistic standpoint, the referent of texts is at the very least more exactly determined if one can show how that referent emerges from the sense of the linguistic structure of the text itself. Consider for an example the recent work on the linguistic structure of parabolic texts by Via, Perrin, Crossan, Funk, and others. In that work, the use of literary-critical analysis for explicating the basic metaphors and plot structures of New Testament parables can also provide a surer way of explicating the expressly religious referential meaning of such texts with a high degree of hermeneutical exactitude. Given Cobb's own commitment to explicit methodological considerations, it is somewhat puzzling to find him relatively silent on this question of the exact relationship between his proposed referential meanings (structure, vision, cognitive beliefs) and the linguistic structure of classical Christian, Buddhist, and prophetic texts.

By formulating this methodological question by means of one explicit theory of interpretation, however, I do not mean to impose an alternative method of interpretation on Cobb's own analysis. Rather, I employ this explicit method only to suggest that the widely shared concern with interpretation of texts should find more explicit entry into Cobb's enterprise. In fact, I believe that such an explication of the *sense* of classical Christian texts would not force a radical revision of Cobb's own referential meanings. Rather, this explication would probably serve to strengthen the claims that Cobb makes for the existential and cognitive referential meanings he develops. In short, the development of an explicitly hermeneutical method to explicate the relationship of the referents of these texts to their linguistic and literary senses would provide more convincing evidence to the wider audience of linguists and hermeneuts for accepting Cobb's various categories (structure, vision, cognitive beliefs). I am left, therefore, somewhat puzzled as to why such an explicit methodological move is not in fact made by Cobb.

This question becomes even more central in importance when one considers the claims of several analysts in the structuralist tradition that there are, in fact, no referents (or 'messages') to religious texts at all but only linguistic senses (or 'codes'). Since Cobb has consistently committed himself to understanding and, where necessary, challenging all the major expressions of modernity, surely this structuralist challenge should also be accepted. For if the structuralist challenge is to be recognized in its full radicality, one must admit, as Paul Ricoeur argues, that the challenge is more radical than that posed by historical consciousness. For the latter, historicist challenge to Christian meanings (a challenge that Cobb fully accepts) is the challenge of relativism. But the structuralist challenge, in its ideological as distinct from its methodological moment, is a challenge to any meaning (*even relative* historical meaning). More exactly, the structuralist challenge is one major formulation of contemporary nihilism. To be sure, in the philosophical moment of his enterprise Cobb does not hesitate to accept and, by means of his own reformulation of Whitehead, to refute the challenge of nihilism. But in the historical-hermeneutical moment of his enterprise, Cobb manages somehow to be silent on the structuralist claim that the principal texts he analyzes have no existential-referential meaning. Such a silence, I believe, is neither desirable nor necessary. In sum, such a silence should be broken in favor of an explicit consideration by Cobb of how the various 'structures of existence,' 'visions of reality,' and 'cognitive beliefs' he articulates are not imposed upon but demanded by the very linguistic and structural characteristics proper to the 'senses' of the text. I hope that these all too brief remarks may encourage Cobb to take up this further methodological challenge as well with his characteristic care and open-mindedness. If he does, I continue to believe that his basic methodology and his evidence will find not refutation but further support.

On the perhaps presumptuous behalf of the many thinkers interested in the central question of theological method, it remains for me only to express my public thanks to and admiration for John Cobb's pioneering work characterized by both careful scholarship and constructive originality. I hope that my own reflections and questions here may serve to suggest some further possible clarifications, expansions, and/or revisions for his method. As such, these remarks may also serve to strengthen Cobb's already singular achievement in ways that he alone can really show us.

NOTES

1. It is probably not an exaggeration to say that thanks largely to Cobb's important methodological study, *LO*, a 'natural theology' freed of caricature became for many theologians a 'living option' again.

2. These components find their most systematic expressions in *LO*, *GW*, and *CNT*; see esp. *LO* 312–324; *CNT* 252–285.

3. As Cobb indicates (*SCE* 16), these categories become clearer from the work of that book as a whole. For clear definitions and uses of them, see 58:81–83 and David Griffin's introductory essay, 7–10.

4. For a clear and succinct expression of Cobb's full commitment to empirical and rational evidence, see 30:95.

5. For the full and subtle determination of this summary expression, see *SCE* 107–136.

6. For a criticism of this concept along the same general lines, see Schubert M. Ogden, "A *Christian* Natural Theology?" in Delwin Brown, Ralph E. James, Jr., and Gene Reeves (eds.), *Process Philosophy and Christian Thought* (The Bobbs-Merrill Company, Inc., 1971), pp. 111–115.

7. See Cobb's own critique of Mascall, *LO* 48–60.

8. For the clearest example, see *SCE* 24–34; 58:81–85; *CNT* 270–277.

9. The phrase 'in some way' can be specified as follows: To be philosophically meaningful, there must be a *legitimate* claim to the universal applicability of the meanings developed. That the concepts 'universal' and 'ahistorical' are not synonymous terms I take to be the major issue demanding clarification.

10. Otto Pöggeler, *Der Denkweg Martin Heideggers* (Pfullingen: Neske-Verlag, 1963).

11. See Ogden, *loc. cit.*, 114.

12. It should be noted that I am not claiming that Cobb holds to this sharp, alternative position. The problem is, rather, how he can logically avoid it without abandoning the model '*Christian* natural theology.'

13. For example, in his refutation of Flew and Matson, D 112–117. Cobb's own method of approach to the question of theism seems better described as far more tentative than Hartshorne's rigorous logical arguments.

SOME CRITICAL REMARKS ABOUT COBB'S
THE STRUCTURE OF CHRISTIAN EXISTENCE[1]

By Traugott Koch
Translated from the German by Clark M. Williamson[2]

I

For some time a renewed interest in the phenomenon of religion, and particularly that of foreign, non-Christian religions, has been observable. This interest comes from an intellectual distance, particularly with regard to 'well-known' Christianity, and primarily demands objective—i.e., unprejudiced—information. What is sought is an impartial, descriptive communication of knowledge, not testimony and proclamation, not subjective engagement. Whoever is of the conviction that such an intellectual distancing from the subject matter of religion is not finally appropriate, insofar as religion strives to overcome such distancing in order to determine a person's life—it is precisely this person who also cannot be closed to that interest; otherwise, the person surrenders religion to irrationality, i.e., to speechlessness: he negates the truth content of religion. Yet, if one tries to pursue this interest in religion today, one will quickly ascertain how little the scholarly and dominant theology is fitted to this end. Nevertheless, deficiency and incompetence with regard to the content of religion are found not only in theology but just as much in the contemporary science of religion. The generally accepted definition of what religion is seems to us to fail to express the function of religion for the comprehension of the world and for the individual and social self-consciousness of man.[3] Into this lacuna steps Cobb's book, *The Structure of Christian Existence,* which seeks to determine the peculiarity of Christianity within the context of a general history of religion. Wolfhart Pannenberg, in his preface to the German translation, energetically recommends this open and comprehensive perspective as a prototype.

With explicit reference, Cobb takes up again Ernst Troeltsch's orientation to the subject (*SCE* 13f): like Troeltsch, Cobb inquires into the specific characteristic of Christianity—into the 'essence of Christianity'— and into the justification of its claims to uniqueness and finality in relation to the other world religions—into the 'Absoluteness of Christianity' (see *SCE* 7, 22). It is unnecessary to emphasize that Christianity is chiefly and principally conceived by Cobb as one religion alongside of others. Cobb argues that the principle of organization of the various religions is the developmental-historical succession; nevertheless, he intentionally separates the followir₰ two themes: in a first train of thought the particularity and uniqueness of Christianity, as that of any other religion, arises in the context of the history of humanity; only afterward in a comparative evaluation can its high rank or absolute superiority be considered and ascertained (*SCE* 137, 16-18). Regardless of the stage of development to which it belongs, each religion—i.e., each of the structures of existence underlying the respective religions—represents in itself "a peculiar and . . . ideal embodiment of human possibility" (*SCE* 16, cf. 18). For the selection and arrangement of the stages, Cobb acknowledges the Christian perspective which he brings with him to the task. Nevertheless, he intends to provide the most objective description possible of each religion and structure of existence (*SCE* 23, 137).

In order to determine the basic identity of Christianity, as that of every other religion, Cobb comes to an important prior decision. In distinction from Troeltsch he holds the view that the uniqueness of a religion or structure of existence is formed and exhibited in its developmental-historical origin, in the original situation of its genesis (*SCE* 109). Its further history brings only the shaping of the original attainment (c.f. *SCE* 143f). Correspondingly, according to Cobb, the specificity of Christianity can be known adequately in its beginnings in Jesus and in the original community. It is only on the basis of this conception that the origination of a new structure of existence is primarily and almost exclusively interesting (see *SCE* 18). The ambiguity of this thesis—which implicitly denies the proposition according to which the 'essence' of a thing is its history—cannot be discussed here; however, for Cobb's whole inquiry it shows the significant connection of a historical theory with a phenomenological topology.

Since for Cobb the origin of religion determines its peculiarity, a religion is understood if its place in the history of humanity is recognized. Cobb adopts the organizing principle of the history of religion. Fundamentally, he conceives history in analogy with biological evolution and characterizes his position as 'evolutionary-historical.' According to this view, human beings have "evolved from subhuman animal forms" and after the conclusion of biological evolution an independent development of structures of human existence begins (*SCE* 17f). This development fundamentally constitutes the history of humanity; in it the plurality of religions becomes arranged, and in this framework the religions are understood. Thereby this theory recognizes the viewpoint of continuity as well as that of discontinuity: in a continuous becoming, a structure of existence permits a wider, new one to come forward as one or more of its elements augments and acquires relevance. Thus each stage makes available the conditions for the next stage of development. Yet the breakthrough to a new configuration emerges discontinuously and brings about a different order of all the structural elements, so that existence then becomes structured around a new central point. Thus an independently new structure of existence originates only through the "crossing of a threshold" (*SCE* 20f, 23, 58, 154).[4]

Consequently, Cobb is cognizant of three—only three—important thresholds of this type in the previous development of humanity: (1) the genesis of man himself—Cobb describes this situation, the 'original condition' as it were, as 'primitive existence.' Then (2) there is the emergence of civilization in the fourth millennium before Christ, described as 'civilized existence.' And (3) there is the time of the 'axial period' in the first millennium before Christ (*SCE* 21f). Cobb takes over from Karl Jaspers the designation and also, to some extent, the characterization of this third stage. With Jaspers, he shares the belief that in this axial period, at least in India, Greece, and Palestine, independently of one another, a self-understanding of man was attained which still determines our present time (*SCE* 22, 53). This notion has a more wide-reaching consequence for Cobb's theory of development: the development of humanity, which previously proceeded in one line, divides into at least three parallel directions, so that the Indian, Greek, and Palestinian religions and structures of existence come to stand at equal rank alongside one another. Only in Greece and Palestine does there develop a further stage in the evolution of human structures of existence: in the former the transition from the pre-Socratic, Homeric existence to Socratic existence; in the latter the rise of Christian existence from the prophetic existence of the Old Testament. Thanks to this presentation of three similarly arranged stages or sequences of development on the ground of a definite axial similarity, Cobb for his position is released from the religious-historical problem, namely, how Buddhism, the Greek understanding of self and world, Judaism, and Christianity can be meaningfully organized in a unified line of development culminating in Christianity. At the same time, the evaluation from which the higher valuation or eventual superiority of Christianity shall result is limited to these three configurations—to the Buddhist, Greek, and Christian types of existence (see esp. *SCE* 139f. (Only in a qualified sense is Judaism still to be included in this calculation of relative value.) What remains is the question how to evaluate these three types. However, on the basis of this presentation, the evaluation of these three types can only be a secondary one; the question of the validity of all pre-axial religions and structures of existence has already been decided, *de facto*, by history itself, through its evolutionary progress (see *SCE* 140).

II

Certainly the main difference from Troeltsch's conception lies in the fact that Cobb—radicalizing Bultmann's example and H. Jonas' interpretation of gnosticism—attempts not only to go behind the doctrines of a religion but to go behind the religion itself as a phenomenon to the constellation of consciousness at the root of it, to the structure of existence occasioning it. We have already heard that this underlies historical change. With this turn toward consciousness, Cobb stands in the modern history of human self-understanding and the Protestant understanding of faith, as this is pre-eminently documented in Schleiermacher's work. Accordingly, man no longer understands himself, even in relation to God, in terms of an objective, prior actuality. In all respects he asserts the right to his own involvement and to his self-assured insight. Whatever shall concern him must be reconciled with his autonomy; otherwise it falls under the judgment of heteronomy and falsehood. Doubtless this turn toward consciousness brings great difficulties for the understanding of a pre-modern, traditional culture and religion, and one wishes that Cobb had reflected more significantly on these difficulties. Indeed, in one place he admits and even stresses that the consciousness of man has not developed by itself, independently of its understanding of the world and God; rather, precisely the latter (e.g., the idea of God as person) was of far-reaching consequence for the self-understanding of man (*SCE* 98). On the one hand, this possibility of self-understanding in relation to the other has to be explicated even psychologically within the general concept of man. On the other hand, this possibility makes Cobb's fundamental premise altogether problematic.

With regard to the establishment of his point of departure in consciousness, Cobb refers to the fact that in the age of secularization religion itself is questionable and the concept of God entirely so and indeed lacking in self-evidence (see *SCE* 14). In fact, the problems of theologians and students of religion are thereby maximized. I think that Cobb must seek to ascertain what religion is in the course of history and what functions it maintains; its inner connection with the historical understanding of self and world is to be thrown into relief so that it becomes obvious the extent to which at least the consciousness of God is not without that of the self, indeed finally how none—neither world, nor self, nor God—is without the other. For instance, on that account, Schleiermacher and

Troeltsch have conceived, each in his way, a concept of consciousness which *constitutively* comprises the religious relation to God. Such thought has its parallels in Continental philosophy since Descartes, which does not conceive of consciousness as purely immanent but grasps it on the part of the human self: on the part of man's capacity to reflect upon himself and to act out of himself. This Continental concept of consciousness or subjectivity emphasizes particularly the human intention to gain the self and it maintains that the human consciousness, correctly understood, is conceivable only with and in its horizon of world, of objectivity, and of intersubjectivity. Cobb, on the contrary, adopts the concept of consciousness of empirical psychology, which aims at the distinctive marks immanent to the consciousness for *itself*. This psychological concept defines consciousness as if its relations were not constitutive; these relations are exclusively understood as the immanent components of consciousness. Accordingly, Cobb describes the development of mankind's consciousness for itself and only coordinates and relates the consciousness so understood and this history of consciousness with the phenomenon of religion and the various religions in their historical becoming. From a definite constellation of consciousness he throws light on the religion appertaining to it—that is the great and illuminating merit of his discussion. However, he does not undertake the task of making evident to what extent consciousness *by itself* implies religion and how the historically definite consciousness at any given time implies the definite religion. Thus the reader finds in great parts of Cobb's book, largely in its fundamental parts (see only the second chapter), an analysis of the evolution of consciousness without a discussion of the essential relationship of consciousness to religion and to the history of religion. *On the whole, this forms the characteristic feature of Cobb's work, that it primarily gives a synopsis of the history of human consciousness, conceived as the augmentation of consciousness, and places the religions in relation to this development.*

Therefore Cobb holds that the deepest and most illuminating way to understand the religions in their heterogeneity is to conceive religions and cultures as 'embodiments' of different structures of existence (see *SCE* 19). In this way a whole culture, differentiated within itself in manifold ways, shall be disclosed "in terms of fundamental and unifying factors" (*SCE* 76). The structure of existence in question consequently functions as the central point of determination which provides the basis for understanding all aspects of this culture. In principle this intention is to be affirmed unreservedly, for it alone guards against a thoughtless amassing of material. Yet Cobb understands this center of a culture as a structure of existence and for him that explicitly means an 'intrapsychic structure' (*SCE* 143). Thereby the psychological constitution of man at the moment is elevated to the conditioning ground of the understandings of the world and of God; in other words, what God and the world are historically depends on how man is momentarily given to himself in his psychical life. Not accidentally, Cobb himself expresses this consistent wording of his methodological procedure clearly in only one place, where he formulates it as follows: the "new existence gave rise" to the "cultures and religions" in question (*SCE* 53). There may be good grounds for this caution of the author, for it is anything but certain that the psychical can be made the conditioning ground of everything else. So at other places he says that a new structure of existence arises "parallel with" a definite sociohistorical development; therefore he speaks of a correspondence between objective, worldly history and psychical constitution (*SCE* 21f; cf. *SCE* 49f, 57). Indeed, the conditioning aspect can be reversed and described in such a way that cultural conditions force a change of the subjective situation (*SCE* 61). The concept of consciousness reduced to the immanent-psychical must entangle Cobb's project in contradictions; thus, for example, Greek man has understood himself in terms of the objective world, he has formed the categories of his self-understanding from his conception of the world—and yet, according to Cobb, this Greek understanding of reality was grounded in a definite 'psychical act' (*SCE*, Ch. 7). In the description of Buddhist existence we are again and again directed to the strict interwovenness of the psychological themes with the ontological question of reality (e.g., *SCE* 62); nevertheless, the position of the psychical consciousness which is attained is said to have 'organized' and 'structured' the world for the Indian (*SCE* 60). It can be seen that the psychological reduction of the concept of consciousness takes its toll.

III

Because of its enormous significance for Cobb's entire undertaking, his concept of consciousness requires still further explication. Without such an attempt, I fear that one will simply not understand the present work. Therefore some further theoretical observations basic to Cobb's position are necessary.

In some places Cobb points out that he participates in the theological development of the process philosophy of Alfred North Whitehead.[5] For our purposes no detailed presentation of this theory is necessary. In the present work Cobb expressly limits the use of Whiteheadian categories "to a minimum" (*SCE* 21). Nevertheless, two principal traits of this theory must be mentioned: (1) Cobb places great value on the fact that this system is in accord, in all its statements, with the results of the natural sciences (*SCE* 149). Who would not value highly such excellence? Yet this harmony also contains the disadvantage that this philosophy, together with this theology, remains true to the objective, 'scientific' way of thought of natural science or, if one will, is imprisoned by it. The subjectivity of man (his consciousness!) and the personhood of God are conceived of just as objectively as the inner structure of a stone. This holds true, even if one takes the theorem of the 'subjective pole' into account. And this is the case in spite of the fact that Cobb knows and realizes that the scientific knowledge of natural science is an 'abstraction' (*SCE* 92). (2) The objectivism of thought manifests itself particularly in the fact that this philosophy understands all reality as the synthesis of simple ingredients, of little particles of events. Each actual entity consists in a multitude of momentary events ('actual occasions'); such an occasion forms itself in the encounter with others, and each actual entity *is* nothing but this occasion.[6] The means by which man or God is distinguished in principle from an elementary particle of microphysics is only the higher aggregative complexity, which results in the fact that one particular event-particle structures the rest—it becomes the dominant one ('dominant occasion'). This means that the organism is centered (see *SCE* 33). In my opinion this concept of reality can be labeled as relational, quantitatively built up atomism.

With regard to Cobb's concept of consciousness, which, as stated, lays claim to the major part of his inquiry: in looking at the experience of man and at his existence—i.e., at the way he is given to himself as subject— Cobb chiefly and fundamentally distinguishes between the unconscious and the conscious part (*SCE* 16, 27). In reality, of course, both parts, while being graded variously according to their portions, are always together (*SCE* 25, 30, 32). The category of the *unconscious* does not have as its content that which is potentially capable of being conscious but which currently escapes my attention and knowledge; rather, the unconscious is equated with the psychical processes which by nature evade conscious knowledge. The transitions and the processes in memory serve as examples (*SCE* 28). Cobb defends the thesis that the predominant part of human experience takes place in this unconscious way and that the unconscious activities have primacy even in rational thought (*SCE* 27f). As a consequence of Cobb's viewpoint the unconscious represents not only the fundamental but also the most primordial aspect of human experience in the evolutionary development. Here we may remark that Cobb's definition of the unconscious does not give it any positive content of its own—as opposed to the psychoanalysis of Freud, for instance, according to which the unconscious is defined in terms of drives. The unconscious as conceived by Cobb can in effect have all sorts of things as its content, but the question is where its contents come from.

In order to understand Cobb's concept of *consciousness* and his conception of the unconscious, one has to realize that he permits consciousness primarily to be defined by its relation to the environment, and that means, to its sense data. This, of course, does not mean that Cobb is an empiricist; he at least completes the empiricist's point of view by referring to the unconscious. But, as pointed out, he thinks of 'unconsciousness' as something that has an existence of its own (intrapsychic) and therefore, in my opinion, he does not develop an appropriate concept of mental acts: he does not conceive of consciousness itself as strictly and always consisting within and out of its intentional acts, which the subject potentially can always understand and in which it is able to understand *itself*. If the relations of consciousness to the different 'given' contents (as not produced by the subject) are taken into view, Cobb describes these relations according to the stimulus-response scheme (see esp. *SCE* 34, 36, 39). First of all, consciousness is not only passively related to the sense data produced by the environment; it at the same time actively takes hold of the environment—accompanied by the aim at survival and the necessity of adaptation (see esp. *SCE* 30). It is obvious that here we have to do with an empiricist concept of consciousness—without intentionality and reference to horizon. The consequence of this concept of consciousness results in the assumption, which Cobb holds as self-evident, that all contents of consciousness which cannot be accounted for by assimilation from the environment are originally in the unconscious and in unconscious processes. Cobb's concept of the unconscious is a residual category.

Nevertheless, according to Cobb, the relation of consciousness to its environment by no means constitutes consciousness in its totality. However, to the extent to which it is defined by this passive and active relationality, Cobb characterizes it as *receptive consciousness* (e.g., *SCE* 26, 39, 42, 49). It represents the underlying and original part of the consciousness —a thesis which is said to be supported by the fact that mere awareness precedes conscious experience (*SCE* 27). The receptive consciousness carries out the assimilation of stimuli and signals, their interpretation and allocation to the organs, the release and regulation of reactions (*SCE* 30, 36f). Cobb also associates intelligence and thereby a great part of rationality with consciousness or a part of consciousness as thus defined (*SCE* 40); for intelligence scrutinizes the contents of consciousness in relation to the environmental data and learns from experience (*SCE* 35, 48f, 56). Of course, the processes occurring in the receptive consciousness must never themselves and as such become known; in this sense they can occur unconsciously and continue to do so.

Alongside of the consciousness which is receptive, related to the environment, Cobb recognizes a second consciousness which, as it were, comprises the mental-inward side, and this he calls *reflective consciousness*. This one is characterized by the following traits: it grasps and conceives meaningful contents, it is realized in symbols and not in signals which merely release reactions, as it is organized by means of these symbols (*SCE* 25, 39f, 41, 47). Here every element of experience stands in a symbolically mediated and articulated context of meaning (*SCE* 27). It holds good for symbolization as well as for the processes of reflective consciousness that can occur unconsciously without knowledge and actually do originally occur in this way (*SCE* 49).[7]

The beginning of an individual continuity of experience, of a subjective-psychical life and of a specific life history, lies in the receptive consciousness when and insofar as the interpretation and organization of contemporary stimuli are influenced by the accumulated experiences of an individual past (*SCE* 37). Nevertheless, it is only as reflective consciousness—through the act of symbolization—that the psychical becomes subjective in the human sense and autonomous, and comes to an inner life.

For thereby it releases itself from the necessary presence of the signified. "The symbol does give to man immense psychic power—the power to bring together past and present in conscious memory"—to anticipate the future—"and to relate and order what is otherwise simply given" (*SCE* 41). No longer captivated by the pressure to survive, this consciousness seeks experiences for their own sake and for the sake of subjective satisfaction. Indeed, this aim at one's own satisfaction, this striving for individual enrichment through experiences of all kinds, drives and guides the consciousness which is organized in symbols and the act of symbolization—and this primarily in an unconscious manner (*SCE* 38–41).

At all times all three constituents—the unconscious, the receptive consciousness, and the reflective consciousness—participate in each human experience. Yet for the momentary historical constitution of the human being, for the structure of existence which has been attained, it is decisive whether it is the unconscious or the receptive consciousness which governs the reflective consciousness and its symbolic capacity. One way or another the psychic life of man has its unity and central point, which structures everything else—and which Cobb defines as the 'seat of existence' (*SCE* 54)—in the reflective consciousness. But, we must assume, the reflective consciousness gains its orientation either from the unconscious or from the receptive consciousness; the 'seat of existence' can, according to Cobb, change from the unconscious to (the receptive) consciousness. The reflective consciousness lacks autonomy of content. And it also is not clear how the reflective consciousness is influenced by the unconscious: is this relation again to be imagined in terms of the stimulus-response scheme?

The major distinction in the development of structures of existence, therefore, consists in whether the seat of existence lies in the unconscious or in consciousness (*SCE* 16, 54, 56). *Primordially* the unconscious prevailed in the symbolically organized, reflective consciousness: man understood himself and his world (which at the same time was a world of gods) in symbol systems in which the unconscious process of meaning expressed itself and unconscious needs find their satisfaction (*SCE* 40, 49). Man thinks mythically and lives in the myth. To put it differently: according to Cobb, myth is the result (!) of unconscious symbolizations (*SCE* 42, 56, 60). Above all, in this primordial phase of humanity the "symbolization based on unconscious processes" dominates over intelligence, over the highest form of the receptive consciousness (*SCE* 41).

With the passage of the seat of existence into consciousness the symbolic capacity, the reflective consciousness, is released from the predominance of the unconscious (*SCE* 49); the receptive consciousness gains influence on the reflective consciousness and its symbolization (*SCE* 48f). However, that means only that it is now determined by intelligence and in that way is rationalized. This new stage of development, rationality, has considerable consequences for both parts of consciousness: now the symbolizations are checked by intelligence, and intelligence—related to the environment as the receptive consciousness—no longer perceives the world in signals but in symbols (*SCE* 48). The reflective consciousness becomes capable of thinking in new meaningful concepts which conform to the observable world (*SCE* 50). Symbolization and, along with it, action can be consciously controlled (*SCE* 57f). Man learned to "observe, calculate, plan, and organize on an entirely new scale" (*SCE* 50). This rational consciousness (*SCE* 57), moreover, includes the fact that man, including his conscious processes, becomes aware of himself, he gains self-consciousness (*SCE* 47); the reflective consciousness attains value also for itself (*SCE* 48f). Only now is man autonomous in his psychic life (*SCE* 49); he actually knows of the autonomy of his subjectivity: individuality and freedom arise. At the level of consciousness attained in this way, the sole differentiating criterion for the various structures of existence that are still possible consists of this question: Where does man locate his self, with what in himself does he identify himself as 'I'? (*SCE* 65, 88f, *et al.*)

As one sees, Cobb conceives the development and origin of the structures of existence as the history of man's becoming conscious, as the increase in consciousness. This history, as outlined by Cobb, reads intricately and sophisticatedly, and yet basically Cobb recognizes only two decisive stages of development: one under the dominance of the unconscious and the other under the dominance of consciousness. But consciousness reaches its highest development as rational. Between these two major phases—the original human stage of 'primitive existence' on the one hand and the rational consciousness of the 'axial period' on the other—is posed a middle stage in which the unconscious and mythical still prevail, while at the same time unconsciousness begins to gain strength. This is 'civilized existence.'

IV

Cobb subsumes the religions under the history of man's becoming conscious.

With regard to the religion of *primitive,* archaic existence, Cobb stresses that the mythical symbols give meaning to the whole of life and thus religion itself is not represented as one fact alongside of others (*SCE* 43, 60, 111). All experiences in their meaning are simply given and are parts of a fixed whole; at that time, differentiations are scarcely made (*SCE* 43). Man exists as a member inserted into a tribe or a horde (*SCE* 55f); his modes of behavior are regulated by means of taboo norms (*SCE* 43f). Cobb understands mythical thinking as projecting from the unconscious and on the basis of unconscious needs (*SCE* 42f, 56, 74f). It must be asked whether these characteristics are not exhausted in negative limitations; in any case, the special world of myth and the function of myth in its own meaning do not become clear. Also not clear is what it means to say that the original locus of religion, of the idea of the gods, is the unconscious. Tillich's position—that myth deals with the powers of origin—is not mentioned. If Cobb accepts the thesis employed in the criticism of religion, according to which mythical thinking 'projects' its gods—this being the origin of God—would not it then be necessary for the concept of projection to be at least cleared or possibly rejected by reasons if theology is to survive after all?

In the structure of *civilized* existence, broader ranges of existence become progressivly rationalized; but the dominance of mythical thinking, particularly in symbolization, could not yet be broken down (*SCE* 47, 50, 53). With the rise of rationality the feeling of isolation grows; moreover, religion maintains, alongside of its continuing function of giving mythical meaning, increasingly the function of overcoming the experience of isolation and separation from the whole (*SCE* 61).

In the *axial* period, the rationality of consciousness, which holds sway until the present, dominates over the mythical symbolization; individuality in common with the consciousness of an autonomous biography arises as well as freedom (*SCE* 54–57). At the same time, however, the conscious control of psychical processes always includes a considerable oppression, particularly of the unconscious (*SCE* 117). Religion primarily has the task of freeing the self-aware individual from the suffering connected with his individuality (*SCE* 61).

Cobb describes the structure of *Buddhist* existence in detail and with much interest of his own. From his statements a fundamental trait of Buddhism is to be emphasized: Indian man, it is true, knows the rational consciousness and its biographical identity; yet he tries to escape precisely from it in order to liberate his I from the course of occurrences and from its sorrowful isolation (*SCE* 63f, 64f, 71f); he tries, above all, to get rid of his I as something that endures in the flux of time (*SCE* 67). Cobb himself expresses doubt whether this attempt with its constant self-negation of the conscious I can lead to a positive end (*SCE* 71). But one hears nothing of the profundity of self-destruction implicit in this.[8]

The pre-Socratic, *Homeric* existence of Greece is characterized by the fact that here rationalization has especially to do with the contents of the receptive consciousness, the data of the objective world. Objective reality is grasped as such, distinguished from the subject, i.e., according to Cobb it becomes aesthetically distanced in a psychic act. Hereafter, Greek man understands himself by reference to this objective givenness. Either he experiences the unconscious, mythical symbolizations as numinous and threatening powers (e.g., fate) or he projects the gods as if they were visible objects and thus arranges them in the aesthetically distanced, beautiful cosmos and in the disinterested beauty of man (*SCE* 74, 77).

Socratic existence completes this objectification, with man perceiving himself as individual subject and identifying himself with his reason—with the reason which he recognizes in the unchangeable forms of the cosmos. The highest and most ethical rationality is connected with a constitutive impersonality of the subject (*SCE* 87f, 90, 104f). As an appendix, one chapter deals expressly with *gnosticism*.

The characteristic feature of the *prophetic* existence of the Old Testament is seen in the way in which man, through the relationship to the one God and through the intensity of his understanding of God, acquires an ethical overall understanding of himself and thus becomes a responsible person endowed with conscience (see esp. *SCE* 100f, 103, 105f).

In terms of content and tightness of argumentation, the description of *Christian* existence may exceed all others. In Cobb's view the central point of the message of Jesus consists in the fact that he renews the sense of the immediate presence of God on the level of the rational self-aware consciousness (*SCE* 111f). For Jesus, in order to be a fully responsible person, consciousness is realized in an existence which has its content wholly in God (*SCE* 112). Only in this way is that conscientious inwardness attained (*SCE* 114) which, at the same time, turns aside from human capacity, even the ethical capacity, and expects everything from the initiative of divine love (*SCE* 116). This structure of existence also characterizes the post-Easter community which conceives that existence as the efficacy of the presence of the Spirit of God (*SCE* 117). Cobb calls this Christian way of existing 'spiritual existence' and defines it comprehensively as "self-conscious self-transcendence" (*SCE* 122). 'Spirit' means that man as responsible subject does not have his center in himself, but transcends and overcomes everything that he is in himself and thereby even himself (*SCE* 119, 123f, 143f). The dependence on God's initiative raises and enlarges the responsibility of the person: man becomes responsible beyond his capacity for all his actions and his whole being. He discovers in himself the difference between will and ability and thus experiences the abysmal nature of sin (*SCE* 121). He must overcome his self-centeredness and yet cannot do this by himself (*SCE* 133f). Cobb does not pass over in silence the precarious constellation of this self-conscious self-transcendence, but emphatically refers to the constant possibility of distorting it into the inhumane (*SCE* 122f, 134f, 141). His brilliant analysis reaches the peak of its forcefulness where he shows that the spiritual existence of the Christian only realizes itself in the freedom of love. For self-transcendence is no new circle around itself only when the I is capable of freedom from concern for itself and of the unpremeditated love of the other. The spiritual I cannot attain such love by means of itself—and yet this love is its only salvation (*SCE* 135). (Cobb dedicates a special chapter to the concept of the historical development of love in its major forms.)

The closing chapter dealing with the theme of the finality of Christianity brings a carefully balanced evaluation of the structure of Christian existence in comparison with the Jewish, Greek, and Buddhist structures. Cobb raises the theme of the absoluteness of Christianity as the question whether and to what extent Christian-spiritual existence has taken up into itself, fulfilled, and transcended all the other structures of existence of the axial period (*SCE* 144). This is answered in the affirmative with regard to the Jewish and Greek structures of existence, but the consideration immediately follows that an indigenous transformation of Judaism toward spiritual existence is only to be hoped for (*SCE* 142), and that the current discussion with the Greek view of man and the world will decide whether Christianity has the power to endure *vis-à-vis* modern reason (*SCE* 147, 150). With regard to the Christian-Buddhist alternative, however (neither of which can be considered as fulfillment of the other), the chance for superiority and continuation in the modern world is open (*SCE* 148ff). Finally, "new modes of Christian existence" are demanded (*SCE* 150).

All the aspects of Cobb's work could not be discussed here. A critical discussion of the presentations of the various religions would have to repeat once again in detail the criticisms raised against Cobb's concept of consciousness and of religion in general. Thus, for example, what God means for the structure of Christian existence is not explained, indeed because the goal-directedness of human self-transcendence is not taken into account. Also, one would like to hear some reflections on the functional involvement of religion with the structural constitution of other regions in life (e.g., politics). And in the concept of each religion, must one not consider its possibilities of promoting inhumanity and of perverting itself into a demonic distortion, which is only too often realized, and hence include the criticism of religion in the understanding of religion? Nevertheless, all the criticisms can only aim at summoning one to discuss Cobb's insights into the structure of the religions and of Christian existence.

NOTES

1.This critical review of Cobb's *The Structure of Christian Existence* (The Westminster Press, 1967) is intended as a continuation of the discussion we had in Mainz (mentioned by Cobb in the Preface) when he was planning this book. This is a translation of a slightly revised version of a review (which appeared in *Theologia Practica*, VII [Jan. 1972]) of the German translation of Cobb's book, *Die christliche Existenz. Eine vergleichende Studie der Existenzstrukturen in verschiedenen Religionen.* Mit einem Geleitwort von Prof. W. Pannenberg (Munich: Claudius Verlag, 1970).

2. [Assistance in the first draft of this translation, made from the German review article, was received from Helga Reitz. This first draft was examined by Traugott Koch, who at this time made some substantive changes in the text and also, in collaboration with J. Metzner, suggested many valuable improvements in the translation. Some further suggestions by David Griffin were also incorporated in the final version.—Note by Clark M. Williamson, translator.]

3. For some frank confessions of the present desolate situation, cf. the article by C. Colpe, "Religion und Religionswissenschaft" in the *Taschenlexikon. Religion und Theologie*, ed. by E. Fahlbusch (Göttingen: Vandenhoeck & Ruprecht, 1971), III, 259–263. With regard to the concept of religion in German Protestant theology, cf. H. J. Birkner, "Beobachtungen und Erwägungen zum Religionsbegriff in der neueren protestantischen Theologie," in *Fides et Communicatio. Festschrift* for M. Doerne (Göttingen: Vandenhoeck & Ruprecht, 1970), 9–20.

4. One may ask here whether this evolutionary conception of history after the manner of biology is sufficient to allow it to become comprehensible that it is man himself as subject who makes his history. In order to clarify this, the concept of consciousness which Cobb uses needs further discussion.

5. Cf. the title of his earlier publication, *A Christian Natural Theology: Based on the Thought of Alfred North Whitehead* (The Westminster Press, 1965).

6. In agreement with Whitehead, Cobb states: "The final ontological individual [i.e., not divisible] is the actual momentary occasion of experience" (*SCE* 69); "an occasion of human experience is [!] human existence at a moment" (*SCE* 33).

7. Cobb takes over the conceptions of the symbolically organized and self-realizing consciousness from Susanne Langer and thereby from Ernst Cassirer's *Philosophy of Symbolic Forms*—certainly without the horizon of objectivity with which it is conceived by Cassirer.

8. Cf. K. Heinrich: *Versuch über die Schwierigkeit nein zu sagen* (Frankfurt: Suhrkamp Verlag, 1964), 121–129: "Exkurs über Buddhismus als Ausweg."

SPIRITUAL EXISTENCE
AS GOD-TRANSCENDING EXISTENCE

By Thomas J. J. Altizer

I

I am persuaded that John B. Cobb, Jr., is now and has been for some years engaged in a fundamental theological turn, a turn in which he will cease to be a primary spokesman for the Chicago or any other liberal Protestant theological tradition, and is rather opening the center and ground of his theological thinking both to the religious worlds of the East and to the truly contemporary modes of thinking and understanding in the West. Not the least of the primary problems which this turn poses is the problem of language and imagery, and above all, the primal problems now posed by that fundamental theological word 'God.' Recognizing as does no other process or liberal theologian that the transcendent, personal God toward whom Christian existence has been directed has faded from our vision (58:91), he is searching for what he calls a new vision which must see "God as a relational process immanently at work in all things, calling them toward life, love, and creative self-transcendence, responsive to all that happens and interacting with it" (58:94). With the fading of the transcendent, personal God from our Christian vision, the very word 'God' has become our most immediate theological problem, and a problem that will not be resolved or disappear until we evolve or become open to a new theological language and imagery. At no other point is the liberal theological tradition more alien to the problem at hand, and the apparent recent success of process or dipolar theology should not deceive us at this point, for its success has been won in an isolated theological and ecclesiastical world which at best has a sectarian relationship to the dominant worlds about and within us.

Cobb is the only major Whiteheadian or dipolar theologian who is open to the cultural, the conceptual, and the human problems posed by the death of God in the modern world, and it could even be said that his theological turn has been occasioned by these problems. Yet as every critical theologian must agree, no theologian has yet become open to the depth of these problems. A recent exploration of these depths is embodied in the magnificent work of Michel Foucault, *Les Mots et les choses,* which is perhaps the first philosophical work to integrate the worlds of Hegel and Nietzsche. In reaching his conclusion, Foucault draws a distinction between the new dawn which was manifest in the nineteenth century and the 'perilous imminence' whose promise we fear and whose danger we welcome today.

> Then, the task enjoined upon thought by that annunciation was to establish for man a stable sojourn upon this earth from which the gods had turned away or vanished. In our day, and once again Nietzsche indicated the turning-point from a long way off, it is not so much the absence or the death of God that is affirmed as the end of man (that narrow, imperceptible displacement, that recession in the form of identity, which are the reason why man's finitude has become his end); it becomes apparent, then, that the death of God and the last man are engaged in a contest with more than one round: is it not the last man who announces that he has killed God, thus situating his language, his thought, his laughter in the space of that already dead God, yet positing himself also as he who has killed God and whose existence includes the freedom and the decision of that murderer? Thus, the last man is at the same time older and yet younger than the death of God; since he has killed God, it is he himself who must answer for his own finitude; but since it is the death of God that he speaks, thinks, and exists, his murder itself is doomed to die; new gods, the same gods, are already swelling the future Ocean; man will disappear.[1]

For Foucault, man is an invention of recent date, and one perhaps nearing its end. And the disappearance of man is not simply in the wake of the death of God but also in profound correlation with it.

Earlier in his analysis, and in the context of speaking of the modern rebirth of philological exegesis, Foucault affirms that this is not a matter of rediscovering some primary word that has been buried in language, but rather of disturbing the words we speak, of denouncing the grammatical habits of our thinking, of dissipating the myths that animate our words, and of rendering once more noisy and audible the element of silence that all language carries with it as it is spoken. Now we are called to destroy syntax, to shatter tyrannical modes of speech, to turn words around in order to perceive all that is being said through them and despite them. Then he can declare: "God is perhaps not so much a region beyond knowledge as something prior to the sentences we speak; and if Western man is inseparable from him, it is not because of some invincible propensity to go beyond the frontiers of experience, but because his language ceaselessly foments him in the shadows of his laws: 'I fear that we shall never rid ourselves of God, since we still believe in grammar.' "[2] This citation from Nietzsche is not without significance, for Foucault identifies Nietzsche as the first to connect the philosophical task with a radical reflection upon language. And it is that reflection which leads to the discovery of a point at which man and God belong to each other, and at which the death of God is synonymous with the disappearance of man. Yet the man who disappears is the man who appeared with the end of metaphysics, an end primarily effected by Hegel, and effected by way of an inversion of the entire field of Western thought. Perhaps when God is truly and finally no longer sayable, then our actual words will be inverted so as to make manifest *all* that is being said through them and despite them.

II

A witness from a different realm, Graham Greene, has recently spoken of his conversion in the first volume of his autobiography. In that very context, he declares that he now dislikes the word 'God' with all its anthropomorphic associations and prefers Teilhard's 'Omega Point.'[3] It is difficult to refrain from associating Greene's dislike of the word 'God' with his account of the process of literary composition:

> It is better to remain in ignorance of oneself and to forget easily. Let the unemployed continue to lurk around the pubs in Vauxhall Bridge Road and the kidnappers drive out of Heidelberg toward the frontier, safely and completely forgotten; we ought to leave the forgotten to the night. If one day they find their way into a book, it should be without our connivance and so disguised that we don't recognize them when we see them again. All that we can easily recognize as our experience in a novel is mere reporting: it has a place, but an unimportant one. It provides an anecdote, it fills in gaps in the narrative. It may legitimately provide a background, and sometimes we have to fall back on it when the imagination falters. Perhaps a novelist has a greater ability to forget than other men—he has to forget or become sterile. What he forgets is the compost of the imagination.[4]

Can Greene, the novelist, teach the theologian that our task is now to forget God? Can God be the compost of our imagination, and compost in the sense that his decaying body is both the source and the consequence of whatever life our words may possess? If we can forget God and leave him to the night, then if one day he happens to return in our language, it should be without our connivance and so disguised that we do not recognize him when we see him again. Is this not a precise formula for our theological task?

Perhaps the most offensive quality of John Cobb's previous theological work is the innocence with which he speaks of God. Can the theologian be so innocent? Or is this truly innocence? Could it be a merely apparent innocence which at bottom is a mask disguising a resolute refusal and evasion of the dead God who embodies the disappearance of man? This question, of course, could be asked of any contemporary theologian who continues to speak of God, including myself, but it has a particular relevance to the theological turn in which Cobb is now engaged. In *God and the World,* surely a transitional work, the primary image of God is that of "the One who calls forward," and God is identified as the source of novelty and the lure to richer actualization. Here, the thesis is established that *"Christian faith is not essentially bound up with the God who is seen primarily as Creator—Lord of history—Lawgiver—Judge* and who has so long dominated the Christian sensibility and the imagination of the West" (*GW* 37). The God whom the Christian knows in Jesus is something quite different from that Creator-Lord. Thus Cobb here demands that the Christian must now as never before, in naming God, *"allow what appeared in Jesus to give meaning and content to the Reality we thereby name."* Significantly enough, in his unpublished "A Personal Christology," Cobb has confessed: "Insofar as I have known God at all it has been through Jesus" (D:7). But what or who is that God whom we can know only through Jesus? Indeed, has a God ever appeared in Christian history, at least in its spoken or linguistic expressions, which makes manifest that God, and that God alone, who is manifest in Jesus?

These questions are asked from the perspective of our own time and history, a time in which the transcendent God of Christianity has faded from our vision, even if he has not been absent from our speech. Here the theologian must make audible that silence for which Foucault calls, for perhaps only the audible silence of the transcendent God can provide a voice through which the God who is manifest only in Jesus can speak. Thus we must forget the transcendent God of our Christian history, and that forgetting must be so radical that we will never recognize the voice or presence of that God again. Can this be what Cobb is now about? If so, one obstacle to his goal will be his apparent bondage to univocal language about God. As recently as 1969, Cobb could declare: "I see the task of theology, in distinction from prayer, praise, and preaching, to be the literal and direct statement of what is intended and believed" (35:98). He associates this aim at literalness with the empirical temper, and more specifically with the Chicago theological school. One noteworthy characteristic of the Chicago tradition, as Cobb points out, is that those who most fully absorbed its empirical temper have been freed from the necessity to rebel (35:96). Startling as this statement may appear, it surely is true, and it leads one to wonder if the empirical temper of Chicago had simply never known the transcendent God of Christianity. If not, then this brings fuller meaning to Cobb's confession that he has known God only through Jesus. But is the God who is known only through Jesus a God who can be spoken of in direct and literal discourse?

One also wonders what Cobb's repeated calls for a new Christian vision can mean in this context. Is that vision manifest in American liberal Protestantism? Perhaps in some sense this is so, but if so it remains theologically unexplored to this day, and above all unexplored in liberal theological language about God. But perhaps the distinctive quality of empirical theology as opposed to liberal theology as a whole is that it says so little about God. In this sense one could even say that only now is Cobb becoming an empirical theologian, and perhaps silence will be his direct and literal way of speaking about God. But how can the theologian be silent about God, how can he forget this primal ground of his thinking, his language, and his experience? If, as Foucault affirms, our language ceaselessly foments God in the shadow of his laws, so that God is something prior to the sentences that we speak, can we turn the word 'God' around in order theologically to perceive all that is being said through and despite this primal word? Can we render once more noisy and audible the silence of a spoken theological language? Perhaps, at bottom, Cobb has been engaged in a quest to speak the word 'God' so as to make manifest this silence. Then we might suspect that not only has his speaking about God been a decisive way to his theological turn, but that in our day it is genuine speech about God which makes noisy and audible the silence of our primary theological word. Not only must we live with this silence, but we cannot speak as theologians unless we make it audible, and doubtless the little that we can make audible is a noisy disturbance of the words which we speak.

III

It is my conviction that Cobb's most significant breakthrough thus far is contained in *The Structure of Christian Existence*. Not only does this book seek out and embody a distinctively modern religious and cultural relativism, but it is written within the horizon of the modern historical consciousness, thereby abandoning an abstract and purely deductive theological language. Here, a wide historical variety of structures of human existence are taken seriously within the context of their own inherent modes and identities, which in itself is theological testimony to the disap-

pearance of a singular and universal 'man.' Is it also testimony to the
death or disappearance of a singular and universal 'God'? Certainly 'God'
is here invisible and unspoken upon the pages that deal with primitive,
Buddhist, Homeric, and Socratic existence. 'God' first truly appears in
the book in the discussion of prophetic existence, which is understood as
a decisive breakthrough into a new structure of existence, a structure that
is realized by knowing Yahweh as the great 'I.' Then man's world is freed
from the sacred meanings of the unconscious, a truly individual human
decision initially appears, and the 'person' first of God and then of man
emerges clearly for the first time in history. This 'personal I' is a transcendent, responsible center, and thus Cobb can correlate prophetic existence with personal existence. At this point Cobb establishes a gulf between himself and his liberal roots, for he intends to understand
Christian existence as transcending individual and isolated personal existence.

Now it is essential to Cobb's position to maintain that, while original
prophetic existence understands God as a person, in the prophetic tradition God's actual present effectiveness is a matter of belief rather than of
immediate apprehension. Thus the central and decisive fact in the appearance of Jesus was the renewal of the sense of the present immediacy
of God. Cobb is troubled by the term 'renewal' in this context, but he
employs it because he is persuaded that in Jesus the full responsible
personhood of prophetic existence was combined, without loss, with an
existence that found its content in the fully personal God. But in what
sense 'fully personal God'? Cobb is careful to note that Jesus' proclamation of the immediacy of God took the eschatological form of the proclamation of the imminence of his Kingdom, which meant the apocalyptic
end of the world. For both Jesus and apocalyptic Judaism, as opposed to
the prophets, there was a total hiatus between what God was and the
actual condition of the world; hence, the nearness of God could only
mean that this world could not stand before him.

> Yet it is not enough to think of Jesus as an apocalyptic preacher,
> however true this may be, for his apocalypticism was quite distinct
> from that of mainstream Judaism. For the latter, the conviction of the
> apocalyptic end belonged with the experience of God's absence and
> remoteness. It was because one *believed* that God must vindicate the
> righteous that one knew that the transformation must come. But for
> Jesus, the apocalyptic message stemmed from the *awareness* of God's
> nearness. Hence, the Kingdom was at hand, and, indeed, at hand in
> such a way as to be already effectively operative in the moment. The
> difficulty of unraveling the elements of futuristic and realized es-
> chatology in the message of Jesus stems from the fact that, far more

basic for him than any conceptual scheme of the sequence of events, was the fact of God's present reality to him and for him. That present reality meant that God was effectively active in that *now*. It meant also that the world as it was constituted in that now was already on the point of dissolution. (*SCE* 112–113)

For Jesus, an apprehension or awareness of the imminence of the Kingdom was a function of the experiential knowledge of the immediacy of God. But can the God who is fully present and active in an eschatological or apocalyptic *now* be identical with the fully personal God who is manifest in prophetic or personal (as opposed to spiritual) existence?

This question might be rephrased by asking how God could be known as a 'personal I' if he is apprehended as being immediately present? Is there not an integral correlation between the great 'I' and *belief* as opposed to *awareness?* Cobb insists that the 'I' of personal existence does not and cannot transcend itself, and it is precisely at this point that the spiritual existence of Christianity transcends the personal existence of prophetic Judaism.

The message of Jesus, on the one hand, and the experience of the Holy Spirit, on the other, broke through this last barrier to total responsibility. The essential demand of God has to do precisely with those dimensions of selfhood which the personal "I" cannot control. To accept those demands and to accept responsibility to live in terms of them is to accept radical responsibility for oneself, and that is, at the same time, to transcend one's self. That means that the new spiritual "I" is responsible both for what it is and for what it is not, both for what lies in its power and for what lies beyond its power. For the spiritual "I" need not remain itself but can, instead, always transcend itself. Thus, spiritual existence is radically self-transcending existence. (*SCE* 124)

If spiritual existence is *radically* self-transcending existence, then certainly the spiritual 'I' cannot be identical with the personal 'I.' How, then, can the fully present God be identical with the fully personal God? It is noteworthy that as Cobb moves more fully into a discussion of spiritual existence the very word 'spirit' seems to replace the word 'God.' This transition is fully apparent in the following important passage:

Although the personal character of the I-Thou relation between man and God was thus preserved, what resulted in the Christian experience of the Holy Spirit was not what is usually meant by the I-Thou relation, for that relation suggests overagainstness, confrontation, speech, and response. The relation of the primitive Christian believer to the Spirit was far more intimate than that. There was no imagery of spatial separation or of demand and obedience. There was, rather, the imagery of two spiritual realities, each fully responsible for itself and self-identical, nevertheless mutually indwelling each other. (*SCE* 118f)

Notice the transition here from God to Holy Spirit to Spirit to two spiritual realities mutually indwelling each other. Surely the word 'God' could not have been employed in this paragraph after its first clause, and if it had been employed in the last sentence, it would actually have inverted its intended meaning!

IV

Even the possibility of speech and response cannot be present in what Cobb identifies as the uniquely Christian experience of 'spirit.' Can he be engaged in a Christian witness to 'spirit' when he then proceeds to engage in a discussion of 'spirit' which limits its meaning to the self-transcending character of Christian existence? Is this discussion possible precisely because it ignores or forgets God? In the final chapter of the book, devoted to the question of finality, Cobb opposes his own relativism by making the claim that Christian or spiritual existence is not only unsurpassable but is also final. And, in my opinion, the following four sentences from that chapter embody the fullest expression thus far of Cobb's theological turn:

> Spirit is defined as self-transcending self. It is the nature of spirit to transcend itself in the sense of objectifying itself and assuming responsibility for itself. Hence, this indefinite transcendence of spirit is also and already spirit. In *this* direction, there is no possibility of further development, only of refinement and increasing understanding of the reality already given. (*SCE* 143f)

Now when we realize that Cobb has previously declared that spiritual existence expresses itself in the imagery of two spiritual realities, each fully responsible for itself and self-identical, but nevertheless mutually indwelling each other, then we must ask if it is possible within this context to speak of 'spirit' apart from 'Spirit.' Surely to speak of "spirit" here is simultaneously and necessarily to speak of 'Spirit'!

Granted that in defining spirit as self-transcending self, Cobb may well intend to limit the meaning of spirit to the self-transcending character of Christian existence. The question is whether or not this is truly possible. If the spiritual 'I' always transcends itself, must not this be a transcendence which not only is open to but also actually incorporates that Spirit with which it therein mutually indwells? Grammatically this is an awkward expression, and it is awkward precisely because if spirit and Spirit mutually indwell each other, then it is no longer possible to speak of a genuine distinction between spirit and Spirit, and hence no longer possible to say 'spirit' without simultaneously saying 'Spirit.' Is this a naming of God, and a Christian naming of God, a naming that allows what appeared in Jesus to give meaning and content to the Reality we thereby name? If so, it is a naming in which the word 'God' must be unspoken or forgotten, and unspoken because with its utterance it is no longer possible to say either spirit or Spirit. Note the significant fact that immediately preceding his definition of spirit as self-transcending itself, Cobb says that in this mode of analysis the way in which God is present to and in occasions of experience has been omitted from the discussion. Then he says:

> Precisely the relationship to God is the decisive category for understanding the distinctiveness of Jesus' own existence or "person" as well as the possibilities of a new reality in the future. In this mode, we can hope for something quite different from anything we now know. (*SCE* 143)

But does this also mean that in knowing spirit we know something quite different from anything we can now know about God?

Is it possible, then, to think of Cobb as a 'last man' who is engaged in a contest with the death of God? Is Cobb's a theological turn which situates itself in the space of that already dead God, thereby accepting the freedom and the decision of the murderer of God? What else could now make possible a theological speaking of spirit which refuses to speak of God? But Cobb still believes in grammar, and is obviously not rid of God, so perhaps his language about spirit is also language about God. If so, this is surely without Cobb's connivance, and it may well be that God is so disguised in this language that even Cobb does not recognize him in this form. Could it be that self-transcending self is also and necessarily God-transcending self? Is it the nature of God to transcend himself in the sense of objectifying himself and assuming responsibility for himself? And is this the God who appears in the *awareness* of immediate presence as opposed to mere *belief*? Is not the great 'I' a selfhood which cannot transcend itself, and cannot do so because it is self-identical with itself? Then the God-transcending self would be the God transcending the fully personal God, and self-transcending self would be a transcendence of *all* isolated and truly individual selfhood. Moreover, this is a way of speaking not only of the death of God but also of accepting the freedom and the decision of the murderer of God. Following Bultmann, and perhaps more deeply his evangelical roots, Cobb places an enormous emphasis upon a truly individual human decision. But has not Nietzsche taught us that a total decision just as total responsibility embodies a willing of the death of God? How could an existence that accepts radical responsibility for itself be an ultimate and final breakthrough if it finds its content in the fully personal God of prophetic and pre-Christian existence and consciousness? How could a final breakthrough be simply a *renewal* of the sense of the present immediacy of God? Is not spiritual existence, as Cobb understands it, far rather an embodiment of the self-transcendence of the personal God (the God who is known primarily as Creator, Lord of history, Lawgiver, and Judge), of God as 'spirit' transcending himself as God? Then, and only then, it might be possible to speak of the finality of Christianity.

V

But as Cobb makes abundantly clear in his recent work such a finality is not a finality in the traditional imperialistic or monolithic sense. A significant clue to Cobb's new quest is the theological seriousness of his dialogue with Buddhism, for this has few if any signs of the older Christian quest to transcend or negate Buddhism, and it intends to take Buddhism seriously in terms of its own inherent and integral identity, and does so in the context of a quest for a new form and identity of Christianity. Cobb's theological position does not share the illusion of older forms of purely Western Christian theology that a God-consciousness underlies an only apparently non-theistic Buddhism, and he is in no way tempted to identify Buddhism as a pure form of paganism or revolt against God. On the contrary, it is rather the Godlessness of Buddhism in conjunction with the purity of its religious way which attracts this theologian who has given so much of his life to a quest for the meaning and identity of the Christian God. It might also be said that it is the modern Western discovery of Buddhism and the East which has been an essential ground of the end of the traditional quest for God. Now we know that the traditional Christian God can be neither universal Lord nor universal Spirit, and Cobb among other theologians today is showing us that an encounter with a purely religious Godlessness can be a decisive way to a new form of Christianity.

Thus far Cobb's encounter with Buddhism is most fully recorded in *The Structure of Christian Existence,* and it cannot be accidental that this is the book which most fully expresses his new understanding of spiritual existence. It might even be said that here it is Buddhist existence rather than prophetic existence which is the real foil or challenge to spiritual existence, and this is, above all, true in terms of the centrality of love or compassion in each of these primal forms of human existence. One won-

ders if a theologian innocent of Buddhism could have reached an understanding of a spiritual 'I' which can always transcend *itself*, or of a spiritual
existence which is a *radically* self-transcending existence. For the self
which is here understood as radically transcending itself is not simply the
sarx of Pauline and Lutheran theology, nor the inauthentic and unen-
gaged man of modern existential theology, nor the guilty self of pride and
sensuality. It is, rather, the personal 'I' of a fully individual selfhood, an
'I' that is fully responsible for itself. Moreover, the transcendence of this
personal 'I' issues in the acceptance of a radical responsibility for oneself,
a responsibility that is identical with compassion, and a compassion that
is possible only by way of a transcendence of one's self. At this point there
are significant parallel points in Cobb's presentations of the meaning of
Buddhist and Christian love in *The Structure of Christian Existence*. The full
practice of the Buddhist way effects the destruction of the individuality
produced by consciousness, and this destruction is equivalent to the
realization of compassion.

> Compassion was the opposite of desire. Desire was the longing of
> some subject for some attainment or possession for itself. It presup-
> posed, therefore, a differentiated world. Insofar as one realized the
> unity in the voidness of all things, desire was impossible and was
> replaced by total openness to all things and undifferentiated good-
> will. (*SCE* 130).

Two pages later Cobb affirms that Christian love transcends prophetic
love because it is a new love of which man is incapable in the free exercise
of his will. The Christian commandment of love transforms the prophetic
commandments of love of God and love of neighbor because the love that
it requires is no longer under the control of the will.

> Especially in Israel, it is clear, love to God and fellowman was central
> to the law as a whole. Nevertheless, that which was commanded in
> these laws could be almost equally well expressed by the commands
> of obedience and justice. Only in Christianity did love as something
> transcending such obedience and justice become in itself the fulfill-
> ment of all that was required. This means not only that the love
> involved was something new, but also that the need for such love was
> now unlimited. (*SCE* 133)

What is the relationship between an unlimited love which transcends
the will and a total openness to all which is a consequence of the destruction of conscious individuality? In his one negative criticism of Buddhism
in this book Cobb says that Buddhism is led to empty the environing
world of real significance for human existence (*SCE* 68n17). But is this
not precisely the ground of its realization of total compassion? And what

significance can the environing world have for an unlimited love which is unattainable by our own efforts? Cobb can even say that the spiritual man can only genuinely love if he finds that he is already accepted, thus he does not need to save himself, and thereby his psychic economy is opened toward others, to accept them as they are (*SCE* 135). But is not such Christian love fully parallel to the world of Mahayana Buddhism, and so much so that 'spiritual man' could here refer equally to Buddhist or Christian? True, Cobb insists that in Christian love, lover and loved retain their full personal, responsible autonomy, and that is certainly inconsistent with Buddhism. Yet is it consistent with a total love which transcends the will? Is not full personal, responsible autonomy a form of will, and of self-will at that? How can a radical transcendence of selfhood retain a personal and autonomous self? One is tempted to say that the Buddhism which Cobb presents in this book is far closer to his own vision of Christian love than is anything which he can say concretely about Christianity.

Or is Cobb now undergoing a decisive change at this point? In an address in 1971, he could say that we now need to envision a post-personal future (53:12). Do we likewise need to envision a post-personal God? Indeed, is such a vision already present in Whitehead himself? Every occasion, for Whitehead, is completed by passing into objective immortality, wherein it is everlasting, and is thus devoid of that perpetual perishing which is the end of all actual occasions. Cosmology, in this sense, is claimed by Whitehead to be the basis of all religions. He even makes the claim that 'everlastingness' (the 'many' absorbed everlastingly in the final unity) is the actual content out of which the higher religions historically evolved. Thus, in the closing pages of *Process and Reality,* Whitehead gives us something like an eschatological vision of a post-personal God and a post-temporal world:

> God and the World stand over against each other, expressing the final metaphysical truth that appetitive vision and physical enjoyment have equal claim to priority in creation. But no two actualities can be torn apart: each is all in all. In God's nature, permanence is primordial and flux is derivative from the World: in the World's nature, flux is primordial and permanence is derivative from God. Also the World's nature is a primordial datum for God: and God's nature is a primordial datum for the World. Creation achieves the reconciliation of permanence and flux when it has reached its final term which is everlastingness—the Apotheosis of the World.[5]

If God and the world are at bottom all in all, and all in all in reciprocal and integral relation to each other, then everlastingness or the apotheosis of the world is just as essential to God as is the eternity of God to the temporality of the world. Here, everlastingness is the actual content of both Buddhism and Christianity, and Whitehead's final vision would appear to be equally rooted in the 'cosmotheism' of Mahayana Buddhism and the Kingdom of God of Christianity. Therein Buddhism gives us a full vision of the primordial ground of everlastingness, just as Christianity gives us a comparable vision of an actual movement to everlastingness. If only Christianity gives us a vision of the salvation of obstinate, irreducible, matter-of-fact entities, which are limited to be no other than themselves,[6] then it is Buddhism which is most effectively mediating to the West today a vision of totality wherein such salvation can be envisioned as an apotheosis. To follow this path is obviously to abandon and leave behind the traditional and personal God of Christianity, but is this not the actual direction of Cobb's new theological project?

NOTES

1. Michel Foucault, *The Order of Things: An Archaeology of the Human Sciences* (translation of *Les Mots et les choses*) (Pantheon Books, Inc., 1971), 385.

2. *Ibid.*, 298.

3. Graham Greene, *A Sort of Life* (Pocket Books, Inc., 1973), 146.

4. *Ibid.*, 159f.

5. Alfred North Whitehead, *Process and Reality* (The Macmillan Company, 1929), 529.

6. Alfred North Whitehead, *Science and the Modern World* (The Macmillan Company, 1925), 137.

PLURALISM AND FINALITY
IN STRUCTURES OF EXISTENCE

By Robert Neville

I. STRUCTURES OF EXISTENCE

The encounter of Christianity with the world's religions is one of the events of most importance to Christians in the twentieth century. Few thinkers have interpreted it with the universal sympathy, clarity, and originality of John Cobb. Among the principal sources of his effectiveness in this regard are his sophistication in abstract metaphysics and his feeling for 'heart' religion. The former makes him an astute critic of abstractions, as Whitehead would say, steering easily around the pitfalls of misplaced concreteness. The latter gives him a strong sense of the meaning of religion in the ways people live; the generalizations with which he interprets various 'structures of existence' ring true to the most important things in life.

These virtues are apparent and polished in Cobb's book, *The Structure of Christian Existence.* Briefly told, the plot of that book begins with the emergence in history of 'axial' man from his primitive forebears.[1] Pre-axial man took the unifying principles of his life from unconscious elements and thus is best understood in terms of his myths, the projections of his unconscious. The evolution of axial man, which took place in China, India, Persia, Greece, and Israel in the thousand years before Christ, involved the development of organizing centers of experience in the reflective consciousness rather than in the unconscious. These new 'seats of existence' struggled in various ways to gain power over the other elements of experience, and different cultures developed different structures of existence accordingly. Cobb details a one-two line of development for India, Greece, and Israel.

In pre-Buddhistic India, according to Cobb, the centering of experience in consciousness brought to focus an awareness of the suffering of an endless, meaningless round of life; the structure of axial existence which was developed, therefore, involved perfecting a distinction between the phenomenal world of change and the ontologically more real world of the unchanging self. Buddhism pushed a step further in declaring the transcendent world of the self to be unreal and empty; although personal virtue consists in compassion for the plight of all, peace consists in extinguishing the desire for surmounting the plight.

In Homeric Greece, the structure of existence for axial man took the form of aesthetic distance from an objective world, enjoying the world for its formed character apart from desire and mythic projection. The development of the Socratic mentality, according to Cobb, made reason the seat of existence, objectifying aesthetic distance and adding a dialectical critical motif to man's relation to the objective world.

The structure of existence for the ancient Hebrews was that of prophetic man, for whom something like the modern notion of the person took predominance over momentary existence as well as aesthetic feeling and rational distance. A 'person,' in the prophetic sense, is one who takes responsibility for his actions, objectifying his perception and reason. The seat of existence for a 'person' may be called his will; the emphasis on voluntary definition of human life is closely connected with man's definition of himself over against a God who makes contracts with promises to keep and a morality to be obeyed. From prophetic man came 'spiritual' man, the Christian structure of existence. The crucial threshold to cross is objectifying the will itself and taking responsibility for one's very feelings. A spiritual man is one who is concerned not only to do what is right but to have a right heart motivating his impulses. Adultery, for Jesus, was not a matter of what one does but of what one wants to do, even if the impulse is inhibited. The spiritual structure of existence involves an indefinite process of self-transcendence, whereby any stage of development is itself objectified and made the subject of personal responsibility.

This brief description of Cobb's thesis overschematizes his subtle and nuanced account. But it gives the general rationale for his historical conclusion. The Greek structures of existence have been incorporated, albeit in subordinate positions, into the Hebraic-Christian structure, forming the Western tradition. The great alternatives today, therefore, are Christianity in its developed form and Buddhism. (Cobb copes more subtly than I have represented here with the problem of the earlier stages —Hinduism, Homeric Greece, and Judaism—resisting absorption into the later stages.) Modern man is faced with a choice between Christianity and Buddhism as structures of existence with which to start. Cobb emphasizes that this is a genuine choice between options that are to all appearances irreconcilable.

Both historically and systematically, the relation of spiritual existence to Indian existence is radically different from its relation to either personal or Socratic existence. In the case of both personal and Socratic existence, consciousness, selfhood, and the power of the soul to transcend and to act upon its world were prized. Spiritual existence carried farther in the same direction a development already affirmed and far advanced. Thus we can speak of fulfillment as well as transcendence or transformation of existing structures. But the Indian sages of the axial period had opposed this whole line of psychic development. To them it was essential either to establish the self beyond the differentiated world, which included the flow of psychic experience, or to annihilate selfhood altogether. Spiritual existence is not the fulfillment of this effort. Nor can the Christian recognize in extinction of his self-transcending selfhood the fulfillment of his existence. Finally, it is impossible to conceive a third structure in which both spiritual selfhood and the extinction of self could be subsumed in some higher synthesis. Buddhism, as the culminating achievement of India, lies side by side with Christianity as an alternative mode of human realization. It stands as the ultimate challenge and limit to the Christian claim to finality. (*SCE* 148)

II. FINALITY

The bottom-line question of all this analysis is what choice finally to make. This is the question of finality. Cobb astutely warns against choosing on the basis of some rational value system, because that value system inevitably will reflect the perspective of one of the principal contending structures of existence. Of course Buddhism is deficient in accounting for history and the fulfillment of the concrete person, he says. And Christianity is deficient in that its ideal of Christ's love is impossible for this world and itself contributes to the suffering to be avoided in compassionate emptiness.

Cobb's own argument takes the general form of saying that Christianity appears from the present point of view to have more fruitful survival value in a world of technological advance and ecological threat. Particularly, because the underlying values of Western technology are winning the world, the importance of personal fulfillment will come to dominate worldwide passions. In another essay, "A New Christian Existence" (58), Cobb deals at greater length with needed developments of Christianity to make it more fit for a genuinely worthwhile structure of existence.

My own view is that the problem of finality is misstated here, however elegantly Cobb has delineated its many parts. The model of choice between exclusive options is unrealistic, I shall argue. Perhaps it reflects a legacy of Barth's 'God's thrown stone,' somewhat surprising in Cobb's tradition. The better model is a more natural one for a Whiteheadian, namely, that a contemporary person seeks to take up a position in wider environment of unintegrated resources. The diverse histories of the resources in his world make them mutually incompatible as they stand in many respects. But so are the givens for any occasion of existence. Taking up a present position requires selecting from among the resources and appropriating them in compatible ways. The free choice comes in the selection and emphasis given to a multitude of resources, not to the wholesale adoption or rejection of complete environments.

All people in the world today are in the problematic situation of having to make for themselves a structure of existence. For Christians the Christian resources are closer to us and more easily integratable with the rest of our environment than non-Western resources; in the same way, the past occasions of our body are closer to us than those of someone else's body. But the cultural resources of structures of existence are *mental* entities, prehended by 'hybrid physical prehensions,' to use Whitehead's term; far more than past bodily states they are malleable and combinable with what appear to be their contraries. It is easier to adopt the mental resources of Yoga than the body postures, because they can be adopted in small doses and in transformed ways: in sitting, either you get both feet on your thighs or you do not. Easterners will find it easier to employ Eastern structures of existence, and Westerners the opposite; but each can appropriate something of the resources of the other.

What I am suggesting is that we are in a situation, worldwide, of constructing a new structure of existence, employing the old diverse structures as data to be selected, weighed, and harmonized. The new structure will be punctuated in different ways by people from different traditions. Whether it will bear the name of one or several of the old structures depends partly on adventitious factors of who writes the histories and partly on real elements of relative dominance. The criteria guiding the development of this new structure of existence are those guiding any creative effort: Preserve as much as possible of the achieved richness of the past. Attend to enriching the relevant present and future environment as much as adaptively possible. Make the environment more stable and supportive of the higher human values, and make those higher human values contain the richest intensities of experience possible. Respect the historical idiosyncracies of individual choices.

III. WHAT ARE THE ISSUES?

Cobb's reading of the historical situation and mine each are hypotheses. Probation of the hypotheses stands logically (though perhaps not existentially) prior to the choice between structures of existence. But how does one test the hypotheses against each other? That they are both readings of the historical situation means that the tests must be empirical in some sense. But the tests are not simply the discovery of more facts. Rather, they have to do with the interpretation of the facts, and the debatable factors in interpretation have more to do with models in this case than simply with facts.

1. As the first step in defense of my hypothesis I would like to put forward the thesis that the belief that something is appropriate for someone logically entails the belief that everyone concerned with the issue ought to believe the same. This is not to say that the same thing is appropriate for all people; but those who are concerned and knowledgeable ought to agree on what is appropriate for whom. Although this very complex thesis cannot be fully defended here, some of its points of argument can be mentioned.

First, the thesis reflects the underlying claim that evidence for a belief has some objective status over against mere assertions regarding the belief. Therefore, if all persons understood a given set of categories couching a statement, even if all the persons differed over the usefulness of the categories, they could agree about whether the evidence as defined by the categories supported or undermined the belief.

Second, although people may begin with different categoreal perspectives, even different structures of existence defining those perspectives, there are objective issues of enriching life that reward or negate those perspectives. Although each perspective defines the values it enjoys, and perhaps does so in a way that no value can be articulated outside some perspective or other, there is an immediacy to value enjoyment that nudges the perspectives themselves. Otherwise there could never be a good reason for developing or altering any of the structures of existence.

Third, this thesis regarding the universality of a claim for appropriateness or truth derives from the Greek structure of existence, and therefore is parochial. But both Cobb and I accept it, and however transmogrified, it seems to have survived the Greek perspective into the Christian, and to have appeal even to those structures of existence originating in India and China.

I share with Griffin an uncertainty about where Cobb comes down on the issue of the relativity of perspectives regarding structures of existence. What should be said seems to me the following. Whereas completed statements (systems and structures of existence) are by definition relative to their worlds, ongoing judgments are by definition partly outside the perspectives that provide their resources; mentality is not finished fact, and therefore cannot be given definite position in a perspective. Only by choice or heedlessness can a judgment on a perspective repeat the criteria in the perspective itself. Contemporary people are right, therefore, in believing either that others ought to agree with them about what is appropriate for various subjects or that evidence ought to be offered to warrant altering the original beliefs.

2. The second step in defending my hypothesis is to suggest that we live in a sufficiently unified world as to constitute a community of inquirers or spiritual pilgrims. The Buddhist is making claims about what is appropriate as an existential structure for human beings, including Christians, and the Christian makes equally inclusive counterclaims. This point is presupposed in the very suggestion that structures of existence are genuine alternatives. If neither felt the other were his fellow, or if the only communication were the hurling of anathemas, there would be no significant contradiction.

This step, coupled with the first, yields the conclusion that Christians, Buddhists, and all other contenders ought to be looking for agreement on what structures of existence are appropriate for the various interested parties. This is not to say that the same structure must be agreed upon as appropriate for all, only that they all agree on the just distribution. I am not at all sure that, in posing his options, Cobb means to suggest that Buddhism is right for some people, Christianity for others; but that would be a logically tenable position.

3. My third step is to point out that this logical possibility is not a historically real one. We simply live in too much a world society, defined by causal interactions if not common culture, to accept that other people are to be humanly addressed according to radically different structures of existence.[2] If we were dealing not with structures of existence but with skin color or even national heritage and ethnic identity, the relativity problem would not be so acute; in fact, that kind of diversity would add richness. But the issue as to structures of existence involves commitments regarding basic visions of reality, a point Cobb has made as well as anyone. Choices regarding structures of existence are not merely cognitive matters, as might be implied if the discussion dealt only with the visions of reality. They also are choices in which the chooser takes responsibility for the kind of human existence he makes for himself. This is as true of the Hindu, Buddhist, Taoist, and Confucianist as for the Westerner. Responsible structures of existence are what define people as

human in relations with each other. The other person's appropriate structure of existence should be seen as appropriate for him from the perspective of one's own structure of existence.

These three steps have been taken in defense of a thesis concerning a logical *ideal*. It would be 'nice,' from a rational point of view, if these universalistic considerations could be realized in the structures of existence aborning. Without them a world community is in grave difficulty, if not impossible. But the conditions for realizing the logical ideal simply may be absent. It might be the case that the only possibilities for making the various old structures of existence mutually relevant would involve abstracting them to the point where they would become mere doctrines, lacking existential force. This would mean in effect that a person would have to choose one structure of existence or none (but not make up a new one out of many), which is Cobb's position.

I want to argue against this, suggesting reasons why conditions do obtain for taking seriously the ideal of developing a new structure of existence both appropriate to the modern world and faithful in the main to the principal cultural traditions. The position should not be overstated. It cannot be argued, for instance, that somewhere the new structure of existence already lies in wait, although an argument from *esse* to *posse* is the strongest kind. Nor do I mean to suggest that the majority of the people in the world are on the threshold of a new structure of existence; my claim is only that the cultural leaders, the pacesetters, are. Finally, I do not mean to suggest any certainty that the threshold will be crossed. On the contrary, various antagonisms might make it impossible. The abyss of savagery is particularly close in this age of nuclear war, economic and social injustice, and the brutalization of nature. At the same time, the impetus to solve these problems fosters, and may indeed require, the development of the delicate but intense sensitivities of a new structure of existence.

IV. THE ORIGIN OF STRUCTURES OF EXISTENCE

The first argument for my conception of the present historical situation is a criticism of Cobb's model for the development of structures of existence. He traces the rise of the current panorama from primitive developments of conscious signals and unconscious symbols through the increasing entry of symbols and their conscious manipulation into consciousness. Axial man, centering the organizing principles of his experience in various foci of conscious life, arose across the globe in different guises. But from this point, Cobb's hitherto genetic account of human nature becomes radically historical. Each kind of axial man developed in ways unique to his tradition, so that, after two or three thousand years, we have the basically pluralistic situation affirmed in the long quotation above.

Is this sudden historical diversity what we would expect for structures of existence? Probably not. Organized and deeply rooted historical diversity is to be expected when the environments within which peoples develop are different and reinforce different cultural artifacts. Geographic and climatic differences give rise to different historical routes where they bear upon cultural development. Particular historical decisions and events also form different environments from which historical divergence takes place. So, for instance, the tropical climate of India makes possible the religious style of the naked ascetic forest dweller, a style impossible in deserts or very cold climates. And the personalities of heroes and contingencies of holy places and events will differ from culture to culture. Admitting that these historical differences account for differences in *modes* of existence, to use Cobb's term, they seem not to be so powerfully relevant for determining the basic *structures* of existence.

The issue is whether the conditions, to which the development of a structure of existence is an evolutionary response, are massively inherited by all men simply by virtue of being men. Is there such a thing as 'the human condition'? Or are the relevant conditions for a structure of existence the sort that are likely to be local to particular cultures? This is an empirical issue, and I shall suggest evidence that the basic conditions are those massively inherited by all cultures.

Suffering is universal, although its forms may be idiosyncratic. Language is universal and, if Chomsky is correct, even its basic forms are universal. Because suffering must be coped with and coping is expressed in language, the symbolic interpretation of suffering is close to the heart of communications that define human life in community. Furthermore, it seems universal that all peoples experience a conflict between their symbolic representations of the meaningful world and symbol-shaking intrusions. Suffering is the most poignant shaker of the domestications of life, but novelty, sharp endings, and unexpected joys also call normal thinking into question. All primitive cultures have sacred ceremonies associated with suffering, birth, death, maturation, and ecstasy, and axial cultures augment or replace these by philosophies and theologies, superinterpretations of the meaning of life's meanings. I argue, therefore, that not only do all peoples have structures of existence, they ideally have structures of existence adequate to these universal conditions.[3]

V. ANOTHER MODEL OF THE INDIVIDUAL

Against this argument it surely will be remarked that the universality of the creative development of structures of existence does not entail the development of only one structure of existence. There may be many adequate structures, and the diversity is to be understood as a matter of historical contingency. To meet this objection I am obliged to make a further argument about the universality of the human response to the conditions occasioning structures of existence. I shall sketch a brief model of the educable 'parts of the soul' and then hang evidence on the model showing that each cultural tradition acknowledges and attends to all parts, with different emphases and historical forms.

Plato in the *Republic* proposed the model of a soul with three parts, each with its own ideal virtue and appropriate form of education. The *appetitive* part of the soul consists of desires, affections, and loves, each a vital response to some erotically attractive value. Movement in life comes from the impulse toward the erotic objects. The *rational* part of the soul deals with the discovery of patterns that make the desires compatible, distinguishing the better from the worse values and articulating an order of life according to priorities. Well-developed reason has dialectical ways of criticizing patterns of compossibility according to real values whose very discernment has been criticized. The *spirited* part of the soul is a kind of aggressive force integrating the other components. When desires are passionate and not feeble, and when reason is developed and critical, not secondhand or dull, spirit integrates the personality by seeing that the desires pursued are those guided by reason. As Plato put it, spirit can get angry at either one's desires or one's reason, whipping them into line. Plato's main point was that each of these parts of the soul has an ideal to fulfill, necessary for personal virtue. Desires must be passionate or there is a deficiency of life. Reason must attain to wisdom or there is a deficiency of possible ways of living, especially good ways in unjust circumstances. Spirit must attain to courage and discipline or the best intentions and the strongest passions will never meet to bear fruit.

Plato's three ideals for the soul illustrate three aspects of personal life that can be developed according to the process model.[4] Desires correspond to the many data providing value and energy to the process, seeking new objectification. Reason corresponds to the function of mentality, providing conceptual propositions, including new ones, for subjective harmony. And spirit corresponds to the drive for unification, restricted by the 'categoreal obligations,' to use Whitehead's term, and perfected by the degree to which the richest desires (most valuable data) are incorporated in the wisest way for mutually enriching objectification.

Any structure of existence, I suggest, involves ideals for each of these parts, and institutions for fostering them, because all parts are important for full human life. In Cobb's terms, each part is a 'seat of existence' and, although the different cultural traditions emphasize and punctuate them differently, all are present. In religious terms, the ideal of spirit is Discipline or personal integrity, the ideal of reason Enlightenment, and the ideal of desire perfect Love.

The development of spirit appears at first to be discipline in the sense of gaining control over desires, thoughts, and actions. Ascetic practices and disciplines are most obviously brought to mind in connection with Yoga, whose stages of development have been carried over into Buddhism through which they met and reinforced meditative practices of posture, breathing, and thought control in Taoism and Confucianism. Ascetic practices in Christianity likewise have involved physical and thought control, down to the days of the Methodist *Discipline.*

The first appearance of the development of spirit, however, gives way in all traditions to the recognition of a special block: the sense of self or ego. In the *Bhagavad-Gita* the self sense *(ahamkara)* leads the person to identify several physical and psychological factors in the world as being 'himself' as opposed to 'other,' and the other things in the world are interpreted in terms of how they affect for good or ill the welfare of that egoistic self. As a result, the person's objective perception is distorted by selective vision, the motives of his actions are perverted by subtle self-seeking, and his thinking is obsessed with the sufferings and triumphs of this fictional ego. Spiritual release consists in giving up attachment to and belief in the empirical ego. One's perception then is undistorted, one's actions directed purely to the good of the end in view, and one's thinking empty of suffering and egoistic triumph. All happenings are the manifestations of God, simple and natural, and all things can be taken in stride. This theme is paralleled in the notion of non-action in Taoism, pellucid sincerity in Confucianism, enlightenment or buddhi in Buddhism, chivalry in medieval Christendom, and in the *Teachings of Don Juan.* [5] The hero of this kind of religious development is the Warrior (Arjuna), who perceives and acts without ego, a pure expression of the essence of things, the Samurai, the Knight Templar, the theocratic ruler.

Even the purest spirit without Enlightenment is amoral and experientially unfulfilled. The universal emphasis on religious experience, on knowledge of the ultimately good and mystical apprehension of the ultimate itself, need not be documented. In some traditions such as Yoga and certain forms of medieval Christian mysticism, the religious experience is connected with a process of discipline. Other strands of religious knowledge emphasize history and moral experience as the arena in which enlightenment is attained, strands often important in Judaism, Christianity, and Confucianism. The Sage gains enlightenment in many ways, and stands as a religious type alongside of the Warrior.

The development of religiously appropriate desires is another universal ideal. On the face of it, this means eliminating selfish and misplaced desires. Deeper, it means developing the passions that embody the divine life. Cobb is certainly correct that this element has received its greatest emphasis in Christianity and its best expression in the life of Jesus. Christianity stresses that all other religious virtues (discipline to surrender the self, enlightenment of all knowledge and faith) are nothing without love. Yet the perfection of the passions, and their articulation as love, is not exclusive to Christianity. It is of the essence of the Bhakti tradition in Hinduism, said to be the highest form of spirituality in the *Bhagavad-Gita*. It is the main thrust of the theme of rectification of the will in Confucianism, and if the Taoists object to it, the reason is not a rejection of the ideal of *Jen*, love, but a rejection of the belief that it can be attained by effort. Even Old Testament Judaism spoke of the God who preferred love to the smell of burnt offerings; Jesus' rendition of the commandment in terms of loving God and man with all heart, soul, and mind was a quotation from earlier sources. All religions have their Saints, the lovers whose divine love has salvific power.

My general contention now is that all axial structures of existence contain themes whose paradigms are Warriors, Sages, and Saints. The structures differ by historical models, and they differ in the ways these are related. In some structures one paradigm may be dominant over the others, but the others are there and play essential roles. To live in such a structure is to define oneself by each of the ideals.

Now the problem for a contemporary structure of existence is to find appropriate new forms of the Warrior, the Sage, and the Saint. More particularly, the problem is to find a way of having these together so as to minimize loss of the old traditions and to maximize the intensity of cultural life in the context of the current environment. My suggestion is that for the development of the new structure of existence we open ourselves to the resources of all the old ones, as an occasion (in process philosophy) enriches itself by broadening its world.

VI. ANOTHER READING OF HISTORY

I doubt that Professor Cobb would object to the examples I have cited. Rather, he would object to the fact that the model presented does not register the uniqueness of the seats of existence peculiar to the different structures of existence. For instance, the model does not reflect the Indian attempt to establish the seat of existence in a consciousness outside the flow of empirical psychic life. It does not reflect the importance of aesthetic and rational distance for the Greeks. And particularly, it does not emphasize the importance of the person and then the spirit as seats of existence in the Judeo-Christian tradition.

This is now the issue. I intend to show how each of these seats of existence is interpretable according to the model given and how, although they are emphasized differently in each tradition, they are all present to a degree.

According to Cobb's account, the structure of the person arose in Israel as both reason and feelings were objectified and subordinated to personal responsibility. A person is one whose will is responsible for his actions. This is to say, in terms of the Platonic model, that spirit (in Plato's sense) has attained a high degree of integration, dominating the shape of one's desires and the use of intellect so that the spirit's own style articulates the person's identity. The aesthetic person's identity is articulated by what he sees; the rational person by what he knows; the spirited person by what he wills in making himself autonomous.[6]

The Christian structure of existence as spirit objectifies even the will so as to make the person indefinitely responsible for all components of his personality. But this is what one would expect from a high development of spirit in the Platonic sense. A spiritual person is one who has attained personal freedom in the possession of his own will.

It should be pointed out that my model for rendering spirit is Plato's, the Greek who was the author of 'Socrates,' in a way of speaking. To say that Plato made reason the seat of existence, subordinating either spirit or eros (highly developed appetites), is to be mistaken about the texts, I believe. Holding a genuinely social conception of reality, Plato believed that reason is the ideal of precedence when action throughout a complex environment is at stake. Spirit is the ideal, in the form of free personal integrity, when the individual is at stake. And eros is the ideal when God's action in the world is at stake: God brings value into the world by having it loved, according to Plato, a notion not far from Christian. On Platonic terms (though of course not in Plato's texts), erotic love would become altruistic agape when its object is God's own love of the world, especially manifested in Jesus Christ.

Cobb argues that the Christian structure whose seat is in personal spirit is alien to the Indian attempt to seat consciousness outside the flow of events. Yet the fact that the method for spiritual development requires the same thing in both cases—the loss of the ego ("he who would save his soul must lose it")—suggests that the difference is overdrawn. The warrior in the *Bhagavad-Gita* who purges himself of self-sense, looking at all things from a conscious standpoint not identified with or attached to any of them, is the person who can act, faithfully valuing the things relevant and serving their intrinsic goods, regardless of reflection back on himself. Although his center of consciousness is not identified with any time-bound psychic state, his identity as an actor is given in his situation and deeds, just as with the Western person. Furthermore, the principles integrating his actions are natural expressions of Krishna, not intrusions of his selfish character. This is not so different from having the 'mind of Christ.'

Now it might be argued that a Western person or spiritual type does not identify himself with his personal career, and that this identification is central to the Western notion of responsibility. Part of this argument may rest on metaphysical beliefs in the soul as an enduring lump-like substance. But both Cobb and I reject this in favor of a process view of the soul as a society of occasions. We would agree with the process tradition in the view that a person's character is the cumulative set of forms each of his occasions presents. A bad spirit, corrupted by attachment to an ego image, would be one overly concerned to reiterate some conception of his past character, and to filter his prehension of the world through that image, in such a way as to sully what could be more richly prehended and to objectify a less than maximal posture. The development of spiritual discipline through loss of self enables a person's character to reflect growth in the realistic maximization of value throughout life without selfish distortions.

The boundaries of self and not-self are fluid and somewhat conventional. I would go beyond many process philosophers in stressing that individual responsibility entails that some past occasions involving commitment must function essentially, not just contingently, in responsible occasions. Minimal requirements for a personal responsible agent would be that certain acts in the past are essential components of the person's present commitments, to be accepted or rejected with moral responsibility.[7] This helps in the understanding of individual responsibility in the Western metaphors, and helps also in making sense of the doctrine of karma. All in all, the process model of the responsible individual works as well for the Indian conception of the person as for the Western. Where the West stresses the responsibility in the continuities, the Indian tradition stresses the perfection of action in the moment. But neither side is lost to the other.[8]

From the Buddhist side, one of the chief points of contrast Cobb draws (*SCE* 139) is that Buddhist love does not involve a self, a lover, and that there is no important distinction between the lover and the beloved. In Christianity, on the other hand, while the ideal of love is equally high and noble, the emphasis is on developing the loving self. But just what is there in this difference?

The Buddhist would say the real self of each person is the Buddha-nature, and the Buddha-nature is the same for everyone. What is loved, however, is not the Buddha-nature *per se,* but the other person as the expression of the Buddha; the ideal activity of love is to attempt to bring the beloved to a realization of the Buddha-nature in him. This is paralleled in Christianity by love of others as the creatures and vehicles of God the logos; the ideal activity of this love is to help the others realize the logos more purely. The Christian calls attention to the identity of the other developing through time, and speaks of the beloved's identity in terms of his time and space determinants. The bodhisattva's attention to his disciples and beloved followers is equally concerned with the details, temporal and spatial, of their spiritual development. Where the Buddhist would say that one must attend to the details of the beloved's individual character to foster the realization of the common Buddha-nature in him, the Christian would say that one fosters the life of Christ in each disciple by attending to the development of his historical character. The Christian would stress the realization of discipleship in coming to terms with one's historical position. But what could say this more plainly than the Buddhist doctrine that all things are empty except historical contingencies apprehended as such? Nirvana is samsara.

It is sometimes said that Indian spirituality locates salvation in flight from the concrete world of historical existence, and Christianity locates it in the perfection of historical existence. Yet both of them see that the only way to grasp historical existence for what it is lies in attaining to a kind of eternal consciousness in the moment, a divine perspective. Both agree that the divine perspective is the most real in an ontological sense and both agree that the historical continuum is where the action is, literally. Some modes of Buddhism emphasize monastic withdrawal, but then so do the Trappists. Some modes of Christianity, especially medieval mysticism, interpret the eternal in the moment on the analogy of sexual ecstasy; Tantrism does the same. Both traditions have meditative strands, activist strands, devotional strands. Although the emphases differ and the mixes look different, similar components are to be found in both. And our present problem regarding the structure of existence is that the particular mixes in each case are inadequate to our times.[9]

I have tried to show in this section and the previous ones that, with a different model of historical configurations from Cobb's, a different reading of the relation between the traditional structures of existence is possible, and plausible. The practical conclusion of this view is that we are not faced with an either/or choice between the Indian structure of existence and the Western one, but rather with a diverse set of resources. The advent of a new structure of existence ought to be open to profit from them all.

VII. CONCLUSION

In this discussion I have tried, somewhat unsuccessfully I fear, to hold attention on the fact that we are talking about existential structures of cultures, not theories to be adopted or rejected. John Cobb does much better in his distinction between the structures of existence, on the one hand, and visions of reality, on the other.

To redress the imbalance in my own discussion I would like to point out that the old structures of existence shaping our world are limiting conditions as well as resources. If the intellectual or mental content were abstracted from those structures, perhaps we could accept, reject, divide, and recombine them as we do ideas. But in fact, to abstract in that way is immediately to leach out the existential power of those structures to enrich our lives on the most basic level. Even if we were to do that, we could not escape the existential hold those old structures have on our lives. No matter what structure of existence I attain to, I will have gotten there as a Methodist from Missouri. There are some places a Buddhist can go I could never reach.

Nevertheless, the structures of existence currently established in diverse cultures are somewhat inadequate to the existential needs of contemporary culture. Each of the major religious traditions seems to be looking back to its own roots, and looking over to its neighbors', in preparation for large-scale developments. Surely the religious syntheses of Vedic and Dravidic cultures in the *Bhagavad-Gita,* and of Hebrew and Greek cultures in Augustine, were no more daring blends of apparent opposites than any of those contemplated now. But we cannot simply will a new structure of existence into being. It arises through deep and mysterious historical processes.

But what we can exercise control over is the development of an appropriate vision of reality. Our control can be critical and dialectical. If we are careful not to confuse theoretical visions with existential structures, there is the possibility that we may wisely influence the latter with the former. This point is one of the chief strengths of John Cobb's philosophical theology.

NOTES

1. Cobb derives the terms and basic analysis from Karl Jaspers' *The Origin and Goal of History* (Yale University Press, 1953).

2. Cobb makes a very useful distinction between structures of existence and modes of existence. The modes are various ways of embodying the larger structures. For instance, there are ancient, medieval, modern, Catholic, Protestant, and Orthodox modes of Christianity, each expressing the life of spirit. Distinctions between structures of existence are much more radical, defining human life in very different ways. To be happy in a world society with different structures of existence is to say some people are human in a different sense from the way we are. To accept different modes of a single structure of existence is only to say there are different ways of expressing a common humanity. I myself have some reservations about the genus-species way of distinguishing structures and modes, preferring kinship relations and family resemblances; but for the present point it is adequate.

3. A very fine extended account of the problems mentioned in this paragraph is John E. Smith's book, *Experience and God* (Oxford University Press, 1968), especially Ch. 6.

4. By 'process model' I mean that generally composed of the themes articulated by Whitehead. Cobb discusses the model in detail in *CNT*, especially Chs. 2 and 3. I present another version in *The Cosmology of Freedom* (Yale University Press, 1974).

5. Carlos Castaneda, *Teachings of Don Juan* (Ballantine Books, Inc., 1969).

6. For an account of will, style, and identity, see my *The Cosmology of Freedom*.

7. This is discussed in detail in *The Cosmology of Freedom*.

8. The impact of Western ideas of evolution on Indian thoughts has brought to the surface a far more historical expression of the Indian conception of life than is found in the ancient texts. Nevertheless, recent writers, for instance Sri Aurobindo and Sri Krishna Prem, have carefully reinterpreted the traditional texts in historically oriented language. A comparison of Aurobindo's philosophy with Teilhard's would indicate that the issues distinguishing India and the West are not strictly bifurcated over the importance of concrete historical life.

9. Cobb's treatment of the differences between structures of existence curiously downplays the role of different orientations to God. Perhaps this is because a discussion of orientations would quickly turn to a discussion of theories about

God. At any rate, I have analyzed the relation between different orientations to God, comparing Indian, Chinese, and Western sources, in "A Metaphysical Argument for Wholly Empirical Theology," in Robert J. Roth, S.J. (ed.), *God Knowable and Unknowable* (Fordham University Press, 1973).

THE COURAGE TO LEAVE:
A RESPONSE TO JOHN COBB'S THEOLOGY

By Mary Daly

I HAVE RESPECT for John Cobb's work, for his sincerity, his will to change, his sense of process and of an open future. This is why I have gladly accepted the invitation extended by the editors of this book to respond to his theology. There are points of contiguity between his thought and mine, and at the same time there is an enormous gulf between us. I will begin with the differences, as I perceive them, and then move on to some important points of agreement.

The chasm between us is expressed by the title of this essay, which is extracted from a passage in *Liberal Christianity at the Crossroads* (*LCC* 108f). The passage is in Chapter 12, "Christ as the Image of Love," which begins with a discussion of the play *One Flew Over the Cuckoo's Nest*, by Ken Kesey. Professor Cobb summarizes the highlights of the play. The story takes place in the men's ward of a mental hospital, "presided over by a castrating nurse." Professor Cobb comments that "McMurphy's Dionysian presence is enough to bring new life to the ward, but it is not enough to give the men *the courage to leave*" (italics mine). Recognizing this, the hero abandons his self-interest and defends the other inmates, knowing that this will result in his own destruction by the dreaded shock treatments. He continues to resist the *female* nurse for the sake of the others, and finally, when he has been destroyed "as a man," one of them, out of kindness, smothers him in his sleep. Commenting upon this vision of the transformation of Dionysus into a Christ figure, John Cobb writes: "I wish I could believe it to be a foretaste of things to come."

I find this extremely troubling. To begin with, Cobb does not seem to acknowledge that the situation in the play is a set of *reversals*. In the real world, the majority of mental patients are in fact women. The idea of genuine power over men being wielded by a 'castrating' female nurse is out of touch with the patriarchal context in which 'medicine' and 'nursing' are practiced. The very role definition of a 'nurse' in this society is one of stereotypically feminine subservience. Nurses, almost all of whom are female, are subordinate to doctors, almost all of whom are male. Moreover, the entire professional institution of medicine and psychiatry is male-controlled—economically, legally (AMA), and ideologically. As Phyllis Chesler and other feminist scholars have pointed out, the mental hospital is in fact modeled on the *patriarchal* family.[1] Therefore the portrayal of men as victims of an allegedly powerful, bullying woman is a travesty. The image of Dionysus turned Christ figure would, in this culture, more realistically be assigned to a strong woman who sacrifices herself for others, although this could hardly be called other than oppressive. The plot, then, is comprised of *reversals* of social reality.

My problem with John Cobb's approach to this play does not end with his non-acknowledgment of its reversals of sexist social reality. I am troubled by his claim that he wishes he "could believe it to be a forecast of things to come." The ethic of Christian love, of self-sacrifice, of being 'the man for others,' has always *meant* the ethic of the *woman* for others. For my 52 percent of the human species this is the ultimately destructive model. To write of it so uncritically and approvingly reveals an unawareness of the deep disease of sexism which Christianity so effectively fosters. As Simone de Beauvoir pointed out, the religious myths of patriarchy are created by men and believed by women. To put it another way, the male power structure *externalizes* itself in the form of phallocratic myth, whereas women *internalize* these myths as the Other, as victims of scapegoat theology.

There remains a separate question which Cobb and other male theologians will have to consider. Since it is destructive—and I must insist that it *is* destructive—to impose an ethical model of self-sacrifice upon women in a sexist society, or to muddy the problem by proposing such an ethic for 'man' in general, there is left only the question of whether such an ethic is appropriate *for males* in a patriarchal society. The question then would be narrowed to the specific dimensions of the situation of males within a sexually hierarchical caste system, i.e., patriarchy. I leave it for John Cobb and his male colleagues to deal with the question of whether "Christ as the Image of Love" is relevant to the members of their sex. Indeed, this can and should be a matter of concern for male theologians, but I would suggest that they can discuss this question authentically only within the limits of this *specific reference to males* and *only* if the *"No"* of radical feminists to the Christ symbol and its implied ethic of sacrificial love is *heard,* understood, respected. I am saying that there is an inherent logic in radical feminism which is *self*-affirming and affirming of our sisters, which says "No" to Christian myths and their psychological, social, and moral implications. This is an ontological logic which says first and foremost "Yes" to ourselves as verbs, as participators in the cosmic Verb, as be-ing, which is becoming. This ontological logic means that we are *seeking* our life force, not losing it. We are finding it, reclaiming it. This logic requires the courage to leave the Christian myth and the societal structures which are its supporting infrastructures, and this courage to leave is very much a matter of self-interest. To use the image of the mental hospital, radical feminism means exiting from the Christian cuckoo's nest. It means naming the self good and sane, which will of course elicit labels of 'evil' and 'insane.' Radical feminism therefore means exorcism of these labels (which are applied to all women anyway), refusal to internalize them. It means unlearning the lesson of self-crucifixion, taking a qualitative leap beyond the death-centered processions of patriarchal religion.

Since John Cobb and I shared the same stage, so to speak, at a lecture series in Portland, Oregon, in 1974, I can anticipate one of his objections to my rejection of Christ as the "Image of Love" for women. That objection is simple: "Jesus was androgynous." I have already pointed out the harmfulness of the 'man [*sic*] for others' image for women attempting to *become* who we are in a patriarchal society. But I fear that John Cobb will try to emphasize the self-affirming elements in this Christ image and still offer it, remodeled, as it were, to the members of my sex. My answer to such an offer is a firm NO! "Jesus was androgynous" is a linguistic/symbolic trap. It is an example of the sexual politics of language. This is not to say that the intentions of those who use it are consciously oppressive. What I am saying is that the usage functions to obfuscate, to oppress. I shall try to explain my position, because I think this explanation is essential for any sort of common understanding.

One of the more easily recognizable threads of the web of deception which is the phallocratic Maya is false polarization into sexual stereotypes. This is obvious in Christian 'sacramental religion' (the Christ-Mary symbolism) and in American civil religion (Gerald and Betty Ford, Nelson and 'Happy' Rockefeller). Moreover, this polarization generates another false dichotomy—that between 'good' and 'bad' women. However, the point I want to emphasize here is that there is another thread of the web of sexist deception which is more insidious and more difficult to recognize, namely, *false inclusion.* This is illustrated by grammar, a primary instrument of sexist conditioning. It characterizes the seductive tactics of liberal organizations such as the ' dical' Left and liberal Protestantism, which 'include' women as appendages to males. In Protestant theology Mary almost disappears, and, in answer to feminist questions about this, Jesus is described as 'androgynous.' The Super-androgyne, the Feminized Male, allegedly includes women, of course. Moreover, non-Christian social theorists such as Herbert Marcuse jump on the bandwagon of women's liberation on the grounds that it will "liberate the woman within the man." Thus, in yet another way, we are 'included,' that is, cannibalized.

When I spoke with Professor Cobb in Oregon I used the term 'androgyny.' I also spoke of the dynamic inherent in radical feminism's logic which is Antichurch and indeed Antichrist, because both the power structure and the symbol system of patriarchal religions, specifically of Christianity (and generally of all the major world religions), legitimate and sustain a phallocentric social system, that is, the sexual caste system. I have used the same terms (including 'androgyny') in my book, *Beyond God the Father*.[2] However, the public discussion with Cobb served to confirm some strong doubts I had been having about the adequacy of the term 'androgyny' to express the concept/reality of psychic wholeness, of integration, which a significant cognitive minority of women have begun to glimpse intuitively, experientially, as realizable. In our search for the right word many radical feminists have experienced the poverty of the language bequeathed to us, and we have come to recognize the manner in which it constricts and even distorts our thought. We have become more conscious of the politics of language.

My own consciousness of the political usages of language was nudged forward quite a bit by Cobb's reply to my unequivocal assertion that the women's revolution is a post-Christian spiritual revolution/mutation. "Jesus was androgynous," he said. At the risk of seeming to belabor the point, I will continue my analysis of this particular instance of semantic mystification, because it is central to an understanding of the politics of naming, specifically to the politics of *false* inclusion. And this understanding is crucial for any response that I could make to his writings. For this assumption that "Jesus was (or is) androgynous" is an unexpressed assumption which affects all of his theological work. I suspect that a similar assumption underlies his God language, and I will discuss this later on. The point now is *to make explicit* a profound problem, which is all the more mystifying because unexamined. To cite from Whitehead (the same citation that appears at the head of the first chapter of *Beyond God the Father*):

> When you are criticizing the philosophy of an epoch, do not chiefly direct your attention to those intellectual positions which its exponents feel it necessary explicitly to defend. There will be some fundamental assumptions which adherents of all the various systems within the epoch unconsciously presuppose. Such assumptions appear so obvious that people do not know what they are assuming because no other way of putting things has ever occurred to them.

As I have become more aware of the politics of naming, I have recognized that the term 'androgyny' is adaptable to such mystifying usage as the expression 'human liberation' has been subjected to. That is, it can easily be used to deflect attention from the fact that women and men at this point in history cannot simply 'get together and work it out,' ignoring the profound differences in socialization and privilege within the sexual caste system. Both 'androgyny' and 'human liberation' function frequently to encourage false transcendence, masking—even though unintentionally—the specific content of the oppression of women and suggesting that wholeness depends upon identification with men. Moreover, even if these terms are not explicitly used, the false assumptions which the usage of these expressions renders more obvious still are at work, unrecognized. The advantage of experimenting with such terms is that we learn from our mistakes. That is, formerly implicit assumptions become explicit.

Some feminists began to feel somewhat less comfortable with the word 'androgyny' when the implications of a small terse fact surfaced to consciousness. This fact is etymological: the first part of the word is derived from the Greek *anēr, andros* ('man'), while the second part is from *gynē* ('woman'). This, of course, carries its own message, similar to the message conveyed by the common use of the expression 'man-woman relationship' and by the liberal substitution of 'he or she' for the pseudogeneric 'he.' A first reaction to this realization was to employ the word 'gynandry,' which, from the perspective of women's becoming, is more appropriate. But it soon became evident that the priority problem in the etymology of the word was only the tip of the iceberg, symptomatic of deeper problems.

In fact, the term 'androgyny' comes to us heavily fraught with traditional associations, that is, associations of male-centered tradition(s). The image conveyed by the term is that of a male who has "liberated the woman within." This fact has been brought home to me in discussions with Christian theologians who, confronted with the problem of the inherent oppressiveness of Christolatry, have responded earnestly that there really is no problem, since "Jesus was androgynous." Whatever this may mean, it has little relevance to the problem of women's becoming *now,* and in fact it distracts from the real issues confronting us. Dressing up old symbols just will not work for women who are conscious of sexist religiosity.

'Gynandry' helps to shift images away from the traditional biases, but only to a limited degree. Placing the female part of the word first does not dissolve the inherent dependency of the word itself upon stereotypes in order that there be any meaning content at all. To put it another way, in an 'androgynous' or 'gynandrous' society it would be senseless to speak of 'androgyny' or 'gynandry,' since people would have no idea of the sex-stereotyped characteristics and/or roles referred to by the components of the terms. Use of these terms can function in a liberating way if they are seen as 'transitional' words, or, more precisely, as self-liquidating words. They should be understood as having a built-in planned obsolescence.

The integration/wholeness that is in fact being experienced/envisioned as well as theorized about by women *now* is wholeness coming from the power of being within women ourselves. Indeed, the titles of journals coming out of the women's movement are indicators of this woman-identified vision of wholeness (e.g., *Amazon Quarterly, Off Our Backs, Feminist Studies, Wicce,* and even *Ms. Magazine*). This vision or intuition of be-ing, of integration, cannot be understood or expressed through male-identified language. When I say 'male-identified language' I mean to include all sex-stereotyped terms, whether 'masculine' or 'feminine.' Indeed, when speaking to audiences I have frequently had the impression that people who are trying to grasp what feminists mean by 'psychic wholeness' are so imprisoned by patriarchal language and its false dichotomizations that they vaguely envisage two distorted halves of human being stuck together—something like John Wayne and Brigitte Bardot Scotch-taped together. They are imprisoned by the fallacy that two distorted 'halves'—whether reified as two individuals, or reified as two complementary 'parts' of the same individual—could make a whole. This reification of wholeness prevents recognition that radical feminism is about *process.*

I must add that this process of women's becoming cannot be circumscribed in the language of non-women, even though the latter may often write and speak about 'process.' The language bequeathed to us does not adequately express the experience of *gynergy* (to use a phrase coined by a feminist theologian, Emily Culpepper). And this brings me to some specific responses to John Cobb. I shall focus mainly on *God and the World.* While I realize that his thought also has been in process since its publication in 1969, I think that the specific issues of concern to me—issues which emerge in consciousness as a result of a specifically gynergetic process—have not yet been confronted in his work.

In *God and the World,* Cobb asks whether it is appropriate to name 'the One Who Calls' by the name 'God.' Having rejected some of the traditional approaches to the problem of God, he defends the understanding of 'God' as the One Who Calls us into the open future. The influence of Whitehead is evident, and indeed I think/feel agreement with the idea of a call into the open future. Yet the many instances of unintentional use of sexist language (e.g., the pseudogeneric 'man,' referred to by the masculine pronoun, and the reference to 'God' exclusively by the masculine pronoun) are warnings to me that this 'open future' would be a strange land and indeed closed to me.

There is a real sense in which I do not wish to belabor the point of sexist grammar. Indeed, the reader might well remark that such a response is predictable from a feminist. It is now evident that grammar is a primary locus of sexist conditioning. (This was less evident in the '60s to most theologians, when Cobb was writing *God and the World*. However, he still had not discarded sexist language in *Liberal Christianity at the Crossroads*, 1973. See, for example, pp. 93, 122–125.) I do not wish to belabor the point of sexist grammar, but rather to look beyond this to a very deep problem, the very problem of naming the Ultimate/Proximate Reality—the Verb in which we live and move and have our be-ing. In *Liberal Christianity at the Crossroads,* Cobb speaks of 'God' as "this tender Cry," this "terrifying Love." Again, I think/feel agreement with these expressions, as I did with "the One Who Calls." However, the context, the very Jesus-centered context of the book, warns me that there is something foreign about this 'Cry.' Once again, I have the sense of being in a strange land. Indeed, Cobb affirms that the Cry is not primarily judge, that it grounds our hope. But I hear nothing that speaks directly to gynocentric hope. Nor do I expect to hear it. This renaming can be done only by women ourselves. The issue, then, to which I want to address myself is the basic issue of whether indeed it is appropriate to name the One Who Calls, the Cry, the Verb which is ultimate/proximate process, by the name 'God.' Cobb appears to answer in the affirmative. At the time of writing *Beyond God the Father,* I also used the term 'God.' I now have some serious questions about the word itself. These questions arise not from a movement on my part toward atheism, but rather from a deepening awareness of the spiritual dimensions of the women's revolution.

A basic problem can be posed bluntly in the following way: Wanted: 'God' or 'The Goddess'? Feminist consciousness is experienced by a significant number of women whom I know as ontological becoming, that is, be-ing. This process requires existential courage to be and to *see.* Courageous vision is itself an alchemistic power; it is revolutionary and revelatory, revealing our participation in ultimate reality as Verb, as intransitive Verb.

Yet the question obviously arises of the need for anthropomorphic symbols for this reality. There is no inherent contradiction between speaking of ultimate reality as Verb and speaking of this as personal. The Verb is more personal than a mere static noun. However, if we choose to *image* the Verb in anthropomorphic symbols, we can run into a problematic phenomenon which sociologist Henri Desroche calls 'crossing.' 'Crossing' refers to a notable tendency among oppressed groups to attempt to change or adapt the ideological tools of the oppressor, so that they can be used *against* him and *for* the oppressed. The problem here is the fact that the functioning of 'crossing' does not generally move far enough outside the ideological framework it seeks to undermine. In the 'black theology' of James Cone, for example, we find a black God and a black Messiah, but this pigmentation operation does not significantly alter the behavior of Jahweh & Son. Cone's black God is as revengeful and sexist as his white prototype. For feminist eyes it is clear that this God is at least as oppressive as the old (for black women as well as for white women). The message in the alteration of symbol is simply about *which* male-ruled racial group will be on top and which will be on the bottom. The basic presupposition of *hierarchy* remains unaltered: that is, the presupposition that there must be an 'us' or a 'them' on top, and a corresponding 'them' or 'us' on the bottom.

Some women religious leaders within Western culture in modern times have performed something like a 'crossing' operation, notably such figures as Mary Baker Eddy and Ann Lee, in stressing the 'maternal' aspect of the divinity. The result has been mixed. Eddy's 'Father-Mother God' is, after all, the Christian God. Nor does Ann Lee really move completely outside the Christian framework. It is interesting that their writings lack the thirst for vengeance that characterizes Cone's all too Christian black theology, which is certainly in their favor. But it is also necessary to note that their theologies lack explicit relevance to the concrete problems of the oppression of women. Intellection and spirituality remain cut off from creative political movement. In earlier periods also there were women within the Christian tradition who tried to 'cross' the Christian all-male God and Christ to some degree. An outstanding example was Juliana of Norwich, an English recluse and mystic who lived in the last half of the fourteenth century. Juliana's 'God' and 'Jesus' were— if language conveys anything—hermaphroditic constructs, with the primary identity clearly male. While there are many levels on which I could analyze her words about "our beloved Mother, Jesus, [who] feeds us with himself,"[3] suffice it to say here that this hermaphroditic image is somewhat less than attractive. Moreover, the 'androgynous' God and Jesus present problems analogous to and related to those problems which occur in connection with the use of the term 'androgyny' to describe the direction of women's becoming. There is something like a "liberation of the woman within" the (primarily male) God and Jesus.

Indeed, it is harder to perform a transsexual operation on the Judeo-Christian divinity than a mere pigmentation operation. This is one reason, no doubt, why Cone is able to achieve a purely black God and black Messiah, rather than a Mulatto, whereas the Christian women mentioned brought forth hermaphrodites, with emphasis on maleness. Indeed, they did something on the symbolic level which is analogous to "liberating the woman within the man." Since they went only this far, they accomplished little or nothing, in social or mythic terms, toward the genuine liberation of women.

One fact that stands out here is that these were women whose imaginations were still partially controlled by Christian myth. My contention is that they were caught in a contradiction (which is not the case in the work of black *male* theologians). I am saying that there is a profound contradiction between the inherent logic of radical feminism and the inherent logic of the Christian symbol system. I would not have said this ten years ago, at the time of writing the original edition of *The Church and the Second Sex,* which expressed hope for reform of Christianity in general and Roman Catholicism in particular. Nor would some women today say this— women who still perceive their identity as both Christian and feminist. Some of these women are new to feminist consciousness and will follow eventually the logic which, I believe, leads to the elimination of such a contradictory dual identity. It is to be expected that others will remain caught in the contradiction while denying its existence.

Both the reformers and those who leave behind Judaism and Christianity are contributing and will contribute in different ways to the process of the becoming of women. The point here is not to place value judgments upon individual persons and their efforts—and there are heroic efforts at all points of the feminist spectrum. Rather, it is to disclose an inherent logic in feminism. The courage which some women have in affirming this logic comes in part from having been on the feminist journey for quite a while. Encouragement comes also from knowing increasing numbers of women who have chosen the route of the logical conclusion. Some of these women have 'graduated' from Christianity or religious Judaism, and some have never even been associated closely with church or synagogue, but have discovered spiritual and mythic depths in the women's movement itself. What we share is a sense of becoming in cosmic process, which I prefer to call the Verb, Be-ing, and which some would still call 'God.'

For some feminists concerned with the spiritual depth of the movement, the word 'God' is becoming increasingly problematic, however. This by no means indicates a movement in the direction of 'atheism' or 'agnosticism' or 'secularism,' as these terms are usually understood. Rather, the problem arises precisely because of the spiritual and mythic quality perceived in feminist process itself. Some use expressions such as 'power of being.' Some reluctantly still use the word 'God' while earnestly trying to divest the term of its patriarchal associations, attempting to think perhaps of the 'God of the philosophers' rather than the overtly masculinist and oppressive 'God of the theologians.' But the problem becomes increasingly troublesome the more the 'God' of the various Western philosophers is subjected to feminist analysis. 'He,' 'Jahweh,' still often hovers behind the abstractions, stunting our own thought, giving us a sense of contrived doublethink. The word 'God' just may be inherently oppressive.

Indeed, the word 'Goddess' has also been problematic, but for different reasons. Some have been worried about the problem of 'crossing.' However, that difficulty appears more and more as a pseudo difficulty when it is recognized that 'crossing' is likely to occur only when one is trying to work *within* a sexist tradition. For example, Christian women who in their 'feminist liturgies' experiment with referring to 'God' as 'she' and to the Trinity as 'The Mother, the Daughter, and the Holy Spirit' are still working within all the boundaries of the same symbolic framework and the same power structure. Significantly, their services are at the same place and time as 'the usual,' and are regarded by most of the constituency of the churches as occasional variations of 'business as usual.'

As women who are outside the Christian church inform ourselves of evidence supporting the existence of ancient matriarchy and of evidence indicating that the Gods of patriarchy are indeed contrived, pale derivatives and reversals of the Great Goddess of an earlier period, the fear of mere 'crossing' appears less appropriate and perhaps even absurd. There is also less credibility allowable to the notion that 'Goddess' would function like 'God' in reverse, that is, to legitimate an oppressive 'female-dominated' society, if one is inclined to look seriously at evidence that matriarchal society was not structured like patriarchy, that it was non-hierarchical.

Would 'Goddess' be likely to function oppressively, like 'God'? Given the present situation of women, the danger is not imminent. Would it function that way in the future? My inclination is to think not, but it is not my intention to attempt to 'prove' this point at this time. The question has a quality of 'abstraction' and remoteness from the present social realities and it is, it seems to me, diversionary. When it is raised, and it is usually raised by men, one senses an 'atmosphere' about the question, an aroma of masculine hysteria, a fear of invading hordes of 'matriarchs' (read: female patriarchs) taking over The Man's world.

There are, however, two points concerning the symbol 'Goddess' which I think *are* relevant to the existing situation. First, it can at the very least be pointed out that whenever the pendulum has swung extremely in one direction (and it *has*—for millennia), it is psychologically/social-ly/ethically important to emphasize 'the other side.' The hermaphroditic image hardly seems satisfactory for anyone. For an increasing minority of women—and even for some men[4]—'Goddess' is becoming more func-tional, meaningful, and loaded with healing associations. As this minority grows, Western society will be shaken by the presence of gynarchic sym-bolism in a new and potent way. It should be noted that women are inclined to speak and write of 'The Goddess,' whereas one seldom says 'The God.' In our culture it has been assumed that 'goddesses' are many and trivial, whereas the 'real' divinity *is* 'God,' who does not even require the definite article. The use of the expression 'The Goddess' is a way of confronting this trivialization, of exorcising the male 'God,' and of affirm-ing a different myth/reality.

A second, and related, point has to do with the fact that the 'self-transcending immanence,' the sense of giving birth to ourselves, the sense of power of being *within* the self and the cosmos which is being affirmed by many women, does not seem to be denoted, imaged, ade-quately pointed to, or perhaps even associated with the term 'God.' With her permission, I will relate a story told to me by theologian Nelle Mor-ton, for whose insights I have the greatest respect. This woman told me that in the past when riding in planes (and feeling fearful about the situation) she often conjured up images remembered from childhood of 'God' as "having the whole world in his hands." Later, this image/prayer? became meaningless. When she was on a plane recently, the ride sud-denly became extremely bumpy and rough. It occurred to her to 'try on' the name/image 'Goddess.' The result, as she described it, was immedi-ate, electrifying, consoling. She sensed a presence and had/heard? the thought: "Just let go. Just sit on the seat and sit on the airwaves and ride." The ride, though as rough as before, became a joyful experience.

Clearly, it would be inappropriate and arrogant to try to 'explain' or 'interpret' this experience of another person. I can only comment that many women I know are finding power of being within the self rather than in 'internalized' father images. As a philosopher, my preference has been for abstractions. Indeed, I have always been annoyed and rather embar-rassed by 'anthropomorphic' symbols, preferring terms such as 'ground and power of being' (Tillich), 'beyond subjectivity and objectivity' (James), 'the Encompassing' (Jaspers), or the commonly used 'Ultimate Reality,' or 'cosmic process.' More recently I have used the expression 'Intransitive Verb.' Despite this philosophical inclination, and also be-cause of it, I find it impossible to ignore the realm of symbols, or to fail to recognize that many women are experiencing and participating in a remythologizing process, which is a new dawn.

It is necessary to add a few remarks about the functioning of the confusing and complex 'Mary' symbol within Christianity. Through it, the power of the Great Goddess symbol is enchained, captured, used, cannibalized, tokenized, domesticated, tranquilized. In spite of this, I think that many women and at least some men, when they have heard of or imaged the 'Mother of God,' have, by something like a selective perception process, screened out the standardized, lobotomized, dull, derivative, and dwarfed Christian reflections of a more ancient symbol and perceived something that might more accurately be described as the Great Goddess, and which, in human terms, can be translated into 'the strong woman who can relate because she can stand alone.' A woman of Jewish background commented that 'Mother of God' had always seemed strange and contradictory to her. Not having been programmed to 'know' about the distinctions between the 'divine' and the 'human' nature of 'Christ,' or to 'know' that the 'Mother of God' is less than God, this woman had been able to hear the expression with the ears of an extraenvironmental listener. It sounded, she said, something like "infinite plus one." When this symbolic nonsense is recognized, it is more plausible simply to conceptualize process as 'infinite,' and to allow the imagination free play with gynarchic symbolism, with 'Goddess.' Nor need 'Goddess' be reified into *one* symbol. Rather, it is a series of manifestations of power of being in all women and in the life-engendering cosmos.

It may appear that the suffix '-ess' presents a problem, when one considers other usages of that suffix—for example, in 'poetess' or in 'authoress.' In these cases, there is a tone of depreciation, a suggestion that women poets and authors are in a separate and 'inferior' category to be judged by different standards than their male counterparts. However, the suffix does not always function in this 'diminishing' way. For example, there appear to be no 'diminuitive' overtones suggested by the word 'actress.' So also, it seems that the term 'Goddess'—or 'The Goddess'—*is not only non-diminuitive* but very strong. Indeed, it calls before the mind images of a powerful and ancient tradition before, behind, and beyond Christianity. These are multidimensional images of women's present and future becoming/be-ing. They represent a sense of sacred presence, of transcendence which is not dichotomized from immanence.

I leave it to Professor Cobb to reflect upon these thoughts on the problem of naming the Call to the Open Future. In a sense these thoughts are beyond *Beyond God the Father*. They also reflect my reflections upon *God and the World*. They are 'in process.'

I should like to move now to some points of contiguity between Cobb's thought and my own. In *God and the World,* the author writes that 'he' who believes in 'God' is entitled to believe in life after death, even though such belief does not entail any assurance. Some of my difficulties with the language are by now clear to the reader. Yet despite these difficulties and the deep mythic/symbolic/political differences which they necessarily entail, I am in deep agreement with the *hope* expressed here. However, rather than writing of 'belief' in the divine spirit as opening up the possibility of 'belief' in other spirits I would choose another word, such as 'awareness.' To paraphrase, I would experiment with a sentence such as the following: "She/he who is aware of the Verb is also aware of eternal life, even though such awareness cannot be 'proved objectively' by technical reason."

'Belief,' as I hear it in its all too traditional context, is fraught with connotations of 'the will to believe'—a distortion which Tillich ably exposed.[5] 'Belief' is too closely linked with heteronomy, with patriarchal Christian authoritarianism. Whether the latter takes the form of Catholic ecclesiastical authoritarianism or Protestant bibliolatry and acceptance of 'the Word' is unimportant. The term is, I think, wrong. Moreover, I perceive its implications as demonic, for the 'believer,' rather than trusting the self, is allowing the self to be possessed by something external to the self.

However, the *hope*, I do firmly agree, is right. Moreover, Cobb's leaning toward experiential evidence, toward a kind of empiricism, does come through, despite his (to me) troublesome usage of traditional Christian terms. The conflict between Christian belief and existential hope is evident throughout his writings (e.g., in his article "What Is Alive and What Is Dead in Empirical Theology?"). Both my agreement with his hope and my alienation from the context in which this is expressed are reinforced by some of his statements. For example, Cobb writes that "belief that this life is all there is can lead to Auschwitz as well as to socialist revolution" (*GW* 101). This strikes me as a remarkably true insight, but I think its expression is weakened by the term 'belief.' For indeed, is it not equally true that *belief* that this world is *not* all there is can lead to Auschwitz? There were, after all, traditionalist Christian theologians in Germany, both Protestant and Catholic, who supported Hitler, and for the most part Catholic bishops in that nation did not oppose him. Moreover, believing Christians have always been ardent persecutors of those who have not shared their beliefs—and of those who have shared them. Heteronomous otherworldly dogmatism breeds dualism, and breeds oppression of 'the Other.' Yet I do share the tentative yet real *awareness/ hope* that this life is *not* all that there is. Without this awareness, nothing makes sense.

I am heartily in agreement with Cobb's insight that rejection of mind/ body dualism must be carefully understood. I agree that "this emphasis

upon unity is useful only so long as a part—and indeed the most important part—of that whose unity is asserted is itself not simply body and
bodily activity as experienced by the sense organs" (*GW* 108). Yet even
at this point of deepest agreement I am made aware of a deep difference.
In the same paragraph he writes: "Christianity, I am convinced, is *most*
concerned about man [*sic*] as self, as 'I,' or as spirit, and in a sense such
that this element cannot be seen, heard, or touched either in oneself or
in others." I must say that I am not convinced that this is true about
Christianity. I am convinced, however, that post-Christian feminist
spiritual consciousness *is most* concerned about woman as self, as 'I,' or
as spirit. Moreover, I am convinced that this element *can* be seen, heard,
and touched in oneself and in others, but not in the banal, enclosed sense
in which 'seeing,' 'hearing,' and 'touching' are understood, that is, misunderstood, by the fragmented false consciousness fostered and forced
upon us by patriarchal power relationships and the myths which reinforce
these. Post-Christian feminist becoming means breaking down the walls
between technical and ontological reason. Moreover, it means something
more. It means something like the development of a new sensibility,
indeed of a new sensorium, *of a new organ of the spirit.* This gynergetic
becoming is, for those who are in touch with it, more than revolution. It
is an ontological mutation.[6] Moreover, I must in all honesty affirm that
I find Christian theology and Christian mysticism unable to speak to this
event. The event is a journey involving both exorcism and ecstasy. Yet
I hear these 'old' words in a new way. Wrenched out of their Christian
context, heard with new ears, they are new words.

  Once again, I affirm John Cobb's ontological sense (even though he
frequently seems reluctant to call it that). I affirm his hope toward an
open future, his awareness of self as spirit—an awareness which gives
meaning to the open future, to the sense of divine presence. Still, the gulf
between us is political and more than this; it is mythic. Yet, paradoxically,
the hope for communication lies precisely in the recognition of this gulf.
As I affirmed in *Beyond God the Father,* the aspect under which the women's
movement opens out to 'human liberation' is ontological. When women
become *present* to *ourselves,* able to affirm "I am," we experience power
of presence. This may be experienced by non-women as power of absence, for we are not there to be objectified, to be used, to agree. We are
not there to be (borrowing Virginia Woolf's phrase) magnifying mirrors,
reflecting men at twice their natural size. This power of presence which
is also power of absence is an invitation to men to experience non-being.
Specifically it is an invitation to experience the inadequacy, the non-
being, of patriarchal power relationships *and myth.* Yet I must add that the
invitation is *not* issued for its own sake, *as invitation.* It is simply a conse-

quence of women's becoming—a process that is taking place whether men can hear the invitation or not.

Cobb and I share, and yet we do not share, a sense of process. This very separation is necessary for wholeness. Yet the separation does not have to seek for legitimation outside of itself. The fact that women are becoming is self-legitimating, and the fact would be muddied by superimposed doctrines of universal human liberation. The gulf between us *is* mythic. I can only let the truth of this fact speak for itself. And, by the way: He who has ears to hear—let him hear.

NOTES

1. Phyllis Chesler, *Women and Madness* (Doubleday & Company, Inc., 1972).

2. Mary Daly, *Beyond God the Father* (Beacon Press, Inc., 1973). See also Mary Daly, *The Church and the Second Sex, With an Autobiographical Preface and Postchristian Introduction by the Author,* rev. ed. (Harper & Row, Publishers, Inc., Colophon Books, 1975).

3. Juliana of Norwich, *Revelations of Divine Love,* ed. by Clifton Wolters (Penguin Books, 1966), from Ch. 61.

4. Kenneth Pitchford chooses Goddess imagery, which occurs frequently in his more recent poems.

5. Paul Tillich, *Dynamics of Faith* (Harper & Brothers, 1957).

6. Françoise d'Eaubonne, *Le Féminisme ou la mort* (Paris: Pierre Horay, 1974).

FROM A BUDDHIST POINT OF VIEW

By Takao Tanaka

A BOOK was published here in Japan in 1958 that contained the reports delivered at the Ninth International Congress for the History of Religions. I had the good fortune to find in it a proposal by Hartshorne. And the proposal was made under the name of "The Buddhist-Whiteheadian View of the Self and the Religious Traditions."

According to Hartshorne, there are three ways in which we may view the Self or Soul. One of them is the doctrine of individual substances as absolutely self-identical through time but non-identical in space. The other is the doctrine of Hindu monism that plurality of selves is mere appearance, since what is called 'Brahman' is the primary reality that is beyond numerical diversity. Each of our-selves is Brahman in which we are all one in some ultimate or non-relative sense.

The last is what Hartshorne calls the 'Buddhist-Whiteheadian' view, and this seems to him most capable of expressing the truth in them all. It is radical pluralism which takes the primary units of plurality to be the momentary experiences or selves. Here we have a definite subject with definite experience. Each new experience means a new total actuality. The numerical novelty of this actuality is not a matter of degree. What we call the rewarded or punished self is, strictly speaking, never the original agent. But this does not mean that we are wholly free from the notion of obligation. Despite, or rather because of, being an original agent, each of our-selves is responsible for the past and the future. If we say here that such responsibility is far beyond our scope and therefore it is sheer nonsense, then where can we find our way under the eclipse of God?

"It is not enough," says Hartshorne, "to say with Zen-Buddhism that the ultimate reality and empirical particulars are identical." To this he adds that there must be the divine awareness, which is, as Whitehead suggests, "always one and always many, always with novel advance moving onward and never perishing." Hartshorne believes that in such conceptions radical pluralism and radical monism, Eastern and Western genius, and universal common sense may find their fruitful meeting ground.[1]

In those days I myself was engaged in studying Whitehead's philosophy. Thus I took so great an interest in this proposal by Hartshorne that I made up my mind at once to set about articulating the thoughts of Dôgen (1200–1253), the founder of the Sôtô School in Japan, with the help of Whiteheadian concepts. After several attempts I wrote an essay to which I gave the title "Dôgen's Religious World-View and Whitehead's Metaphysical Cosmology."[2] But can this essay be a Whiteheadian Buddhist natural theology? Can there be such a theology at all in regard to Buddhism as the doctrine of No-God?

Now, it is necessary to scrutinize two questions:

I. Would a Whiteheadian Buddhist natural theology be possible?

II. Would a Whiteheadian Buddhist natural theology be desirable?

I. WOULD A WHITEHEADIAN BUDDHIST NATURAL THEOLOGY BE POSSIBLE?

First of all, can there be a Buddhist theology? According to Cobb, there can be. In what sense is it possible? He defines theology in the broadest sense. By 'theology' he means "any coherent statement about matters of ultimate concern that recognizes that the perspective by which it is governed is received from a community of faith" (CNT 252). This definition contains three conditions: (1) coherent statement, (2) ultimate concern, (3) community of faith. But we should here notice the fact that Cobb's definition of theology requires no accounting for God's existence.

Buddhism is, in fact, a doctrine of No-God. But insofar as it cannot do without concern with man and his possibility for illumination or salvation, Cobb admits it to be theological (CNT 255). There will be no need to dwell upon the fact that Buddhism is a doctrine of illumination and salvation. But in order to make this clear, I want to give here one or two examples.

In Buddhism, the Buddha is, as it were, an illuminated illuminator. He is an illuminated subject of illumination. In this illumination, the Buddha finds his place and time to realize himself, and at the same time every other thing finds its place and time to realize itself. In this situation, each and every thing is a Buddha as an illuminated illuminator. The world of such illumination is what is called the 'Buddha's-Land.' In Buddhism, a Buddha is no other than 'one-among-many.' As such, a Buddha is a companion of ours. This is one of the main perspectives in the Kegon sutra.

According to Dôgen, whose vision of reality was deeply indebted to Kegon thought, to learn to realize the way of Buddha is to learn to realize true self, and to learn to realize true self is to learn to realize all the worlds. All the worlds are, in Buddhism, a body of true self. True self or Buddha shares, without fail, the awareness and behavior with all the worlds and with all living things. In these formulations we will be able to find the Buddhist metaphysical ground for the possibility of man's salvation as well as of his existence. Such being the case, I myself, at least, should like to say with Cobb that there is no need for hesitancy in speaking of Buddhist theology.

Next, can there be a Buddhist 'natural' theology? Cobb conceives natural theology as the area of overlap between philosophy and theology, and, while it need not be naturalistic, it looks for its primary data to nature—to what is universal, recurrent, and widespread—rather than to the specifics of history (*SCE* 8). But if we say that natural theology should be the product of unhistorical reason as a universal human power, then Cobb will reply once for all, "There is no such thing" (*CNT* 261).

The structure of natural theology is, anyhow, both theological and philosophical. It is theological in the sense that the theologian's selection of anyone's philosophy expresses his particular perspective formed in a community from which he speaks. At the same time, it is philosophical in the sense that he should try to give expression in terms of norms to matters of theological importance (*CNT* 266f). But Cobb asks a natural theologian to accept two criteria for the evaluation of available philosophies when he attempts to construct natural theology. One of them is that consistency and coherence, where they are possible, are to be preferred over inconsistency and incoherence. The other is that there are no reasons whatever for accepting as a natural theology a position hostile, for example, to Christian faith (*CNT* 265).

In Buddhism, the possibility for our existence and salvation is deeply grounded upon the fundamental principle of universal 'No-Self.' This principle of No-Self has come to hand through the great struggles in radical doubt about seeking true self in any substantial forms whatever. In this sense, Buddhism is, in itself, philosophical. No-Self is essential to nature. It is universal, recurrent. We can find its evidence in us and in each and every thing around us.

To be sure, the principle of universal No-Self has played a destructive role in purification of taints originated from illusion. But Buddhist theologians also have been engaged in arranging as well as in cleaning.

They have tried reinterpreting various teachings and doctrines and reorganizing them, from the standpoint of universal No-Self. Thus we can give not a few examples which satisfy the conditions of natural theology demanded by Cobb.

Last of all, can there be a 'Whiteheadian' Buddhist natural theology? Cobb believes that it would be possible for us to construct such a natural theology. But Cobb asks the theologians to select a philosophy according to its compatibility with their fundamental vision of reality as well as to its philosophical excellence. Here Cobb does not expect that adherents of other faiths should simply accept his choice as a common basis for joint reflection (*CNT* 282). Nevertheless, there are many points of contact with the East in Whitehead's extraordinarily comprehensive and original philosophy. For example, in it we can find the emphasis on immanence, the rejection of any substance underlying the succession of experience, the relation of man to nature, and the primacy of aesthetic categories in the understanding of ethics. And all these modes of thought have affinities to this or that Asiatic philosophy or religion (*CNT* 282).

But after all, Whitehead is a Christian. Here if we take it for granted that to be a Christian is one thing and to be a Buddhist is another, there will be no possibility for mutual understanding between them. But Whitehead stands more closely than we can imagine to the Buddhist doctrine of No-Substances when he criticizes the idea of absolute monism in Western metaphysics. And while I was, as mentioned above, engaged in Whitehead's philosophy, I recognized that there were some affinities between his world view and Dôgen's. Thus, I myself admit with Cobb that it might be quite possible for a Buddhist to construct a Whiteheadian Buddhist natural theology, however strange it may sound.

And further, here in Japan we have the philosophy of Nishida (1870–1945), which has not a few affinities with that of Whitehead. According to one of the disciples of Nishida, if Whitehead's idea of God as an everlasting entity—this seems to be the most vulnerable point in his system—were replaced by what Nishida calls 'absolute nothingness,' then we would be able to detect in the thought of Whitehead elements that are deeply in touch with Nishida's philosophy. Whitehead's system may be, as it were, a book sealed with seven seals. But the seven seals do not remain unbroken forever for those who have learned Nishida's philosophy. I will here point to some of their affinities.

1. *The standpoint of both Nishida and Whitehead is a thoroughgoing objectivism.* According to Nishida, apart from the world's self-expressing process there can be no self-consciousness experienced in us. Truth emerges when and where each of us is to become a world's self-projective point through our thoroughgoing self-negation. In order to make this under-

standable, he is fond of referring to Dôgen's phraseology: "To learn the Self is to forget the Self, and to forget the Self is to be proved by All." And further, he sometimes refers to a Christian phraseology: "It is only through absolute negation of the Self that it is possible to live in God."

What Nishida calls 'action-intuition' takes place in us in the form of a perspective point in which the Self mirrors the world and the world mirrors the Self. He regards this 'action-intuition' as fundamental in knowledge. It will be synonymous with 'immediate experience.' But it does not mean that he stands by pragmatism's side. And he also protests against Kantian apriorism. In the case of Nishida, what is objective is already involved in what is subjective, and what is subjective is already involved in what is objective. The objectivity of our knowledge is to be grounded on the self-consciousness as the process of the world's self-expression. This is the reason why Nishida says that his standpoint is a thoroughgoing objectivism.

Something like this tone heard in Nishida's world view we will be able to hear in that of Whitehead. According to Whitehead: "In a certain sense, everything is everywhere in all times. For every location involves an aspect of itself in every other location. Thus every spatio-temporal standpoint mirrors the world."[3]

In this view of the world, Whitehead finds the ground of his 'philosophy of organism.' He says that his organic philosophy interprets experience as meaning the self-enjoyment of being one among many, and of being one arising out of the composition of many.[4] From these statements it will be clear why he protests against various forms of the 'bifurcation of nature.' It is not the case with him to say that what is sensuous is merely subjective. It is real as sense-object. What seems to have been experienced in the subject has been experienced, to tell the truth, in the object, and what seems to have been found in the object has been, in fact, found in the subject. He makes much of the fact of immediate experience. But this does not mean that he lays stress on the process from subjectivity to objectivity, but he himself finds in the immediate experience the process from objectivity to subjectivity. This is the reason why he inverts Kant's philosophy. "The philosophy of organism," says Whitehead, "is the inversion of Kant's philosophy," and "For Kant, the world emerges from the subject; for the philosophy of organism, the subject emerges from the world."[5] In this sense, his standpoint is also a thoroughgoing objectivism.

2. *The philosophy of Nishida and that of Whitehead are both the philosophy of the 'world.'* According to Nishida's world view, the Self is, as mentioned above, a "self-projective point of the world." Thus, the Self is not the Self that stands outside the world and looks at the external world. It is the Self

that exists in the world, mirrors it, and acts in it. It is the Self in which the world has its own self-projective point. In this sense, the philosophy of Nishida is the philosophy of the 'world.' The same is true for White-head's philosophy by reason of his world view.

3. *It is not that I am, therefore I experience; but that I experience, therefore I am.* In Nishida's philosophy, reality is more than mere given data. What is given is what has been formed. Reality is where we 'are' and 'act.' Acting is not a mere fact of will; it is 'forming,' that is, it is the making of things. But the formed has already entered the environment and has already become a part of the past. Thus, the process from the formed to the forming is that from the past to the future.

This rhythm of process will be heard in Whitehead's cosmology. The term 'superject' is central in his philosophy. It is not that there is a feeler first of all and then feelings take place, but that feelings take place first of all and then there is a feeler. And this process from feelings to a feeler is that from the past to the future

4. *The individual is a creative factor of the creative world.* The creative process of the world has its foci in the individuals. Insofar as we partake of this creative process, we are engaged in the formation of things. When we are forming things, we are physically acting and at the same time we are forming our-selves. Nishida often uses his own phraseology "seeing in becoming physical." In fact, it is through our physical body that we are able to enjoy our-selves as the creative factors of the creative world. Our 'body' belongs to the order of nature which is the universal formative logos. Thus, the body is logical, instrumental, and technological.

Whitehead also recognizes both the individuals and the world as crea-tive. According to him, the actual world is a creative process, and the process is the becoming of novel, and self-creative, actual entities. This is a complex process of appropriating into a unity of existence the many data presented as relevant by the physical process of nature.[6] And we can read his following phraseology: "It is by reason of the body, with its miracle of order, that the treasures of the past environment are poured into the living occasion."[7]

5. *We owe to the sense of Deity the obviousness of the many actualities of the world and the obviousness of the unity of the world.*[8] According to Nishida, the world does not have its unity and identity within itself. If that were true, the world would lose the character as the process of creativity. Thus the world must have its unity and identity in the absolutely transcendent. This fact means that the individual many are confronted with the tran-scendent 'One,' and at the same time that thereby each of them becomes more and more individual. Here we will be able to find at once the direction to the unity of the world and the direction of the individual

many of the world. They are in the opposite directions. Despite and just because of their opposite directions, they are coexistent and coefficient in the absolute present as the eternal now in which the direction from the past to the present and the direction from the future to the present are simultaneous. That absolute transcendent is, in fact, this absolute present. The self-determination of the absolute present is, as it were, the determination-without-a-determining-one. It is spiritual in the sense that it is the mirroring-without-mirror. The Oriental religion of 'Nothingness' teaches that the 'Soul,' as it is, is the 'Buddha.' According to Nishida, this is neither mere spiritualism nor mere mysticism. It means that 'All is One.' But this does not mean that all are one without differentiation. It is that One by which All that is, is. He calls this the unity of opposites.

The sense of 'Deity' arises from here. According to Whitehead, Deity is that factor in the universe whereby there is importance, value, and ideal beyond the actual. "The unity of a transcendent universe, and the multiplicity of realized actualities," says he, "both enter into our experience by this sense of Deity."[9]

Here, for a moment, we listen to what he says: "Everything has some value for itself, for others, and for the whole. This characterizes the meaning of actuality. By reason of this character, constituting reality, the conception of morals arises. We have no right to deface the value-experience which is the very essence of the universe."[10]

Our experience is thus always a value experience. Our value experience implies failure as well as success. Whitehead says: "The intertwining of success and failure in respect to this final experience is essential. We thereby experience a relationship to a universe other than ourselves. We are essentially measuring ourselves in respect to what we are not."[11]

Just as between the unity and the many Whitehead sees the contrast of opposites, so also between success and failure he sees the contrast of opposites. In Whitehead's world view, the way in which we lose sight of the contrast of opposites will lead to the way in which we lose sight of God.

So far I have mentioned some affinities between the philosophy of Nishida and that of Whitehead. It will be desirable that I should further take up their differences. To be sure, we are able to detect them. But they are not always insurmountable. Here I will discuss one of the fundamental modes of thought from which their differences arise.

According to Whitehead, there are two senses of the 'one'—namely, the sense of the one which is all, and the sense of the one among the many. We are, each of us, one among others; and all of us are embraced in the unity of the whole.[12] Any of them mirrors within itself the other two and it-self. As such, each of them is an organism as a whole. An actual entity is an epochal whole. As such, each actual entity has temporal extension. Here Cobb suggests, "The temporal extension happens all at once as an individual unit"; or, "In terms of physical time the occasion must be said to become all at once" (*CNT* 186). A whole which happens "all at once" also happens, I should say, "once for all." It is by reason of its "once for all" that an actual entity other than God, even though it is an epochal whole, must perish.

But God as a whole does not perish. Whitehead suggests that there are two sides in God. One is the primodial nature of God. It is eternal. According to Cobb's interpretation, this means that it is wholly un-affected by physical time, the nature of which lies in 'perpetual perishing,' or by process in the sense of the 'before-and-after' within the becoming of an actual entity. The other side is the consequent nature of God. It is everlasting. God, for Cobb, is an everlasting whole in the sense that "whatever enters into the consequent nature of God remains there forever, but new elements are constantly added, while God always envis-ages all possibility eternally" (*CNT* 187). Thus, God as a whole is ever-lasting. And here he seeks the ground of the divine absolute self-identity.

Whitehead's conception of God as non-temporal does not mean, Cobb thinks, that God has no process whatever in himself. 'Before' and 'after' are to be relevant terms for describing this process. And further, on the basis of some philosophical objections to the notion of God as a single actual entity, Cobb presents God as a whole in the form of a 'living person,' namely, an "infinite succession of divine occasions of experi-ence" (*CNT* 188).

The notion 'living person' does not always demand that of 'substance' and any visible 'form.' In this sense, I have no objection to Cobb's view of God. A person has its self-identity in a contrast of contrasts. In White-head's philosophy, the notion 'contrast' means the opposite of incompat-ibility. The opposites have their meanings in a unity of them, namely, in a contrast. Everything is, in a sense, a contrast of contrasts. God is, in the ultimate sense, a contrast of such contrasts of contrasts. Donald W. Sher-burne says, "The more an actual entity can hold the items of its experi-ence in contrasts, and contrasts of contrasts, the more it elicits depth and intensity for its satisfaction."[13] On this basis we can read Whitehead's passage: "All the opposites are elements in the nature of things, and are incorrigibly there. The concept of God is the way in which we understand this incredible fact—that what cannot be, yet is."[14]

Why is it possible in regard to God that what cannot be, yet is? If I might give an answer in place of Nishida, I should say that its possibility is due to the fact that God has no standpoint whatever. God is a standpoint-without-standpoint, in which all standpoints are denied and at the same time from which all standpoints do emerge. Such a standpoint-without-standpoint is not anything like this or that. In this sense it is, as it were, 'Nothing.' In a sense, God is Nothing. God is not a thing that belongs to this or that. Because of his nothingness, God does not give any self-persistent context to this or that standpoint. The absolute 'One' has nothing in itself. In the self-denial of such an absolute one there is the ground of our absolute immediate self-enjoyment of concrete experience. Our Selves come into being as individual many which emerge in virtue of the self-denial of the absolute one. In this way, the absolute one has its self-identity in its self-denial, namely, in individual many. And therefore our Self has its self-identity in that which is beyond, and, at the same time, at the bottom of our Self.[15]

As above, the notion 'nothingness' is the ultimate category of categories in Nishida's philosophy. To be sure, 'creativity,' 'many,' and 'one' are the ultimate categories for Nishida as well as for Whitehead. Nishida, furthermore, adds the term 'nothingness' to them. But this does not mean that Whitehead's 'ontological principle' is no longer in need. Nishida admits the fact of efficient and final causation. But he thinks that the process from the past to the future is to be made possible only through the self-determination of 'absolute present,' which is, as he says, using an old phraseology, an infinite sphere, the center of which is everywhere, the circumference nowhere.

II. WOULD A WHITEHEADIAN BUDDHIST NATURAL THEOLOGY BE DESIRABLE?

Whitehead rejects 'the fallacy of dogmatic finality' in the following terms: "The Universe is vast. Nothing is more curious than the self-satisfied dogmatism with which mankind at each period of its history cherishes the delusion of the finality of its existing modes of knowledge. Sceptics and believers are all alike. At this moment scientists and sceptics are the leading dogmatists. Advance in detail is admitted; fundamental novelty is barred. This dogmatic common sense is the death of philosophic adventure. The Universe is vast."[16] Without presupposing this fact that the universe is vast, we cannot expect any fruitful result from the encounter of Christian and Buddhist theologies. According to Cobb, Whitehead can offer great aid to the West in its task of rethinking its faith in the light of the reality of the great religions of the East (*CNT* 283). Here in Japan most Buddhist theologians have, more or less, been interested in Nishida's philosophy. But this does not mean that there is no need for us Buddhists to construct a Whiteheadian Buddhist natural theology. And, between the philosophy of Nishida and that of Whitehead, it is not true to say that if one is right then the other must be wrong. I should like to say that the more we understand Nishida, the more we understand Whitehead, and at the same time, the more we understand Whitehead, the more we understand Nishida. Through investigating this possibility of their mutual understanding, I expect that the East and the West will be able to encounter each other. And there we should find God as a contrast of contrasts. For this reason, a Whiteheadian Buddhist natural theology would be desirable for the East as well as for the West.

Cobb's effort to develop a Christian natural theology is made through investigating Whitehead's philosophy by dint of a Christian vision of reality. One of the reasons why he has chosen Whitehead's philosophy as the basis on which he would propose to develop a Christian natural theology is the fact that in Whitehead's works there is a fully developed alternative to nihilistic tendencies of modern thought (*CNT* 15). This is also the case with a Buddhist natural theology. By the way, the Buddhist doctrine of 'nothingness' may be, as has often been, taken as nihilistic. But this is not true. Buddhism would like to share the Whiteheadian 'principle of relativity.'

Both Nishida and Whitehead seem to have cherished an idea that at once Buddhism and Christianity would have to experience a radical reformation once more. And they both suggest that such a reformation must be scientific. In his last paper, Nishida writes the following words: "I agree, in general, with Berdyaef in almost all his views expressed in his 'The Meaning of History.' But his philosophy does not go out of the limit of Boehmean mysticism. New era should, above all things, be scientific." As a matter of fact, there will be little use of Buddhists' trying to have a large share in building up a new era without paying attention to science. Whitehead also expects the reformation of the two main traditions of the world religions. According to him, science has become the third tradition in our modern world. This tradition has not been brought up in the school of dogmas but in the school of experience. The reformation will not be able to do without this school of experience, the door of which should be always open to the 'creative advance' of the world. In any case, in order to have some share in forming a new era, our natural theology must enlist the aid of a creative and scientific view of the world. Whitehead's philosophy is at the same time creative and scientific. Thus it is desirable that our Buddhist natural theology should be a Whiteheadian Buddhist natural theology.

But we cannot pass over the fact that there are several points at issue in constructing a Whiteheadian Buddhist natural theology. From the Whiteheadian point of view, Cobb proposes some questions about Buddhism. Here I will take up one of them. It is about the relation of the past to the present. According to Cobb, a certain kind of Buddhism is involved in a subtle illusion in which much Western philosophy has had a share. We are apt to be led to empty the environment of its real significance for human existence when concentrating on experience in the mode of 'presentational immediacy' (*SCE* 68).

Cobb's criticism leveled against Buddhism refers to the Buddhist pretension that the present occasion alone is ultimately responsible for how it prehends its predecessors. What makes his criticism right is the word 'alone' found in the context. It is not the case with Cobb as well as with the Buddhists that there is no self-determination in this present occasion. His view is, like that of the Buddhists, that the ultimate ontological individual is a momentary occasion of experience (*SCE* 71). But, as he points out, in Buddhism, especially in Zen Buddhism, there has surely been such a tendency to exaggerate the capacity of an actual occasion of human experience to determine its own relation to its predecessors. This tendency is prone to lead the Buddhists to turn away from what Whitehead calls 'efficient causes.'[17]

The Whiteheadian point of view shows us how each actual occasion comes into being against the background of the whole past of the world. The past is composed of innumerable occasions that have had their moments of subjective immediacy and have perished. Though perished, they have not become simply nothing. Rather, they have their own mode of being, which Whitehead calls 'objective immortality.' They are effective as objects to be prehended by new occasions (*CNT* 38). This determination by the past is real, although it is not absolute. What I have been in the past and what the world as a whole has been may narrowly limit what I can become in this next moment. But within those limits it is still my decision in that moment as to how I shall react to all these forces impinging upon me (*CNT* 39). In this way, the causal efficacy can be regarded not only as a process from the past to the present but also as a process from the world to the individual. In this case, however, we should not put it out of sight that it is left to new occasions to decide how to react to the past.

In fact, this conception of the universal causation of the world would finely be expressed in a Zen Buddhist phraseology: "There has taken place the world just in the opening of a flower." According to Dôgen, it is an illusion to find and enjoy All by means of proceeding from Self to All, and it is an illusion to find and enjoy Self by means of proceeding from All to Self. But the notion of this universal causality of the world may lead us to assume the substantiality of the world. It would be almost impossible to evade such an assumption when we look for the fundamental ground for our existence only in the world-in-itself. But there we could not find any possibility for our salvation. To get rid of this difficulty, Buddhists sometimes try to seek their deliverance from worldly existence by reducing the environment to mere momentary congeries of elements lacking all significance for existence. Through this kind of reduction, the emotional life can be disengaged from attachment to and involvement in the world (*SCE* 68).

Such a Buddhist view of the world may be, as Cobb points out, a result of concentrating on experience in the mode of 'presentational immediacy' without paying any attention to 'causal efficacy.' To be sure, the world of sensa is contemporary with the world of the subject in the sense that it belongs in and with the world of the subject. But it is not true to say that hence there is no object at all in experience (*CNT* 45). If we Buddhists say that we can find no reality in objects as the past or as the world from the viewpoint of the self-in-the-world experience in the mode of presentational immediacy, then we must admit Cobb's criticism that we are committing the error of reducing the past to mere nothingness and hence of disregarding causal efficacy.

In any case, Zen Buddhists would like to give priority to the present over the past and the future. In this case, however, they may do so by reason of the Whiteheadian definition of 'contemporaneousness.' Whitehead's definition of contemporary occasions teaches us how they happen in causal independence of each other as well as in mutual independence of each other. This definition has respect only to the internal process of self-enjoyment or self-adjustment of a contemporary occasion. Thus it does not mean the reduction of causal efficacy to inefficacy. According to Whitehead, the vast causal independence of contemporary occasions is, however, a cosmological fact. "It provides," says he, "each actuality with a welcome environment for irresponsibility."[18] Here I must confess that I have an idea, though it is not yet sufficiently warranted, that in Whitehead's definition of 'contemporaneousness' there could be a clue to Nishida's conception of 'absolute present.' The reason for my confession lies in the fact that in the contemporaneousness there is nothing substantial, and that there emerge self-creative actualities. That in which there is nothing substantial and from which self-creative actualities emerge; this is what Nishida calls 'absolute nothingness.'

NOTES

1. "The Buddhist-Whiteheadian View of the Self and the Religious Traditions," *Proceedings of the IXth International Congress for the History of Religions* (Tokyo: Maruzen, 1960), 298–302.

2. In *Zen no Honshitsu to Ningen no Shinri* [The Essence of Zen Buddhism and the truth of the human being], by Hisamatsu Shin'ichi *et al.* (Tokyo: Sobun, 1969), 213–270.

3. Alfred North Whitehead, *Science and the Modern World* (The Macmillan Company, 1925), 133.

4. Alfred North Whitehead, *Process and Reality* (The Macmillan Company, 1929), 220.

5. *Ibid.*, 135f.

6. Alfred North Whitehead, *Modes of Thought* (The Macmillan Company, 1938), 205.

7. Whitehead, *Process and Reality*, 516.

8. Whitehead, *Modes of Thought*, 140.

9. *Ibid.*

10. *Ibid.*, 151.

11. *Ibid.*, 141.

12. *Ibid.*, 150f.

13. Donald W. Sherburne (ed.), *A Key to Whitehead's Process and Reality* (Indiana University Press, 1971), 216.

14. Whitehead, *Process and Reality*, 531.

15. Nishida's last paper: "Logic of Topos and Religious World-View."

16. Lucien Price, *Dialogues of Alfred North Whitehead* (Little, Brown & Company, 1954), 7.

17. Dôgen protests against the tendency of Zen Buddhists to turn away from the principle of this 'efficient cause,' referring to Nagarjuna's words: "If the causality were to be broken, there could be no present world and no future world."

18. Alfred North Whitehead, *Adventures of Ideas* (The Macmillan Company, 1933), 251.

COBB'S THEOLOGY OF ECOLOGY

By Charles Hartshorne

WHEN I READ Cobb's book on Whitehead's philosophy I thought: "This is splendid. But I knew he could do it." When I read his book on ecology I thought: "This is indeed splendid, but I did not know he could do it." I *should* have known. To be sure, to anticipate that Cobb would write such a book one must have anticipated the great increase in general awareness of environmental problems that made it natural for a very gifted, clearheaded theologian to turn his attention to ecological matters.

I can scarcely remember when I began to think about pollution. Anyone who has not done this in the preceding decades can hardly be interested in nature at all. I recall as a youth (about 1914) swimming in a mountain stream in Pennsylvania whose waters were brownish from the tannin put into them by a tannery upstream. In its rocky bed and rushing torrent it was a magnificent stream—only, so far as we could tell, devoid of trout, whereas the tributary streams, which were clear, had trout. I also recall, several decades ago, hearing an expert on China reply to the question, What about the population increase in that country? "I can't see any solution to that problem." I recall too W. H. Sheldon, the inventor of the "Sheldon Types" anthropology, long ago objecting to some philosopher or theologian of repute (I rather think it was Whitehead): "What has he to say about population?" implying that unless a man faced that issue he could be dismissed. In such ways I have been somewhat alerted to these questions for a good while. Still I scarcely dreamed of such a book as Cobb's *Is It Too Late? A Theology of Ecology.*

Cobb begins, with characteristic lucidity, where one should begin. Even Malthus did not quite do this. He compared population increase with food increase. But he did not take sufficiently into account the temporary relief given by the settling of the Americas and other slightly inhabited areas, and did not foresee various effects of technology. Nor did he realize that food is not necessarily the most critical factor, which might rather be wholesome air and water.

Cobb faces us, on page one, with the rock-bottom principle that no geometrical increase of a species can go on forever, or even for many centuries. Not only would the earth fail to provide standing room, the solar system and even our island universe could not do so. At the recent rate of increase, by the year 2300 there would be a thousand times as many people and by the year 2633 a million times as many as now. Cobb does not go on with the calculations, but not many centuries would be required to make the human species comparable in mass to the now known universe! The conclusion seems as certain as anything we can say about the future, and it is that the recent rate of increase will be drastically slowed down, probably before many decades have passed. It is also certain that the slowdown will consist of one or both of the following: fewer births, more deaths, annually. Since not many would prefer that there be more deaths, it is sheer logic that we must prefer a reduction in births.

Cobb is aware, as Malthus could scarcely be in his age, that pollution is the ultimate threat. Long before standing room would be gone, breathable air and drinkable water would be but a memory. And many food resources would have been used up or poisoned out of existence. Cobb is also aware that starvation on a large scale is happening here and there in the world even now. He relates the 'green revolution' in India to the introduction of potatoes into Ireland, which led first to a great increase in population, then to a potato blight and mass famine. He is aware, too, that better distribution and increase in production of wealth will in some respects make things worse. For it is the well-to-do, those living luxuriously, who contribute by far the largest amounts of polluting wastage to the environment. It is the industrialized countries that do most of the polluting. Yet the poor and agrarian countries, as their populations grow (thanks to modern hygiene), pollute too. Thus the problem is, in substantial part, too many people. And while technology can eliminate some forms of pollution, it always introduces new forms, thermal pollution of air and water if nothing else. It is basic physical law that there is a price for everything, including every form of power and every luxury. People want and to some extent need power, the more people the more power, and the more power the more pollution as the minimum price. We can perhaps lower the present per person price, but we cannot eliminate it.

Our theologian realizes that there are those among us who resent emphasis upon the ecology-population relationship, and who see this emphasis as distracting from the worst immediate evils of unjust distribution and unemployment. Here we are given a brilliant allegory: a ship on a long voyage has steerage and first-class accommodations. In the steerage there is crowding, malnutrition, disease; on the upper decks there is plenty of room and many luxuries. The victims in the steerage complain and contemplate revolt. Some concessions are made, but the discontent does not abate. More violent means are required to maintain law and order. Meantime the ship has sprung a leak. The officers are too busy maintaining order to attend to the leak. Violence, specially by the officers, increases. Cobb's question is, Shall we go on in this style, 'where we are now,' or shall we cooperate to deal with the leak? The ship begins to list a little.

The next chapter, "Let the Engineers Handle It," takes up the easy way out: trust to technology. Cobb gives the Aswan Dam as an example, which has had some good and some very bad effects. He warns us that, no matter what the engineers do, we shall have to change our way of life as well as our gadgets. Three objections bring out the limitations of the merely technological solution. First, there is the beauty and intrinsic value of non-human life on this planet, that wondrous process which went on for billions of years before man. Engineers as such have nothing to say about this, and are, if anything, its enemies and detractors. They and those who think like them speak of a natural forest or swamp as, of itself, mere wasted space, needing 'development,' which tends to mean destruction of a great wealth of non-human forms of life and beauty. Second, there is the ugly fact that technology tends to be closely associated with military power. Engineers tend to think in terms of economic potential and military—that is, destructive—capacity. Third, the technological attitude makes a sharp distinction between ends and means, and inclines us to see all of non-human life, and much of human life, as mere means to some more or less abstract end, such as military victory, or individual or community wealth. But life is the absolute end. It is never rightly taken as mere means. This applies to all forms of life.

As Cobb is aware, Asiatic philosophies and religions have differed from our Western tendency to regard the rest of nature as nothing but means to our human ends. Reverence for life as such is pervasive in the Orient, but has not been so in the West. Here Cobb, rightly, I hold, thinks that Christianity needs to reconsider its basic values. He does not say so, but I think it could be argued that Western science makes the extreme form of Christian exaltation of man as the sole valuable form of life rather ridiculous since it implies that divine purpose took billions of years to get to something of any value. Schweitzer is introduced as a guide to the needed reconstruction of theology.

The ultimate clue Cobb finds in Whitehead's metaphysics, according to which every singular instance of creativity, which for Whitehead is the same as reality in its concreteness, has its intrinsic value or satisfaction and contributes directly to the divine life. Man is merely the supreme, rather than the sole, contributor on this planet. To me it seems clear that no other metaphysics can so clearly ground an ecological attitude, that is, an attitude of respect for the whole web of life by which each item in the web is sustained and made possible. Cobb has developed this implication of process philosophy and theology exceedingly well. This development is the heart of the book.

In spite of his command of metaphysical abstractions, Cobb is nicely balanced in the attention he gives to practical and specific implications. He 'gets down to cases,' giving vivid suggestions as to how our habits may have to change to meet ecological requirements.

I offer no criticism of this book. I only wonder how it can be brought to the attention of the many readers it deserves.

SOMATIC ETHICS: JOY AND ADVENTURE IN THE EMBODIED MORAL LIFE

By Charles H. Reynolds

I

ALFRED NORTH WHITEHEAD his monumental work in metaphysics and in the philosophy of culture and society with an apparent blissful distance from the characteristic concerns that receive attention from ethicists.[1] Although Whitehead was interested in the metaphysical origin and explanation of *value* as a social reality, there is little in his writings that is directly relevant to the discussions that have characterized recent ethical theory. One will not find a justification scheme for ethical statements, a theory of virtue, an analysis of the concept of morality, an explicit answer to the question, Why be moral?, a theory of justice, or a way of resolving the dispute between act and rule utilitarians—or between act and rule deontologists—anywhere in Whitehead's writings. Yet these are representative of the issues that have been at the forefront of the discussion in twentieth-century ethical theory.[2]

Whitehead ignored ethicists and their issues in developing his system of thought, and one must observe that ethicists have returned the favor, for ethicists characteristically ignore the work of Whitehead. Indeed, we appear to have here an unbridgeable chasm.[3]

If those of us concerned with ethical theory are to read Whitehead and his interpreters, therefore, we will do so for reasons different from those that generally lead us to read our fellow ethicists. Certain writings of John Cobb are instructive in assisting us to apprehend what some of these reasons might be. Cobb is not convinced that we have here an unbridgeable chasm (see esp. *CNT*, Ch. 3).

Whether or not it proves to be bridgeable, however, we need a careful and critical study of the differing philosophical assumptions underlying the apparent abyss that now separates process thought from most of contemporary ethical theory, including assumptions about self-identity and moral responsibility, affective and cognitive

116

moral perceptivity, the social formation of moral agents and moral autonomy, the isolated will of the moral agent and the social nature of
the moral self, etc. A probing analysis that maps these differences as
they are focused in process thought and most contemporary ethical
theory is essential if a fruitful discussion across our apparent chasm is
to be undertaken.[4] In the absence of this more fundamental analysis,
one can at best make some tentative suggestions, as Cobb has done,
concerning how a rapprochement here might best be accomplished.[5]
Along this line, we can investigate some of the advantages we stand
to obtain from relating the rigor of contemporary ethical analysis to
the social background of Whitehead's process metaphysics. One can
intuitively see that each of these traditions of fundamental inquiry has
something to receive and to give when a constructive and critical dialogue between them is established.

The thesis of this essay is that an ethics essentially faithful to process
thought will be a somatic ethics, an ethics of the socially embodied moral
self in constitutive interaction with a socially embodied moral God. An
important role is given to eros and the aesthetic imagination in developing what it means for a moral agent to be a socially embodied self. The
somatic perspective is such that joy and adventure are internal elements
in ethical theory and interpreted as essential to the moral life. But if
somatic ethics is to be a full-scale theory of ethics, able to assist us in
answering metaethical, normative, and tactical questions,[6] and not a partial, fragmentary theory, it will provide us with a way (1) to justify certain
normative rules and principles for our individual and institutional morality, (2) to specify the principles of selectivity at work in this justification,
and (3) to focus the frame of reference by which this justification is
achieved.

II

Cobb has not claimed to find an explicit ethical theory in Whitehead's
work. He observes that Whitehead had a "notorious lack of interest in
ethics" (8:621). In this connection Cobb attempts to develop an ethical
theory that is harmonious with Whitehead's expressed views and that will
supplement Whitehead's work by treating questions neglected by him
(*CNT* 113). In pursuit of this constructive intention, Cobb opens a conversation with the formative persons and issues in recent ethical theory.

I am in essential agreement with the project that Cobb has initiated and
with its execution to this point. His writings represent the best extant
bridge between process theology and contemporary ethical theory. Cobb
will, it is hoped, continue to pursue some of the questions he has raised

on these matters, especially the relationship of Kant's ethical theory to his own and Whitehead's basic philosophical orientation (*CNT* 123).

In adumbrating a somatic ethics, my intention is to supplement Cobb's work in a way similar to his own efforts to complement that of Whitehead. The role of eros in this tradition of thought discloses an important dimension of what is involved in our being social selves as moral agents. This dimension of our experience needs to be accounted for more adequately than is generally done as we formulate our theories of religious ethics. An ethic that gives an important role to eros, unlike most current approaches to religious ethics, invites us to a life of adventure and joy. But not to a joy that denies suffering or to an adventure that renounces sacrifice. It is indeed an ethics.

The socially embodied communications between God and persons, elicited by the divine eros and confirmed by real internal relationships, provide us with a perspective for understanding God as an Ideal Participant in our given social reality.[7] Somatic ethics affirms for its basic background[8] the notion of a sympathetic, unitive power beyond us and operative upon us that in part constitutes us as social selves and that in part persuasively conditions our social reality. This vision of God is of One who stands over against us as a fully transcendent moral judge while also being an intimate companion and friend. Or, as H. Richard Niebuhr once so clearly put the implications of this vision of God,

> The simultaneous, unified knowledge from within and from without that we may ascribe to God is indeed impossible to men, but what is simultaneous in his case can in a measure be successive for us.[9]

God can know us from 'within' and from 'without' in that God fully participates in our social reality and (in a different aspect of God's reality, as the unconditioned One) has a distinctive reality that is totally independent of our social life.

Whitehead in part prepared the way for this development of a theological somatic ethics by interpreting eros as a constitutive characteristic of God's reality.[10] To discern the import of what is here intended, imagine yourself as being drawn toward, and as consenting to letting yourself be drawn toward, everything that has reality in a loving, other-affirming way, in that way which the sensibilities of Jonathan Edwards tasted as being-consenting-to-being in general, a consent that respects and affirms the individuality and diversity within all being. It is this aesthetic vision of a loving and persuasive divine consent to creative individuality that focuses the primal background for a theological somatic ethics. While this aesthetic vision of a primal background is of critical importance for our discerning of the import of God's social reality for somatic ethics, it is essential nevertheless that we not be beguiled into simply identifying aesthetics and ethics.

Cobb has interpreted this moving principle of consent that pervades all reality, i.e., Whitehead's notion of eros as a function of the Primordial Nature of God, with the aid of the theological category of *Spirit.* Confidence in and reliance upon the moving power of Spirit can, as Cobb affirms, provide us with a ground of hope when we are bedeviled by complacency and despair. In Cobb's words:

> Since what makes for life and love and hope is not simply the decision of one individual or another, but a Spirit that moves us all, I do not have to suppose that my own efforts are of great consequence in order to believe them to be worthwhile. I can recognize that they may even be futile or misdirected and still persist in them as long as no clearer light is given. For I see what I do as part of something much greater, something in which each person participates to whatever extent he sensitively responds to the insights and opportunities that come his way. Belief in the Spirit is belief that I am not alone. That in working for life and love in hope, I am working *with* something much greater than myself; that there are possibilities for the future that cannot be simply projected out of the past; that even my mistakes and failures may be woven into a healing pattern of which I am not now aware. . . . That Spirit, of course, is the God of whom we have been speaking. (*TE* 144)

This Spirit that moves us all and lovingly establishes a bond of community within all social reality is a manifestation of eros as a constitutive factor in God's reality.

III

Eros has characteristically been left ungeneralized and has frequently been ignored or maligned in theological ethics. Most Christian ethicists have played down eros, perhaps intending thereby to elevate the importance of agape.[11] This may also in part be related to the limited emphasis placed upon the aesthetic imagination in most interpretations of Christian ethics. For it is, after all, the lure and drive of eros that generates our entertainment of the regulative categories for our being and doing, except and insofar as this activity is not simply the internalization of prevailing cultural patterns. Once this creative role of the aesthetic imagination for ethics has been recognized, it is indeed understandable why eros is typically downplayed in ethical theories that emphasize calculated rational choice among cultural options objectively presented to individual moral agents.

Eros is dynamic and indeterminate. Agape, by contrast, whether understood as a dispositional characteristic of the moral agent or a moral norm for action, is easily at home in what must be called conventional interpretations of theological ethics.[12] This domestication of agape has been achieved by severing agape from eros, and thereby from the generative aesthetic imagination, thus distancing agape from an urge toward creative advance into novelty, i.e., from adventure. Once domesticated, agape is quite easily adapted to the orientation of conventional ethics which focuses on the rational will and choices of isolated individuals. Gone is that sense of community fidelity which issues from feeling oneself in unity and solidarity with both near and distant humankind, both close and far social reality.

Quite naturally, moral vision becomes a critical problem in ethics when the sense of community with others and with all social reality has been lost.[13] For while agape may provide certain motivational and/or justifying reasons for a discrete individual's moral decisions, when severed from eros it is isolated from the generative source of moral vision, the aesthetic imagination. Thus impoverished, agape ethics does not challenge the prevalent assumptions in contemporary Occidental ethics about the point of departure for developing a theory of ethics, or about the nature and agenda of constructive ethical theory. A full and robust theory of love, a theory that would indeed challenge such assumptions, needs the attractive, luring, binding indeterminate and driving vitality of eros together with the steadfast, determinate, and equal-regarding characteristics of agape. Process theology understands God as the embodiment of this full and robust notion of love. This complex understanding of God as love provides a richer background for theological ethics than is to be found in traditions of thought that focus primarily—if not exclusively—on the transcendent, free, powerful, and benevolent will of God.

Process theology understands God's power in terms of God's love, not God's love in terms of a freedom to exercise power in a benevolent and beneficent manner. It is this difference in fundamental assumptions that distinguishes process theology from the classical Occidental theological tradition. A notion of participation is at the heart of process theology's understanding of God.

This rich and complex understanding of God as participant in social reality has its anthropological correlate. The social nature of the moral self as understood in process thought is quite at variance with the emphasis on the naked rational will of the individual who is to decide in the moment what she or he is to do that is prevalent in most contemporary ethical theory, including Christian ethics. Given this important difference, we are in a position to understand the claim that "the absence of an ethics written by Whitehead is to be explained by the fact that he does not distinguish 'ethics' from 'social philosophy.' "[14] One might more appropriately claim that instead of Whitehead's not having an ethics, he simply understands ethics quite differently than is typically the case in the mainstream of contemporary ethical theory. Just as Spinoza can be considered 'drunk with God' or an 'atheist,' depending on one's theological assumptions, Whitehead is or is not an ethicist, depending on one's assumptions about what constitutes ethics. Taking this position, Richard Davis argues that *"Adventures of Ideas* must be understood to be an ethical work in the same sense as Plato's *Republic.* "[15] Although this comparison strikes me as too sharply drawn, the general claim that underlies it may well be correct, for Whitehead does imply an alternative perspective on the nature and function of ethics. His focus on the social nature of the moral self that underlies his social philosophy enables him to appreciate the moral nexus of political and social institutions in a way that most current theories of ethics are simply unable to do. For if persons are viewed as having merely external relationships to institutions, as is the case where the focus is on will and choice, then institutions are assigned a non-constitutive role in the moral life. It is quite different when the social nexus in which the moral self is formed is discerned as inclusive of those institutional associations to which persons are considered internally related. We have here differences that are rooted in the respective philosophical anthropologies that underlie process thought, with its focus on the embodied social self, and most contemporary ethical theory, where the focus is on the isolated individual's moral choice. It is precisely here that those of us in theological ethics who are eager to relate our discipline to concrete institutional life have the most to learn from process thought.

Even so, I agree with Cobb that Whitehead's social thought needs to be supplemented by treating questions of ethics neglected by him. Maybe it is overly superficial to say that Whitehead's socially embodied selves must nevertheless individually deal with Kant's question, How can I know what I ought to do? I find it instructive that Cobb extends and develops Whitehead's work by turning to Kant for assistance in dealing with the issue of how we are to discern our moral obligations (*CNT* 123f). Cobb is probably correct in assuming that one who takes this tack does not need to establish first of all that Whitehead's interest in ethics as social philosophy and value theory is somehow compatible with a concern for this additional question of ethics. Cobb assumes that Whitehead's general metaphysical scheme is sufficiently adequate and inclusive to enable one appropriately to formulate the Kantian question, even if Whitehead himself did not do so. A constructive position, which is what Cobb offers, is the ideal way to confront the issue. The difficult challenge is to focus the additional questions of ethics in a way that is compatible with the Whiteheadian metaphysical scheme. While it is not yet evident that this is possible, since the full and constructive position has yet to be developed, it is a promising departure that could possibly provide us with the fullness and unity of a moral vision that has thus far escaped formulation in the modern world. The remainder of this essay provides a sketch of how a theological somatic ethics may augur precisely this inclusive moral vision.[16]

IV

Initially, without clarifying or specifying what is involved in the claim, let us assume that in God's sustaining relationship with us we are presented with 'claims of rightness' that are experientially present to all somatic selves. Let us further assume that these claims of rightness are included somehow in the ideal aims (or initial subjective aims) that God continually presents to all gradations of social reality and that persons experience these claims as somehow demanding moral excellence or flourishing.

Now given the above heuristic assumptions, can we specify a theoretical way of discerning the moral intentionality of God? To answer this question we must first determine what it would mean for God to intend moral excellence or flourishing. Confidence that God is on the side of moral excellence or flourishing, granted that we intend to live a life that is affirming of God, could provide a motivational reason for us to be and do what we think is morally good and right and virtuous. But such confidence does not give us a reason to believe that what we think about such matters is also what God intends that we think.

What, then, might it mean for God to intend 'moral flourishing' for all persons at all times? Is it possible for one to attempt theoretically to answer this question in a way that respects God's distinctive reality? The typical answer to this question is an emphatic "No!" It is, however, an answer with certain unusually interesting implications that are generally not examined. For if God's distinctive reality entails that we have no theoretical way of knowing God's moral intentions for us, or perhaps God's appreciative evaluations of us, then for our public ethics we have no recourse but to develop the most adequate non-theistic ethical theory that we can. Otherwise, theological ethics is necessarily a form of imperialistic particularism. This is what 'confessionalism' in theological ethics finally amounts to, and I suggest that it has been a normative critique of this position that has underscored the passion for the autonomy of ethics in the Occidental philosophical community. But an affirmation of the autonomy of philosophical ethics does not in any way address the extremely and perplexingly difficult question of whether or not it is possible for us to discern the moral intentionality of God. One might indeed hope that a non-theistic and autonomous ethical theory would spell out God's intentions and mode of evaluation, but that hope would admittedly be uninformed. Yet how easy it has been for this hope to become an assumption, and furthermore an assumption not accessible to critical evaluation. The irony is that a procedure intended to protect God's distinctive reality can easily have the opposite implication, as it permits human evaluations to function as the ultimate court of appeal—that is, as divine—and then to be carelessly identified as having divine sanction. It is clear, then, how idolatry can be one consequence of a negative answer to our question, with the abstract emptiness of what Paul Tillich called the 'Protestant principle' being another. These two consequences have the same locus of origin as they both depend on our being unable to specify the moral intentions of God.

One peril of being defensive about idolatry in theological ethics may in itself ensure that one will find oneself in nothing other than an idolatrous perspective. Insofar as this is indeed the situation that theological ethics is in today, it behooves us to venture forth and risk specifying an answer to our question. We simply must do so in a way that is informed by what it is that makes God's reality distinctive. This will ensure that an appropriate affirmation of God's transcendence will ineluctably be associated with whatever proposed answers to our question we proffer. This will be to avoid idolatry in the proper theological manner.

It matters little whether one falls back on the moral vision of a particular religious source or some secular source (or some combination of these, as Christian ethicists tend to do) to work out one's ethical theory once the perspective of the fully inclusive theological moral vision is dismissed as inaccessible to our understanding. When the geography of the ethical is less than fully appropriate to all social reality, adventure in the moral life is proportionately circumscribed. Only a moral vision grounded in a radically monotheistic vision of God can provide the full comprehensiveness appropriate to the moral life itself. To refuse to affirm this distinctive theological perspective in the spirit of respecting God's transcendence is simply one more example of good motives having unfortunate consequences.

We become imprisoned by our limited, conventional theories of ethics when our theological convictions do not permit us to venture in faith and fully generalize our moral vision as an aspect of the nature of God. Such a move does not in any way require that we must claim for ourselves the capacities that we would consider definitive characteristics of God as the embodiment of our moral vision. On the contrary, our limited perspective for moral judgment and our limited capacity for moral venture become fully apparent only when contrasted with the supreme instances of these capacities and perspectives as present in God.

V

A complex, multidimensional vision of God centers the symbolic background for the somatic ethics adumbrated in this essay. The religious symbolic background of an ethical tradition conditions the moral consciousness of persons raised within that tradition and shapes, at least indirectly, the theoretical interpretations of ethics generated by scholars of the given tradition. Consider, for example, the profound impact of classical Western theism as symbolically understood and presented on the ethical theory of Kant. Elizabeth Anscombe has claimed, and I think rightly, that a religious background has shaped the meaning of moral terms used within the Occidental ethical tradition.[17] She argues that the very meaning of terms such as 'duty' and 'obligation' has been historically associated with an understanding of God as lawgiver. Given that the modern mind no longer associates moral obligation with this vision of God, she holds that Occidental culture is now without a meaningful sense of moral duty and obligation. Hence her own proposal to develop an ethics of virtue rooted in the notion of human flourishing.

Somatic ethics is an alternative constructive proposal, but one that recognizes the need for fundamental rethinking of what ethics is about. Now Whitehead, and the process theologians who have further developed his understanding of God, proposed a vision of God different from that found in the classical Western tradition. Although this is not the place to pursue the matter, part of the difficulty in understanding Whitehead's 'ethics' may be rooted in this fundamental theological shift. For if shifts in the background religious symbols of an ethical tradition can change the meaning of ethical terms associated with that tradition, it is also quite possible that such a change could lead to a radical shift in what would be meant by ethics itself. This is what Anscombe certainly implies. And this would be consistent as well with John Rawls's claim that alternative theories of ethics are dependent on alternative theories of society.[18]

A fundamental theological background transformation occurs when eros is considered, as in process thought, an important constitutive dimension and characteristic function of God. Once this transformation is introduced into our vision of God, we can then conceive of God as having the capacity for venture into novelty. God as envisioned in the classical

Occidental theological tradition did not have this capacity for adventure. Is it any wonder, therefore, that adventure in the moral life would be downplayed in an ethical tradition in which the One who is understood as a source and ground of morality experiences no adventure? The possible import for theological ethical theory of this shift in background is a matter that deserves critical attention.

A recognition of the changing, dynamic dimension of God that is central to process theology must not, however, be permitted to obscure another aspect of God that process thought also enables one to explicate as part of the basic symbolic background of theological ethics: i.e., the sense in which there is that in God which does not undergo change as God experiences novelty. This is the abstract constant character of God, that which maintains the identity of God even as novelty and adventure are experienced as real.

God as understood in process thought is simultaneously an adventurous, changing, responding socially embodied self who internally experiences novelty by suffering the experiences of all others and an unchanging, stable, socially embodied self with a constant character that is the same yesterday, today, and forever. This is what it means for God to be 'dipolar,' and what makes it possible for God to know us from 'within' and from 'without,' as a removed spectator and a participating agent. Predicates signifying venture and stability, disinterestedness and involvement, can both appropriately be applied to God as they specify different aspects of God's nature. This enables us to conceive of God as a personal agent with a non-personal (or perhaps better, an impersonal) character. Once this move is understood, we are then in a position to handle a problem that has recently baffled some theological ethicists, i.e., how a personal God can be the source of an impersonal moral demand.

W. G. Maclagan in an important study has argued that the notion of God as personal cannot satisfy the moral necessity that 'ought' be interpreted as an impersonal, objective demand.[19] "The concept of God as person," Maclagan maintains, "is not simply unnecessary in this moral context; the context positively repels it."[20] Thus, says Maclagan, "the term 'God,' if our use of it is not to misrepresent the nature of moral demand, must be understood to refer to some *non*-personal Being."[21] Maclagan is, however, most unhappy to leave the matter here, for he recognizes that religion, with its concern for a God who hears prayer, seems forced to think of God in personal or anthropomorphic categories.[22] Thus we must "somehow think of God as both personal and impersonal"; but when we attempt to do this, says Maclagan, "what results seems not to be integration so much as a working conflation of the personal and impersonal."[23] Hence he concludes that "we must be content to assert, without comprehending, the unity of personal and impersonal natures in God."[24]

Process theology can provide Maclagan a way to resolve his conceptual muddle. The abstract constant character of God is the locus in God for the objective, impersonal moral demand. This way of understanding 'claims of rightness' (duty, ought, and obligation) has not, however, to my knowledge been developed in process thought. Cobb, for example, relates what Whitehead called our experience of that "rightness in things, partially conformed to and partially disregarded" to the impact upon consciousness that issues from the failure of a subjective aim to accord with an ideal aim given by God (*CNT* 249). Yet it is not evident that Whitehead's ideal aims (or initial subjective aims) can be experienced as 'claims of rightness' in a way that is distinguishable from a lure or claim of goodness. It thus appears that some addition is required in the Whiteheadian metaphysical scheme if rightness is to have the same kind of objective quality as goodness. Without this addition, I am unable to see how the metaphysical scheme can provide the full social background that is needed for a comprehensive ethical theory. For even granted the validity of Anscombe's historical thesis about the meaning of obligation terms, we do continue to need, as Frederick Carney has shown, a way of taking account of our experience of moral obligation.[25] Even if as theological ethicists we can no longer account for the experience of moral obligation simply in terms of God being a commanding lawgiver, we nevertheless need to develop an alternative theological way of grounding the notion. My suggestion would be that we further explore the possibility of grounding the experience of moral obligation in the abstract constant character of God.

As theological ethicists we must not permit ourselves to be constrained by the resources that we appropriate for our work. In areas where these resources are inadequate for the work we need to accomplish, we must simply make the adjustments that our interpretations of theological ethics require. To locate the ground for our experience of objective claims of rightness in the abstract constant nature of God may even provide us (and I presently think that it does) with a fruitful way of formulating an ontological theory of natural law. This issue will have to await exploration at a later date.

Just now I want to indicate how the complex vision of God that process theologians have explicated makes it possible for us to conceive of God as an ideal moral judge and as One who can intimately experience participatory relationships with other socially embodied selves. Process thought makes it possible for us to claim with consistency that God is always independent, fully informed, impartial, and loving as God appreciatively suffers and evaluates all novel experiences. This suffering of novelty does not necessitate that God has to cease being an ideal moral judge.

We can, however, conceive of God as an ideal moral judge only by fully generalizing our moral vision. As we have clear theological and philosophical warrants for generalizing our moral vision in this way, we have a procedure for at least beginning to spell out what it means for God to intend 'moral flourishing' for all persons at all times. Moreover, we have a procedure for doing this that does not do violence to the distinctive reality of God, as it is only a fully transcendent God who can serve as the ground for a fully generalized moral vision.

To be sure, we can but faintly imagine what it means to seek 'moral flourishing' at a given time for a given person as it is intended for that person by a fully informed, impartial, and loving transcendent God. Yet we mean here by 'moral flourishing' nothing other than "what would be intended by a fully informed, impartial, and loving transcendent God." We must still venture forth and risk our own moral intentions and evaluations knowing that we certainly cannot claim these transcendent capacities for ourselves. Yet there are ways that we can unpack this definition of moral flourishing to yield important elements of a decision procedure to guide our moral deliberations. We can also use the decision procedure that follows from this definition to justify certain of the virtues, duties, and goods operative in conventional interpretations of morality as indeed properly to be regarded as valid elements of morality. They are those which according to our considered judgments, informed by the transcendent perspective of the ideal moral judge, warrant being taken as valid.

Perhaps the sense of awe that tends to overcome one with any attempt to generalize fully the moral point of view provides the explanation, but, for whatever the reason, process thinkers have been most reluctant to proceed in the way here being proposed. For example, while Cobb comes close to this position when he defines intrinsic value as "that which is, in fact, preferred on full disinterested considerations" (*CNT* 122), he does not explicitly develop this insight in relationship to his understanding of God. He does not fully generalize his definition. But can anyone other than the transcendent One give *full disinterested consideration* to anything? Is not any non-theological vision of *full disinterested consideration* necessarily a parochial and limited one, i.e., not what it claims to be? Moreover, is not any truly adequate theory of this type in fact theological, whether it intends or claims to be theological or not? As theological ethicists therefore we should not hesitate to ground our basic definition of 'intrinsic value' or 'moral flourishing' in our vision of God.

Or again, when Cobb formulates his 'final ethical principle,' he states it as: "An ethically developed man ought to act in that way in which he would will, on full consideration of all relevant factors, that all men should act, given just these factors" (*CNT* 124). Cobb, however, leaves this principle overly vague by not providing us with a way of specifying the meaning of 'full consideration' and 'all relevant factors.' Moreover, if, as Cobb appears to affirm, each individual is free (from the point of view of morality) to resolve these matters for himself or herself, then we have here a vicious form of ethical relativism. Cobb can only avoid the relativism of what appears to be his present formulation of a 'final ethical principle' by fully generalizing his notion of 'full consideration of all relevant factors' in such a way as to remove all particulars from its logic.

The relevant factors are precisely those that would be considered relevant by the One who has a fully informed, impartial, and loving transcendent perspective for such evaluations. In making our own determinations on such matters, we venture forth and attempt insofar as possible to view moral issues from the perspective of this type of moral vision. Certainly this leads us to realize that we cannot be fully informed as we make our actual moral decisions. Therefore, if we are in disagreement with a neighbor on a moral decision, we suspect that it may be due to our factual disagreement about the moral situation in question. We are open to the exchange of additional information on the matter. We then review the facts as understood, with an eye toward locating the source of our disagreement. Likewise, we realize that it is unusually difficult for us to be impartial in our moral decisions. The theory under discussion helps us to be on guard against the way our self-interests can pervert our moral judgments and decisions, causing them to be in error. And so on for the other characteristics of a moral vision that is an aspect of our vision of God, being God in the exemplary role of ideal moral judge and agent.

By conceiving of God as an Ideal Participant in all social reality, this adumbration of a theological somatic ethics intends to assist us in reaching agreement on what indeed are the relevant factors for making moral decisions. This approach to ethics is essentially compatible with process thought, and even requires a dipolar understanding of God. An appropriation of this type of theory could assist Cobb in escaping the relativism of his present position and yet would continue to leave his ethics open for the kind of creative novelty that he rightly does not want to surrender. An attractive feature of the somatic ethics here being proposed is that it can explain and justify the need for a continuing *aggiornamento* in our moral commitments—including our understanding of moral rules and principles—in a way that does not commend anomie or antinomianism.

To illustrate this dynamic dimension of somatic ethics, let us consider our relationship with nature. If we believe that a transcendent, loving, fully informed, and impartial God evaluates nature as having only instrumental value for human beings, then we can feel justified in using nature in whatever way appears to suit our human purposes. But if this belief changes and we come to think that God appreciatively treasures the beauty and grandeur of nature as intrinsic values, then, providing that we continue to take God's evaluations as a model and directive for our own evaluations, we have a motivating and justifying reason to cultivate an appreciation of the intrinsic values of nature ourselves. The change in consciousness justifies the change in our morality.

VI

A vision of God that makes it impossible for us to conceive of how our being and doing could contribute to the joy and beauty of God leads to a barren and austere sense of how one lives a life in affirmation of God. By contrast, to contemplate the way the God of somatic ethics experiences the rich diversity of all social reality in a way appropriate to every particular experience of joy and beauty is itself joyous and beautiful. The way God can enjoy with full adequacy the joyous feelings of all creatures has received insufficient reflective attention in religious ethics. Yet it may be that a vision of God that can provide us with a sense of God's own beauty is essential if we are to formulate a comprehensive religious ethics. For perhaps the *summum bonum* is nothing other than the adequate appreciative enjoyment of all experiences of joy and beauty and morality by the One who is alone endowed with the capacities essential for maximizing the beauty of this enjoyment with a unitive consent that affirms all that is experienced as worthy of being experienced. To sense this Edwardian aesthetic affirmation, and to affirm its import for somatic ethics, is to avoid the beguiling trap of utilitarianism for an ideal participant perspective. To affirm the beauty of the ideal participant is to live for all social reality in a way as to maximize joy and beauty and morality, knowing that God as ideal participant always experiences our being-good-for-others as a good-form-of-otherness, as an excellence of otherness that persists while also contributing to the realization of the *summum bonum*.

For a somatic ethics that takes its departure from this vision of God as socially related to all reality, indeed as embodied in all social reality, there is clearly no reality that falls outside the range of God's care and appreciation. All social life is valued and has value. In our relationships with all forms of life, we are engaged with that in which God is embodied as a dimension of the divine life. God's feelings reciprocally feel the feelings of all that feels, including the various gradations of feelings in nature with its fullness of scope and variety. All life has intrinsic value for a God who values in this way, be it a tree, a bird, a fish, a fetus, or a person. If we are to justify cutting down trees, shooting birds, catching fish, aborting fetuses, or killing persons (and I think that each of these practices can at times be justified), then we are to do so in spite of the intrinsic value that is lost in each of these practices, not because trees, birds, fish, fetuses, and persons are sometimes completely devoid of value. All life can have intrinsic value even if certain forms of life have the potentiality for more substantial contributions to the highest good than do others, as is clearly the case. This greater potential does not, however, entail that these higher forms of life have a license to destroy at will the lower forms. Any unappreciative destruction of life, whatever its level of development, can only be indicative of an estrangement from the social sources of one's own capacities for sharing in life. Any wanton destruction of life issues from a failure to understand and appreciate one's own sociality and its forms of embodiment.

The primal vision of a theological somatic ethics, that vision of a loving God in constitutive interactions with all social reality, will, it is hoped, inspire and sustain in us a desire to share with God in the celebration and appreciation of all life, for somatic ethics recognizes all life as valued and as having value. Conventional morality does not typically treasure life as intrinsically valuable, does not include in its vision a notion of the divine eros that gently nurtures a thrust toward excellence in all social reality. Conventional morality tends to affirm operational definitions of moral concepts. Valuable life is defined as life that is useful. In such a frame of reference, it also makes sense to think of useless life, of life that does not perform any desired operations, and therefore of life without value.

The somatic vision of a socially embodied God in loving relatedness to all that is ignites an extension of our care for other being that is in keeping with one thrust of the Christian tradition. As Cobb has stated so well, "the extension of concern to all living things is neither a movement backward nor away from our Christian heritage. It is a movement forward in the inner transformation and further development of this peculiar tradition" (*TE* 50). Somatic ethics, then, is grounded in a vision that requires a justification for destroying or limiting any life, as it views God as affirmative of the possibilities inherent in all life. Any limitations or negations of life must finally be justified with reference to a fully generalized understanding of the moral point of view, i.e., from that inclusive perspective whereby God is recognized as an interested participant, while still an Ideal Participant, in all social reality.

In the theological somatic ethics suggested in this essay, we do not have to choose between (1) a mode of ethics that emphasizes joy and adventure in life, but is unable to justify moral rules and principles warranted for stability in our social relations; and (2) a mode of ethics that can justify moral rules and principles to facilitate our social living, but has no place for joy and adventure. Yet many complexities associated with affirming the rich and varied aspects of a full and comprehensive somatic ethics have not been investigated in this essay.

NOTES

1. By ethicists, I have in mind such persons as Philippa Foot, R. M. Hare, Paul Ramsey, John Rawls, Frederick Carney, James Childress, and Richard Brandt.

2. See William Frankena, "Ethical Theory," in Richard Schlatter (ed.), *Philosophy* (Prentice-Hall, Inc., 1964), 347–463.

3. Unfortunately, persons who have understood themselves to be working out a Whiteheadian ethics in theology have generally not been in conversation with the 'ethicists' mentioned in n. 1. Their work has not therefore provided a way to bridge the chasm.

4. The journal *Process Studies* encourages this type of work and the recent launching of it is certainly to be applauded.

5. Although Cobb is less interested in establishing such a conversation than he is in developing an ethics that is compatible with Whitehead's metaphysics, his work nevertheless is of such a quality as to stimulate this kind of dialogue.

6. See Arthur Dyck, "Questions of Ethics," *Harvard Theological Review,* 65/4 (Fall 1972), 453–482.

7. See Charles Reynolds, "A Proposal for Understanding the Place of Reason in Christian Ethics," *Journal of Religion,* 50/2 (April 1970), 155–168.

8. On the importance of 'background' for moral beliefs, see P. R. Foot, "Moral Beliefs," *Proceedings of the Aristotelian Society,* 59 (1958–59), 83–104.

9. H. Richard Niebuhr, *The Meaning of Revelation* (The Macmillan Company, 1941), 88.

10. See especially Alfred North Whitehead, *Adventures of Ideas* (The Macmillan Company, 1933) 253, 277.

11. For an excellent analysis of interpretations of agape in recent Christian ethics, see Gene Outka, *Agape: An Ethical Analysis* (Yale University Press, 1972).

12. By "conventional interpretations of theological ethics," I mean those interpretations where the author assumes, without seriously questioning, the currently prevailing specialist and academic sense of ethics. One of the givens currently in this approach to ethics is that ethics focuses primarily on individual choice situations.

13. See especially Stanley Hauerwas, *Vision and Virtue: Essays in Christian Ethical Reflection* (Fides Publishers, Inc., 1974).

14. Richard Davis, "Whitehead's Moral Philosophy," *Process Studies*, 3/2 (Summer 1973), 80.

15. *Ibid.*

16. The position I developed in the essay "Elements of a Decision Procedure for Christian Social Ethics" is presupposed in some of the argument that follows. See *Harvard Theological Review*, 65/4 (October 1972), 509–530.

17. See Elizabeth Anscombe, "Modern Moral Philosophy," *Philosophy*, 33 (1958), 1–19.

18. John Rawls, *A Theory of Justice* (Harvard University Press, 1971), 9, 121.

19. W. G. Maclagan, *The Theological Frontiers of Ethics* (London: George Allen & Unwin, Ltd., 1961).

20. *Ibid.*, 170.

21. *Ibid.*, 171.

22. *Ibid.*, 179.

23. *Ibid.*

24. *Ibid.*

25. See Frederick Carney, "The Virtue-Obligation Controversy," *Journal of Religious Ethics*, 1/1 (Fall 1973), 5–20.

A LIBERAL LOGOS CHRISTOLOGY:
THE CHRISTOLOGY OF JOHN COBB

By Wolfhart Pannenberg
Translated from the German by David P. Polk

THE CHRISTOLOGICAL SKETCHES of the preceding decade usually begin with the historical Jesus, in order then to justify the Christological dogma as an exposition of the human-historical reality of Jesus but also critically to evaluate that dogma through the use of this criterion. The classical Logos Christology of the early church is not easily reconciled with such an approach, since conversely it interprets Jesus from God hither and hardly raises the question of how one is to justify the assumptions about the divine Logos from which it proceeds. The personalistic interpretation of the Logos Christology by dialectical theology, which found in the Logos only the hypostasized divine word of revelation, has contributed rather to the discrediting of present attempts in this direction. For it becomes visible therein that the classical function of the Logos Christology—the exhibition of the universal validity of Jesus through the connection of his historical form with the philosophically accessible principle of world order—is not readily attainable in present theological thinking. Since 1964, I myself have criticized as a hopeless venture the connection of the figure of Jesus with the question of the order of the cosmos, a question now dealt with through the knowledge of laws by the natural sciences,[1] and I pleaded for a replacement of the Logos concept by the notion of revelation, which in any case concerns Christology's 'point of departure.'[2] Even so, as a second step, Christ must certainly be thought of as mediator of creation, for only thereby is he genuinely conceived as one with God, as participating in the all-determining reality of God.[3] And only thereby is the universal validity of the figure of Jesus to be legitimately grounded. This substantially amounts to a demand for a renewed Logos Christology, which interprets the historical figure of Jesus in continuity with God's relation to the world in general.

John Cobb has now produced such a Logos Christology, entitled *Christ in a Pluralistic Age*. It is noteworthy that precisely a liberal theologian like

Cobb has taken such a step, for liberal theology has ordinarily concerned itself with stripping away the divinization of Jesus in the early church's Christology (or what appeared to it as such) as a secondary coat of paint over his true, historical humanity. Even Cobb will permit no diminution of the full humanity of Jesus (*CPA* 130ff). His sympathy for Piet Schoonenberg's defense of the human personality of Jesus is probably grounded primarily therein (cf. *CPA* 271, 166f). But he correctly considers it necessary, beyond that, to ask about Jesus' distinctiveness, specifically in regard to his relation with God—in regard to a "concrete particularity of the divine presence and action in him as there is in each of us" (*CPA* 130f). Only such a distinctiveness of his relation to God can ground Jesus' authority for us. Whereas Cobb was content in an earlier essay to characterize this distinctiveness anthropologically (cf. *CPA* 13), it is now developed in the form of a Logos Christology (*CPA* 135; cf. 138ff). Cobb arrived at this posture through the natural philosophy of Whitehead, which enabled him to expound the universal significance of the words and work of Jesus with a forcefulness that is unattainable through a merely anthropological interpretation.

With such a procedure, certainly, there is even already presupposed a definite concept of the 'Logos,' whose presence in Jesus is asserted. How Cobb justifies in an authentically theological manner his concept of the Logos as "the power of creative transformation" (*CPA* 131) does not become very clear from his statements. That is a problem which he shares with the Logos Christology of the early church. The initial chapters of his book, which exhibit the principle of 'creative transformation' in the histories of Christian art and Christian theology, cannot furnish any theological justification for that as the Logos or messianic principle which appeared in Jesus. They certainly show the significance of the principle of 'creative transformation' for the self-understanding of modern art, and also its actual efficacy in the history of modern theology. But derivation from the history of Christianity does not yet assure, here as elsewhere, that one thereby has to do with a Christian motif, much less the central Christian motif. Considering the ambiguity of all processes of secularization, it could also be understood as a falling away or detachment from its Christian origin. Accordingly, Cobb emphasizes correctly: "This account of Christ in art and theology cannot stand alone. Christ is indissolubly bound up with Jesus" (*CPA* 62). Part Two of the book is therefore supposed to demonstrate that the principle of 'creative transformation' exhibited in Part One has in fact appeared also in Jesus Christ, and, to be sure, in him completely for the first time. But even here the basis for the applicability to Jesus of the previously developed concept of the Logos as 'creative transformation' exists only in the reference to Jesus' consciousness of full power of authority as the authority of a man who dares to act in God's place. "This suggests that in some special way the divine Logos was present with and in him" (*CPA* 138). This grounding, on the contrary, already presupposes the previously mentioned Logos concept.

Now it could be easily asserted that Cobb's actual justification for the Logos concept which he employs is given not at all through historical-exegetical argumentation but on the basis of philosophy. Here the concept of the Logos is only another name for the cosmological function of Whitehead's God, namely, his 'primordial nature,' by virtue of which, according to Whitehead, God gives to every event its ideal possibility, its 'initial aim' (*CPA* 225; cf. 229, 76f). Therein the idea of creative transformation is grounded, the new is brought forth, the future is granted (*CPA* 70f), and thereby the possibilities of the past are realized (*CPA* 69)—therefore transformed without being destroyed. While this aspect of God, which for Cobb can be presupposed, is called 'Logos' by him, he establishes only a conjunction with traditional Christian language which justifies theologically what would be philosophically required besides, namely, to describe structurally Jesus' fulfillment of existence in the sense of this general philosophical assumption. Does the Logos concept therefore furnish here only a justification for interpreting the figure of Jesus in the sense of Whitehead's metaphysical principles?

One will have to add at least that Cobb considers an inner, essential relationship between Whitehead's philosophy and the Christian faith to be a matter of fact (*CPA* 229). Cobb finds this essential relationship above all in the notion of divine love (*CPA* 229, 248). Of course Whitehead in his principal work[4] first speaks of a divine love toward the world in reference to the divine preservation of the values independently realized by the finite processes, whereas Cobb already interprets as an expression of God's love the divine presentation of ideal futural possibilities (the 'initial aim') for the self-actualization of creatures. For this he refers not to Whitehead's principal work but to another of Whitehead's few references to the notion of God. In *Adventures of Ideas* the primordial nature of God is "pictured as the love that lures man to adventure" (*GW* 84).[5] Whitehead does in fact speak there of the divine love, though not in reference to God's relationship to the creation but in the sense of an erotic impulse in God himself toward the actualization of ideal possibilities, whereby God's infinity is actualized in the world process.[6] One must judge that this notion is not simply identical with the Biblical notion of the forgiving love of God, for this is creatively bestowed upon the world, whereas Whitehead has rejected precisely the notion of creation.[7] His concept of divine love points on the one hand to God's own essential realization, but on the other hand, as love toward the world, it points to the preservation of the values produced by the finite processes themselves.

A similar idea results in regard to the reference to the future, which is central to Cobb's concept of 'creative transformation' (70f). The Christology relies here on the detailed explanations in *God and the World* (1969) concerning the divine 'call forward' toward a possible fulfillment of creatures in the future (*GW* 42ff). God is that one (*GW* 63) who "calls us forward in each moment into a yet unsettled future" (*GW* 55). Cobb connects this assertion with the notion of God's love: God is "a lover of the world who calls it ever beyond what it has attained by affirming life, novelty, consciousness, and freedom again and again" (*GW* 65). This notion is undoubtedly impressive, and it seems to me to be thoroughly in agreement with the understanding of God in the Bible. But can it really be attributed to Whitehead, as Cobb believes (*GW* 66)? I doubt it. So far as I can see, Whitehead has given the future no ontological status, not even in his doctrine of God. He has even explicitly said of love that it does not concern itself about the future.[8] Therefore the correlation between love and hope has simply not been thematized by Whitehead. And although in *Adventures of Ideas* he also depicts the creative synthesis of all events as an 'anticipation,' and is even conscious of the new qualification of the present through the future that is grounded in that synthesis,[9] the thesis of a constitutive significance of the future for what is present, as suggested by the term 'anticipation,' does not lie within Whitehead's field of vision. One may not consider unimportant the fact that certainly this aspect is *implicitly* present in Whitehead's formulations. It is not accidental that Whitehead has not developed these implications. Had he done so, he would have had to change his concept of actual entities as present or past occurrences. But that would have required a revision of his entire system. On the other hand, precisely because Whitehead has not investigated the constitutive significance of the future for the present, he has developed his problematic doctrine of timelessly subsisting, abstract possibilities (eternal objects) over against what is actually real (actual entities). The timelessness of eternal objects actually *replaces* the missing reflection upon the constitutive significance of the future for present and past events.

How then does Cobb, in his striving for a theology along a Whiteheadian track, come to his vision of the God who calls the world to its future and *therein* is lovingly devoted to it? It appears that he has read Whitehead through the spectacles of the so-called 'theology of hope' and of Teilhard de Chardin.[10] Thereby Cobb could rightly suppose that he is only working out explicitly the specific matters which are somehow implicitly present in Whitehead. But so far he seems to be overlooking the fact that such an explication amounts (at least implicitly) to a revision of the metaphysical foundations of Whitehead's thinking. Without doubt one can also thereby learn yet a great deal from Whitehead, but in such a way that one moves beyond Whiteheadian scholasticism, which appears to me still to be a danger in process theology.

This is not the place to develop more exactly the suggested revision of the foundations of Whitehead's philosophy.[11] It is sufficient in the space of this contribution to point to the tensions arising in Cobb's Christology from the fact that, on the one hand, he develops a theological vision stimulated by Whitehead but leading beyond him, while, on the other hand, he narrowly attaches himself again and again to theorems expressly expounded by Whitehead.

The first difficulty of this sort already steps forth in the introduction of the concept of the Logos as 'creative transformation' without justification from the historical particulars of Jesus' own history. Cobb's expressed vision of 'creative transformation' as origin of the contingently new in the world, but also as an expression of God's love toward the world—which works in Teilhard's sense as a creative unification by overcoming the isolation of the individual—would be thoroughly appropriate for such a justification.[12] It could be developed out of the Biblical understanding of the historicity of God's relation to the world, and out of the revelatory function of the history of Jesus which is to be decided in connection with the whole of this divine history. But Whitehead's philosophy suggests another conception of 'creative transformation,' which conforms to Whitehead's explicit statements about the initial aim presented by God to each event for its self-constitution. Now this initial aim, taken for itself, is not at all futural but is an ideal possibility, an 'eternal object.' It first becomes the transformation of extant reality through the way in which the self-constituting occurrences, through their own creativity (!), include their initial aim into the process of their self-constitution, making it their subjective aim. And this concept certainly is not grounded in the history of Jesus. It can only be substituted for it in the sense of a positive analogy.

Through this substitution, Cobb's Christology gains significant advantages. Whitehead's philosophy is one of the few detailed philosophical interpretations of the natural world which our age has produced, and among the sketches put forward it is perhaps the most significant. Of course, one may not thereby close one's eyes to the one-sided partialities clinging even to it, as has so often happened in the history of theology where one has made a decision for this or that philosophy and then followed its theorems dogmatically. Cobb rightly considers it to be a goal of his book "to seek a positive account of the kind of experience that is expressed in varied religious contexts rather than to reject them as incomprehensible or as doing violence to the facts" (*CPA* 117). The question is only whether his close attachment to Whitehead's philosophy always allows him to pursue this objective. In that he connects the figure of Jesus with Whitehead's philosophy through the concept of the Logos, the universal cosmic significance of the history of Jesus becomes articulatable in an imposing way. That must be a goal of all Christology. But perhaps Cobb, through the wholesale acceptance of Whitehead's natural philosophy, attains this goal too easily, without the difficult work of a critical transformation, in the light of the history of Jesus, of the foundations of the philosophical system from which he proceeds. The ease with which Cobb attains the cosmic perspective of a Logos Christology could be purchased at too high a price, namely, on the one hand, through the fact that particular tensions between Cobb's authentically Christian statements and Whitehead's fundamental philosophical ideas are only verbally disguised (as has been shown above in respect to the notion of love and the efficacious working of God as originator of the new), and, on the other hand, through the fact that particular aspects of the history of Jesus must be eliminated, especially the realism of his proclamation of the near end of this aeon with the arrival of the Kingdom of God. Indeed, John Cobb seems to perceive just therein a superiority in Whitehead's thinking, in that his philosophy permits theology to be released from problems of the end of the world that are bound up with Jesus' imminent expectation, since this imminent expectation has apparently been refuted by the continuation of history (cf. *CPA* 225, 250). But not only for contemporary Christendom does clinging to the notion of an end of the world and of history stand in tension with the non-Christian understanding of the world. On the contrary, that was already the situation of Christian thinking *vis-à-vis* the classical systems of Greek philosophy, and precisely the adherence to a realistic eschatology, and therewith to the notion of an unrepeatable historical process irreversibly running toward its end, enabled Christian thinking to achieve a 'creative transformation' of the philosophical heritage of antiquity.

The most important limitation in Cobb's diagnosis of the history of Jesus through the philosophical scheme of Whitehead might consist in the fact that the Kingdom of God is no longer presented in the dynamic of its coming, as the field of force of the divine future determining the present.[13] Cobb himself judges this dynamic to be broken for us, two thousand years later: "We do not anticipate an imminent coming of a new order or a new age in which the ambiguities of our world will be superseded" (*CPA* 225; cf. 249ff). It is true that the imminent expectation of

Jesus and primitive Christianity has not been fulfilled in its original sense. But in this connection Cobb curiously does not consider the event that made this delay of the eschaton bearable for early Christianity by guaranteeing to believers the presence of future salvation already now, in the midst of this world of death: the resurrection of Jesus. One can say that the imminent expectation of Jesus has thereby encountered a transformation, grounded in historical experience, which nevertheless remained in fundamental continuity with Jesus' message of the world-altering dynamic of God's future. Instead of following this development and interpreting its meaning, Cobb tries to formulate the presently authoritative content of Jesus' message through immediate adherence to Whitehead's conceptual standards, especially to his concept of the Kingdom of Heaven. Although one can certainly agree with Cobb that this notion of Whitehead has been deeply influenced by the New Testament, I am not able to acknowledge that it is 'homologous' (*CPA* 227) with the New Testament. Cobb sees the antithesis himself: "In the New Testament the Kingdom of Heaven will come no matter what we do. For Whitehead it will preserve and redeem our actions no matter what they are" (*CPA* 227). In the New Testament the futural Kingdom of God is the majesty of the coming God himself, from which nothing that is present can escape. It is not only a guarantee for the immortality of the outcome of all temporal events in spite of their transitoriness. Cobb tries vainly to reconcile this antithesis by indicating that in both conceptions the human decision has a central significance (*CPA* 227f).[14] That is the case for many views of the world, but what matters is the character that is ascribed to this decision before which humanity presently is placed. In the New Testament, this is the majesty of the God of Israel, to whom alone the future belongs, so that only through being joined with him can humanity hope for salvation. On the other hand, Whitehead's God preserves in one way or another the positive content of our experiences and actions. Accordingly, there is no interest in God's coming, in his future.

Only at one point is Jesus' orientation to the future of God's lordship in accord with Whitehead's philosophy, and Cobb propels this point again and again into the center of his interpretation: that is the implicit futurity of the ideal possibility for realization that is presented, according to Whitehead, to every occurrence. The person of Jesus is accordingly represented as an exception to the general circumstance that every occurrence makes the ideal possibility presented to it (initial aim) into the object of its own self-actualization (subjective aim). Cobb finds the uniqueness of Jesus in the fact that Jesus has made his God-given initial aim, the Logos, into his subjective aim without distortion (*CPA* 140ff). Therefore in Jesus is not found the "usual tension between the human aim and the ideal possibility of self-actualization that is the Logos" (*CPA* 139f). In this sense Jesus' 'I' is constituted—or rather co-constituted[15]—through the presence of the Logos in him (*CPA* 141), and this means for Cobb that in Jesus there was no tension, no opposition of his 'I' to God (*CPA* 140f).

Part Two of Cobb's Christology ("Christ as Jesus") reaches its zenith in these explanations. Cobb began here with Jesus' words (Ch. 5), in order thence to press forward through the question of their efficacy (Ch. 6) and of the basis for their authority (*CPA* 131ff) to the distinctiveness of Jesus' person (Ch. 8). However, in this process of argumentation—for which the parable of the Pharisee and the publican serves as a guide—Jesus' message of the Kingdom of God is now limited to the question of Jesus' personal relationship to God. Thereby the future of the Kingdom of God for humanity shrinks to the futurity of the God-given ideal of individual self-actualization for Jesus' person. To be sure, Cobb also says something about the content of this ideal of existence, which became constitutive for Jesus' self-consciousness. In conjunction with Machoveč he states that Jesus not only proclaimed the Kingdom of God but *"incarnated this lived future* in his entire being" (*CPA* 138). However, Cobb does not engage in a more exact analysis of this fact, but employs it merely as an illustration for the formal thesis, then developed in orientation to Whitehead's doctrine of the subjective aim: "Jesus existed in full unity with God's present purposes for him" (*CPA* 141). Thereby Jesus' unity with the Kingdom of God that he proclaimed is simply characterized as unity with the Logos, in the sense that "his very selfhood was constituted by the Logos" (*CPA* 139). However, a more exact analysis of the matter of the relation of Jesus to his proclamation, described in connection with Machoveč, would have to demonstrate, *first,* that the mission of proclaiming God's Kingdom which constituted Jesus' selfhood had a content *distinct* from Jesus' individual existence, namely, the future of God's Kingdom as it concerned the whole world; and *second,* that it thereby concerned not simply the Logos but the *lordship of the Father.* But Jesus knew himself to be in no way identical with the Father. It is erroneous to conceive of Jesus' relation to God as such an identity that in it there "would not be the confrontation of an 'I' by a 'Thou' " (*CPA* 140). In his humanness Jesus knew himself to be so very different from the Father that he rejected the address "Good Teacher" with the remark: "No one is good but God alone" (Mark 10:17f). This is central for the whole of Christology; for according to the Gospels, that Jesus had made himself equal to God was precisely the accusation of Jesus' opponents. His self-distinction from God, the Father of the coming Kingdom, was the condition for Jesus' unity with God, which he had as 'the Son' in obedience to the Father, and had in only that way.[16]

Unfortunately, Cobb has not taken notice of this matter which is so fundamental for the whole of Christology. He has not gone into the fact that Jesus' relation to God is first of all a relation to the *Father* and, as such, should be characterized by means of differentiation. Only in this roundabout way does Jesus' own unity with God as 'Son' become understandable without diminution of his full humanity. Insofar as Cobb endeavors to think of Jesus' relation to God as an immediate relation to the Logos, along the track of the Christological debates of the early church, he not only misses the historical phenomenon of Jesus' existence but also gets entangled in the dilemma which has accompanied the Logos Christology of the early church since the conflicts of the fifth century, the dilemma of Monophysitism and Nestorianism. It is a self-deception if Cobb intends through process philosophy to be fundamentally beyond this dilemma that penetrates the entire Christological tradition. This dilemma has not only been a consequence of 'substantialist' categories of thinking, as Cobb presumes (*CPA* 167). It is rather the consequence of every attempt to think of Jesus' unity with God immediately as Jesus' relation to the Logos, instead of in reference to Jesus' relation to the Father. Cobb is closely connected thereby with the model of the ('Nestorian') Christology of separation. It is significant in that regard that the Logos can only have value as 'co-constitutive' (*CPA* 141) for Jesus' selfhood, because Jesus "freely chose to constitute his own selfhood as one with this presence of God within him" (*CPA* 173). Which is the subject of such a free choice? The man Jesus already united with the Logos? Then his unity with the Logos is not first grounded through this act of choosing. Or was the man Jesus, not yet united with the Logos, the subject of that free choice? Then the man Jesus was not one with the Logos from the outset. Christology avoids this dilemma only when the *Sonship* of Jesus is understood as a qualification of his whole person in the light of his relationship to the *Father*.

Jesus' self-distinction from the Father is also central to the Christian doctrine of the Trinity, and here also the inattention to this fact, which is to be exegetically established, has problematic consequences in Cobb's conception. To be sure, his theology has acquired a fundamentally positive relation to the doctrine of the Trinity through the introduction of the Logos concept (cf. *CPA* 13). As Jesus is seen together with the Logos, so the Spirit is seen together with the future of the Kingdom of God, so that the Spirit is the presence of this coming Kingdom of God as Christ is the presence of the Logos (*CPA* 261f). This idea is convincing, but it does not by itself establish a complete doctrine of the Spirit—as Cobb himself says (*CPA* 263). The distinction of Logos and Spirit as thus formulated is suggested by Whitehead's distinction of the primordial and consequent nature of God. On the other hand, no point of departure is produced by Whitehead's doctrine of God for the distinction of the Son (as also of the Spirit) from the Father, nor for the Biblically attested relationships between the three persons. Therefore it is probably not accidental that these elements are also missing in Cobb. It would be difficult to arrive at a fully developed doctrine of the Trinity without a thorough revision of Whitehead's metaphysics. Especially serious is the lack of a distinction between the union of Father and Son appropriate to the historical facts concerning the appearance of Jesus. This lack manifests itself in the sentence already quoted, that for Jesus' mode of existence, united with the Logos, no personal oppositeness to God, as an I to a Thou, is to be assumed (*CPA* 140); and the same lack appears in Cobb's critical reflection upon the development of the doctrine of the Trinity, that perhaps only the Father should have been conceived as a hypostasis, with the Son and the Spirit on the contrary as two modes of his activity (*CPA* 260): such touches of a Dynamistic Monarchianism might be inferred from Whitehead's statements about God. A Christian trinitarian doctrine of God would no longer be attainable along this path. Not only the point of departure of the trinitarian understanding of God but also Jesus' own divine sonship depends on the personal self-differentiation of Jesus from the father.[17]

The interpretation of the figure of Jesus as incarnation of the Logos, in the sense of Whitehead's doctrine of the initial aim, is perhaps also responsible for the restriction of Cobb's Christology to the person of Jesus as that is expressed *in his words,* in distinction to *the history* of Jesus. The relation between the appearance of Jesus with his message on the one hand and his fate on the cross (as also his resurrection) on the other hand is curiously not discussed in this Christology, although in 1969, in *God and the World,* Cobb had found in Whitehead an access to the theological understanding of the cross as an expression of God's participation in the suffering of the world (*GW* 97). It is unfortunate that this notion, generally held in Christology, has not been developed further in reference to the suffering of the Son sent by God to proclaim the nearness of his Kingdom, and in reference to the significance of this suffering for the world. To do that, it would certainly be necessary at least to work out the connection between Jesus' 'words' and his specific authority more precisely than has been done by Cobb. To be sure, Cobb emphasizes incidentally, in conjunction with his exegetical authorities (*CPA* 104), that Jesus' notion of love is grounded in his eschatological message of the coming of God's Kingdom. But he does not enter into the question of the extent to which the same holds true for Jesus' claim of authority.[18] Unfor-

tunately this question is often overlooked even in the exegetical literature, as Jesus' consciousness of the full weight of authority is dealt with
as a remnant of the old dogmatic view of an immediate divine presence
in him. But on this question hangs the possibility of recognizing the
connection that leads from Jesus' message to his crucifixion: his claim to
authority was inextricably bound up with the ambiguity that it could seem
that he made himself God. But this ambiguity, arising in consequence of
the appearance of Jesus, is not analyzed by Cobb, nor is the confirmation
by the resurrection of Jesus' claim to authority. The entire historical
process which is bound up with Jesus' claim to authority is displaced by
the already discussed expositions of Jesus' structure of existence.

The history of the efficacy proceeding from Jesus—in which Cobb
returns to the question of Jesus' authority—also becomes thematic only
in a singularly reduced form, namely, in a reduction to the problematic
of the salvation of the individual. It is concentrated upon justification,
which is first presented in Jesus' parable of the Pharisee and the publican
(*CPA* 107ff), then constitutes the key to the description of the efficacy
proceeding from Jesus (Ch. 6, "Life in Christ"), and finally is taken up
once again in reference to the explanation concerning Jesus' authority
(*CPA* 143f): these now appear as an attempt to ground precisely the same
efficacy of Jesus which emanates from that parable (*CPA* 143). In particular, Cobb develops a series of noteworthy insights on the theme of justification—namely, on the dialectic of publican and Pharisee (*CPA* 109), the
dissimilarity between the Pauline notion of justification and that of the
parable (*CPA* 111), and the present ineffectiveness of justification faith
(CPA 113f). Cobb tries to provide an answer to this latter experience
through a consideration of the Pauline notion of a 'field of force' (*CPA*
116ff) proceeding from Jesus Christ, which occasions in us a conforma-
tion to Jesus and so also a participation in his righteousness (*CPA* 122f).
However, thoughtful and beautiful though these explanations may be, it
yet remains peculiar that Cobb limits the question of the efficacy proceeding from Jesus completely to the individual's self-understanding and
scarcely goes into the rise of the *church* as a consequence of the history
of Jesus. To be sure, it is occasionally mentioned that in early Christendom the church—alongside of the teaching of Jesus and bound up with
it—was experienced as an expression of the 'field of force' arising from
Jesus (*CPA* 128ff). But this historical observation remains inconsequen-
tial. Subsequently it is once again mentioned that the Kingdom of God
proclaimed by Jesus was connected with the rise of a new human community (*CPA* 222), but again no connection is established with the factual
rise of the Christian church and its history. Elsewhere Cobb even emphasizes the systematic circumstance that faith and hope *require* a community

"that expresses the field of force generated by Jesus" (*CPA* 185). But again there is no talk of the church in this connection. Instead of this, in connection with Paolo Soleri, the twelfth chapter develops the utopia of a new city which is characterized by an intensive living together of human beings.

The neglect of the church as the decisive, world-historical effect of the history of Jesus—if one is already inquiring into the effects proceeding from Jesus—is all the more astonishing inasmuch as Cobb opposed with sharp criticism (reminiscent of Teilhard) the phenomenon of a Christian individualism. He says that the call of Jesus, which was directed toward a "community of perfect openness," has *de facto* brought forth instead "the strongest and most isolated individuals in history" (*CPA* 110), who have brought the whole planet into the orbit of that history which measures time from Christ's birth. According to Cobb, this individualization united with alienation (*CPA* 184f) must be overcome (*CPA* 42)[19] by a turning from I to we (*CPA* 215; cf. 220). But Cobb does not go into the fact that the religious independence of the individual, grounded upon the justification faith (*CPA* 109), is only a product of Protestantism and an expression of specifically Protestant piety. His presentation, oriented toward the parable of the Pharisee and the publican, of the 'Christian structure of existence' (*CPA* 109) as a continually renewed effort to overcome one's own self-justification does not by any means simply describe Christian piety, but is characteristic only for a quite specific type of Protestant pietism, which certainly is also characterized by the individualism criticized by Cobb. But how does it happen that Cobb considers this Protestant pietism simply to be the Christian form of existence? Does not even his own presentation remain closely bound up thereby with the individualism that he criticizes? Does he perhaps come to terms more with his own tradition of piety here than with the objective, historical phenomenon of Christianity and its development? Cobb's criticism of the isolation of the individual, as it has actually evolved in this Protestant piety, would not at all need to call up the Buddhist dissolution of the self as the corrective. This criticism could be grounded within Christianity upon the continually effective presence of the Catholic tradition and its orientation in the life of the church. It is interesting that such a notion lies farther than Buddhism from Cobb. He could have exhibited the unintended loss of the unity of the church in the Reformation as a presupposition for the development of the individualistic piety correctly criticized by him. He could have concretized his legitimate longing for a new form of Christian community into the demand for an ecumenical renewal of a church encompassing all Christians. But instead, Cobb finds a symbol of his hope for a new community in the utopian city planning of Paolo

Soleri. However, must not an inner renewal of human social life precede every modification of its external form, if this is not to work dehumanizingly? And in the understanding of the Christian tradition, is not the Spirit, through which the Kingdom of God already becomes present (*CPA* 261f), given to the church? Should Cobb's legitimate critique of the individualism of a privatized Protestant piety not lead to the notion of penitence, in respect to the continuation of the separation of the church? In any case, this may be the only field where theology and Christian engagement today could yet—beyond bare rhetoric—create really fundamental changes which, in their consequences, could even change society.

Perhaps the reason that Cobb did not thematize the church as an object of Christian hope is to be sought in the fact that for him the church is an expression of the particularity of Christianity, and therefore does not seem to be sufficient as a criterion of the universality that corresponds to the cosmic relevance of Christ as incarnation of the Logos. The application of this criterion permeates Cobb's entire book. Already the generalization of the title 'Christ' in the first two chapters, which at first glance seems strange, exhibits this tendency: even where Jesus Christ is no longer an object of artistic representation, he remains efficacious as the principle of 'creative transformation' determining the artistic productivity.[20] And even where Christian theology relativizes its own Christian tradition and religion, with the desacralization of the tradition it remains true to the Christian spirit. In contrast to the closedness of its own cultural tradition, cultural pluralism thus becomes the expression for the universal validity of Christianity: precisely in its engaging in the pluralism of the present situation of humanity it confirms its universal validity. I wish to agree with this tendency in Cobb's exposition and I consider in this sense even his sketch of a Logos Christology to be a positive contribution in the right direction, in spite of all the individual criticisms expressed. The original function of the Logos concept in Christology was indeed to make explicit the universal relevance and truth of the confessions concerning Jesus Christ. In a similar way, Cobb correctly turns also against every attempt to shield the Christian faith against critical discussion through "special pleading" (*CPA* 26f), to assure it of independent certainty (*CPA* 238f). Perhaps even the ecclesiastical form of Christianity appears to him as an expression of such a particularity shut in upon itself. I do not believe that such a judgment would be correct. A Christianity without a church can only lead to the impasse of individualism or to the identification of Christianity with a conservative or revolutionary civil religion. The church itself must receive the element of pluralism into itself. That is, primarily, in regard to the plurality of the Christian confessional traditions, the ecumenical task of the present, perhaps the greatest task and opportunity of the present generation of Christendom. But an ecumenical church, which, mindful of its own provisionality in comparison with the eschatological future of God's truth, has taken into itself an element of pluralism, will also find a new relationship to the extra-Christian religions and cultures of mankind—as Cobb discusses again and again, especially in regard to Buddhism—and, to be sure, without renouncing its own identity. Only in this way will the Christian church be able to be in the full sense a "symbol and instrument of the unity of mankind," as the Second Vatican Council and similarly the World Council of Churches in Uppsala (1968) have characterized its essence.

The becoming of a new form of a creedal church must be the central object of the inner-worldly hopes for the efficacy of Christ. Cobb rightly places the theme of hope at the middle of the third and concluding part of his Christology. Regarding this subject—without debating the facts of the matter more closely, to be sure—what is Christologically at stake thereby is the return of Christ and the present efficacy of the Lord who will come again and who has already been elevated to Messiahship in the hiddenness of God. The locus of such present workings of the Christ who comes with God's future is primarily the church. Therefore the Christian hope must be directed toward the fact that the Spirit of the coming Christ unites and renews the church. This is unrestrictedly bound up with the hope—which Cobb designates as transcendent—in the Kingdom of God and the resurrection of the dead. It is surprising that Cobb considers as competitive (*CPA* 243f) the different contents of hope, the immanent and transcendent forms of Christian hope as well as the hope in the Kingdom of God and in the resurrection of the dead. Hope for Christ's bringing about the unification and salvation of his church—with which, to be sure, Cobb does not deal—is closely connected to hope for the Kingdom of God and for the resurrection of the dead. But especially these last two contents of hope cannot be separated from each other without losing their full meaning. In the interconnectedness of the resurrection hope and the Kingdom of God hope, the interdependence of the individual and social destiny of humanity finds its expression.[21] And just because the union of these two aspects is definitely realized in no political order, the church is required as a symbolic representation of that messianic future of humanity. A competition between these contents of Christian hope cannot exist except, at most, in relation to Whitehead's special interpretation of the 'Kingdom of Heaven' and to Soleri's utopia of a futural city, insofar as these take the place of the church as a prefiguration of the reign of God.

NOTES

1. Wolfhart Pannenberg, *Jesus—God and Man* (The Westminster Press, 1968), 166f.

2. *Ibid.*, 168.

3. *Ibid.*, 168f.

4. Alfred North Whitehead, *Process and Reality* (The Macmillan Company, 1929), 532.

5. Cf. Alfred North Whitehead, *Adventures of Ideas* (The Macmillan Company, 1933), Chs. 19 and 20.

6. Whitehead, *Adventures of Ideas*, 226: "We must conceive the Divine Eros as the active entertainment of all ideals, with the urge to their finite realization, each in its due season. Thus a process must be inherent in God's nature, whereby his infinity is acquiring realization."

7. Whitehead, *Process and Reality*, 526: "He does not create the world, he saves it." Certainly this rejection of the notion of creation is directed against a traditional interpretation of creation which thought of creation as a completed, primordial act. Whitehead's antithesis would lift up the fact that precisely the process of redemption, in its own right, is to be thought of as creation. But Whitehead himself has not done that, and such a notion is also not feasible apart from a thoroughgoing revision of his philosophical principles—because Whitehead conceives of God and world in mutual interdependence (*ibid.*, 527ff), and that is unifiable with no concept of creation.

8. *Ibid.*, 521: "It does not look to the future." For a different view, see Cobb, *CPA* 85ff.

9. Whitehead, *Adventures of Ideas*, 268; cf. 194f. But according to Whitehead, the character of every occurrence as an anticipation of the future is not an expression of a constitutive significance of the future for the present, but to the contrary is an expression of the necessity which the present occurrence imposes upon the subsequent future.

10. Cf. Cobb, *GW* 43ff. Moreover, Cobb himself remarks there: "The intense focus of attention upon the future, characteristic of much contemporary theology and bound up with its understanding of Jesus Christ, is foreign to both Whitehead and Bonhoeffer. Neither the God who works slowly and quietly by love nor the God who helps us by his suffering can be readily identified with Pannenberg's Power of the future."

11. Cf. my critical remarks in "Future and Unity," *Hope and the Future of Man*, ed. by Ewert H. Cousins (Fortress Press, 1972), 64, 72f.

12. To be sure, I would prefer to speak of 'creative formation.' Transformation is only a partial aspect of the intended dynamic. Also the form which preceded the transformation has already been attributed to the working of the Logos, and

the determination of the relation between form and transformation is precisely what is crucial. Cobb does make a valuable contribution in that regard, however, in that (in connection with Whitehead) he conceives of the emergence of new occurrences as a condition for the realization of the contribution of the past to the ongoing course of events (*CPA* 70). Of course, not all new occurrences have equally such a positive function for that which is. Moreover, the concept of 'creative transformation' or 'creative formation' is by no means simply identical with the concept of the Logos, because it signifies God's creative activity altogether, working together in the Father, Son, and Spirit. To that extent, it is more encompassing than the Logos concept, which in turn is to be defined as a partial aspect of creative transformation or creative formation (see below, note 17).

13. My explorations into the concept of a field of energy (cf. *Theology*, 75 [1972], 15), cited by Cobb (*CPA* 253), differ from Cobb's use of this idea insofar as Cobb uses the concept for the saving efficacy proceeding from the historical Jesus (*CPA* 116f), and indeed in the sense that occurrences have aftereffects for the future (*CPA* 118). However, a field of energy is not a function of occurrences but, to the contrary, the occurrences are functions of the field. Accordingly one would think not of the historical but of the risen Christ, who is identical with the future of the one resurrected for the world, as the field of force which determines the present existence of the Christian—which is probably closer to the meaning of Paul.

14. The wider point of comparison appears to me to be just as problematic also: "In both cases the primary [?] implications of the expectation are to reinforce and undergird as important those actions which would also appear as good from more general considerations" (*CPA* 227). Jesus argues not from a basically creaturely consciousness but the reverse: Only in the light of God's eschatological future does the meaning even of everyday reality, the meaning of creation, become clear. However, that the content of his message also appears as good under more general points of view is unlimitedly valid only within the context of the Christian tradition. Already Nietzsche and Marxism realized the effect of these important limitations.

15. Co-constituted—for according to Cobb, even in the case of Jesus the appropriation of the initial aim remains an act of human self-actualization: Jesus freely chose to allow his selfhood to be constituted through God (*CPA* 173).

16. On this point, see Pannenberg, *Jesus—God and Man*, 334ff.

17. One should also differentiate the concept of 'creative transformation' in the sense of the distinction between Father and Logos, which, strictly speaking, already characterizes a collaboration of Father and Son in the act of creation. It might be considered whether it is not precisely the aspect of the immanence of form into the creatures which is associated with the Son or Logos in this event.

18. Cf. Pannenberg, *Jesus—God and Man*, 61 and 251f.

19. In his Christian evaluation of the Buddhist criticism of the self (*CPA* 205ff), Cobb indeed declares himself rightly against a dissolution of individuality and, instead, for its enlargement (*CPA* 219f) in relation to the community (*CPA* 213f). Only the substantialist interpretation of the self as a subject must be dissolved (*CPA* 214). Cobb justly wishes thereby to preserve the interest that has found its

expression in the Christian emphasis upon the individual (*CPA* 215). However, the question is not only of the interest in the personal responsibility of the individual, but of the love of God bestowed upon the lost individual with eternal love: Therefore in Christianity the individual can no longer be subordinated without reservation to the system of the society.

20. Whether one may perceive in this process a completion of the incarnation (*CPA* 62) is nevertheless doubtful: The history of Christian art presented in connection with Malraux describes a process of the dissolution of Jesus into the Logos (or into an efficacy of the risen Christ), whereas the concept of the incarnation characterizes the entering of the Logos into the historical figure of Jesus. Also the generalization of the title 'Christ' into the designation of every immanence of the Logos (cf. *CPA* 63, 87) requires at least a more exact grounding and differentiation, if the specifically messianic meaning of the title 'Christ' is not to disappear.

21. Cf. my explanation in "Future and Unity," in Cousins (ed.), *Hope and the Future of Man,* 69ff. Cobb presents my interpretation one-sidedly, in that he discusses it only under the aspect of the resurrection hope in distinction from hope for the Kingdom of Heaven (*CPA* 239ff, 250ff). My adhering to the bodiliness of resurrection—which, alongside the binding of the resurrection of the dead with the end of our time, forms the major item of Cobb's critique of my interpretation (*CPA* 252ff)—represents in my eyes not so far-reaching an opposition to Cobb's Whitehead-oriented interpretation as the question of the constitutive significance of God's future for the present. If it is sufficiently considered that every actual event remains present in all its aspects to the eternity of God, then the bodiliness of the resurrection, which actualizes this divine memory of temporal events in a creatively new manner, should cause no insurmountable difficulties for understanding.

RESPONSE TO TRACY

THE OFTEN overwhelming sense of the relativity of all my efforts to apprehend and express truth, which leads me to positions that Tracy criticizes, is repeatedly nourished by discussions in which I find that others see my theological program as misdirected and my affirmations as meaningless or irrelevant. My hope for some transcendence of relativity is restored by Tracy himself, who understands me so well, shares my concerns, and prods me to advance. For his identification of areas of unclarity in my thought, and of others to which I need to address myself, I can only be grateful. I particularly appreciate his help in sharpening distinctions, and I look forward with pleasure to working as a colleague with a person of his abilities and insights who agrees to such a large extent as to the nature of the theological task.

Of the many important questions he raises I shall limit my response to one—the justification of speaking of a *Christian* natural theology. Tracy quickly removes the initial layer of reasons for interposing the word 'Christian'; that is, he shows that serious people will not suppose 'natural theology' to be free of historical conditioning. Hence there seems to be no further need to guard against that misunderstanding. Second, Tracy shows that historical conditionedness of an insight does not preclude that what is seen is universally true. H. Richard Niebuhr stresses this point, and Whitehead's understanding of philosophy is entirely congenial to it. It is my position as well. If the adjective 'Christian' modifying 'natural theology' seems to deny this, then it should, as Tracy proposes, be dropped.

Nevertheless, I believe that the integrity of my position requires me to keep the label 'Christian,' and I will explain, dealing in more detail with Tracy's analysis. Tracy distinguishes between philosophy as articulation of a basic cultural vision and philosophy as critical, self-transcending argumentation. He agrees that if philosophy is used only in the former way, then it would be appropriate to speak of *Christian* natural theology, but he rightly sees that I would not be satisfied with that. If I appeal to philosophy as critical, self-transcending argumentation, then, he argues, I should not use "Christian" as a qualifying adjective.

My response to this distinction is that all real thinking, and *a fortiori* all philosophy, is never simply articulation of a given vision. Thinking in its very nature is origination of ideas, and in some measure it always attains truth. No philosophy "is explained without remainder in terms of its particular cultural world view" (above, 31). Only a historian of culture would try to articulate its basic vision.

If all thought is a transcendence over the given toward truth, then the question can only be how radically it succeeds in transcending, or what is left untranscended. Tracy suggests that Samuel Alexander, Lloyd Morgan, and Pierre Teilhard de Chardin do not transcend their culture, whereas Heidegger, Whitehead, and Hartshorne do. I could support these judgments in general as a matter of degree, but only that. I believe that in spite of their great originality no aspect of the philosophies of Heidegger, Whitehead, or Hartshorne achieves the level of transcendence which Tracy seems to attribute to them. To avoid abstract and formal discussion, I will take examples Tracy offers of transcendent grasp of truth by Heidegger and Hartshorne and view them in the light of intercultural discussion, specifically with Buddhism. Before claiming that we have transcended our Western vision, we should examine a non-Western one.

Tracy takes as his example from Heidegger the ontological difference between being and beings. This is a good example, and when we look to the East we find quite similar metaphysical insights made almost as a matter of course. Indeed, Heidegger is widely appreciated in the East for his affinities to Chinese and Buddhist thought. But the question is whether Heidegger's grasp and formulation transcend the Western vision of reality and achieve universality. And here the answer cannot be simply affirmative. Heidegger's use of the word 'being,' as he knows, is shaped by interaction with the whole Western tradition of its use. In that tradition being is primary in its relation to non-being or nothingness, and this relation to nothing enters into the deepest layers of the meaning of the word even as it is used by Heidegger. Buddhists are astounded by this Western preoccupation with being. For them Absolute Nothingness is primary and all thought of being is shaped by that primacy. The Buddhist might formulate something like the ontological difference as that between events and Absolute Nothingness, although the mere translation into a Western language already alters the meaning. This by no means indicates that Heidegger is wrong. Buddhists would be the first to hail his insight as progress toward truth. But they can only see it as progress by Westerners toward a truth that is better grasped in quite another way. If the word 'metaphysics' is taken to mean the transcendence of cultural vision, then I would speak of Heidegger's insight as a brilliant breakthrough of and within *Western* metaphysics. The time may come when, through intercultural dialogue, Western metaphysics will be purged of its need for this qualifying adjective. But if dropping the adjective implies that Heidegger is correct, and therefore that the Buddhist apprehension of Absolute Nothingness is false, then we are not ready; for we have not yet studied, much less existentially understood, the Buddhist insight sufficiently to declare its error.

Tracy's example from Hartshorne is the ontological argument. Let us set aside continuing questions about the structure of the argument and assume that it proves that 'Perfection exists.' What has been proved? That depends on the meaning of the words. The word 'exists' is notoriously obscure. Any full clarification of a meaning of this word involves us in the development of a complete philosophy. That its meaning should entirely transcend cultural differences is extremely doubtful. But let us set aside that difficulty as well. What about the meaning of perfection? Hartshorne discusses this problem brilliantly. The argument does not work, he knows, unless there is a coherent understanding of perfection. Perhaps his greatest contribution to philosophy is his detailed development of the requisite understanding of divine perfection. But is his view of perfection the only possible coherent view? It will seem strange to a Buddhist, laden as it is through and through by Western valuations. If asked to describe perfection, the Buddhist will describe Emptiness instead, and what the Buddhist means by 'Emptiness' is not what the Christian means by 'God.' Does the argument then prove the existence of both God and Emptiness, or does it rather show that the ontological argument is still an aspect of *Western* metaphysics, where Western notions of perfection and existence can be assumed?

My conclusion is that, whereas all philosophy worthy of the name is self-transcending argumentation, we are not yet at the point in global history where such distinctions as 'Western' and 'Eastern' can be dropped. I share Tracy's desire to reach that point, but I doubt that this can be done through an interior Western discussion alone. If we think of our deepest insights as simply metaphysical truths and refuse to describe them as Western metaphysics, we are still too likely to suppose that we can transcend our cultural conditionedness without exposing ourselves to the East.

This is *not* to belittle the achievements of Heidegger, Whitehead, and Hartshorne in their transcendence of the received Western tradition. The degree of their transcendence is amazing and providential, and White-head especially offers an excellent bridge of understanding between East and West. Indeed, I believe that there can be a Whiteheadian natural theology for Buddhists as well as one for Christians. But the Buddhist natural theology based on Whitehead will not be the same as the Christian one. For example, it will say nothing about God and a great deal about creativity, which, at least in my version of a Christian natural theology, was slighted. The whole valuational tone will also be very different. The use of different but consistent features of the same conceptuality to formulate natural theology for both Christianity and Buddhism will lift the Christian-Buddhist discussion to an entirely new level. Perhaps in time the two natural theologies can merge!

My vision is that thought advances chiefly in any culture not by building a solid foundation and then erecting an edifice upon it, but by opening new vistas that alter the understanding of the place one stands and alter also the place itself. The alteration is never total, but we cannot know in advance the respects in which the place we now stand will remain unchanged.

An important question is what vistas will be opened to us. Reality is immensely complex, and there is no way of simply examining it as such or in general. What we see depends on what we look for and where we look for it. We have supposed in the past that modern science has a specially privileged and appropriate access to reality, and its acceptance by the East seemed to show that it was not culture bound. We have thought that its immense results in technology demonstrated its unique truth. The success of medicine, for example, was taken to prove that Western biology, chemistry, and physiology are on the right tracks. But we now discover that ancient Chinese medicine also works, although it is based on quite different empirical facts about the body associated with a theory that Westerners find unintelligible. I understand that ancient Indian medicine also works with a still different theory and practice. This does not mean that Western science has not attained a great deal of truth, but it does mean, I think, that the vistas it has opened on the physical body are not the only ones that lead to truth. Today, instead of saying simply 'scientific medicine' to describe what our doctors practice, it is more accurate to say 'Western scientific medicine,' leaving open the possibility that there are quite different Chinese and Indian forms. It is hoped that this relativization of our Western science will not lead to contempt for its methods or achievements. Instead, Western scientists should be challenged to develop and extend their science by peering into unaccustomed vistas. If they do so, the results will be not simply the addition of new information but unforeseeable changes in the whole scientific view of reality. Undoubtedly, much from the past will emerge through the change relatively intact, but what will be changed, and how, can only be learned through the process.

My reasons for reluctance to abandon 'Christian' before 'natural theology' are similar to those I have suggested for introducing 'Western' before 'metaphysics' and 'science.' I believe that persons with other interests, habits, and structures of existence open different vistas on the one inconceivably complex reality. What Buddhists see is, with unknowable limitations and qualifications, there to be seen. What they see seems inconsistent with what Christians see, but it is my conviction that ultimately it is not inconsistent, and that we can understand how both Christian theism and Buddhist atheism are true. In the process Christian theism will be transformed in ways that cannot be foreseen in advance. Whether Buddhists will experience the same necessity to internalize the Christian vista is not yet clear. If they do, there will emerge a new form of Buddhist natural theology. Even if Christian and Buddhist natural theologies eventually merge, the result would be a Buddhist-Christian or a Christian-Buddhist natural theology still needing to internalize threatening truths apprehended in other traditions.

RESPONSE TO KOCH

KOCH'S REVIEW of my book *The Structure of Christian Existence* is basically sympathetic and appreciative of my general purposes. It combines rich detail of exposition with a fundamental critical thesis. This thesis is that my inadequate conception of consciousness leads to confusion throughout the book. This appears especially in my failure to recognize that "the consciousness of God is not without that of the self" (above, 42). I have not developed a "concept of consciousness which *constitutively* comprises the religious relation to God" (above, 43). As a result I have essentially omitted God from my book.

Clearly my omission of God, in distinction from discussions of beliefs about gods and God, reflects a different understanding from Koch's of the nature of consciousness and of religion. For Koch, consciousness universally includes consciousness of God, and the several religions realize this element in consciousness in diverse ways. This follows a long and honorable tradition in which, as Koch notes, Schleiermacher is a key figure. Partly because Koch's close identification of religion with experience of God is widespread, I subordinated the term 'religion' in the book. If religion has to do with God, then Buddhism is not a religion. Also, in my judgment, the Hindu Brahman is so profoundly different from the Hebrew Yahweh that it is misleading to translate both as 'God.' In short, I prefer to speak of the diverse Ways or great traditions, recognizing that they are not all oriented to what either I or Koch calls 'God,' and I prefer to avoid the question as to whether, for that reason, some are religions and others are not.

More generally, I think, Koch believes that the structure of consciousness as described in the continental tradition is an absolute in terms of which any history of consciousness should be explained. My view, on the other hand, is that our present mode of consciousness is a late emergent in the evolutionary-historical process. Of course, our disagreement is not total, since Koch can acknowledge some development, and I assume some constancy, but the difference remains substantial. Koch finds me entangled in contradictions in that I sometimes emphasize the priority of intrapsychic changes over the givenness of the objective world, and sometimes stress the primacy of the outer in determining the inner. My view is that in different traditions the inner-outer relation has in fact been structured differently, whereas Koch believes, I think, that this is fixed by the nature of consciousness itself. He thinks that, because I am writing the history of intrapsychic changes, my consistent view should be to treat the outer as secondary, whereas my actual view is that certain psychic structures render the outer primary.

The different consequences of our views of consciousness show up most sharply in respect to Buddhism. I am positively impressed that the Buddhist effects a radical alteration of consciousness with respect to its self-identity through time (although I question whether some formulations of the Buddhist goal do not demand the ontologically impossible). Koch is struck by "the profundity of self-destruction implicit in this" (above, 50). In this reaction he follows a long tradition of Western Christian and humanist horror at the Buddhist goal of 'extinction' of the self, a tradition which perceives this process only in terms of what is lost. I am convinced that we need a more open-ended view of self and consciousness which allows us to see that the Buddhist goal and achievement is a brilliantly positive one. This may be impossible if we remain with the continental doctrine.

Since Koch stresses that the crux of his objections to my treatment relate to my view of consciousness, it is unfortunate that his use of this term is made to cover two notions that are, for me, quite distinct. There is, on the one hand, the psyche, and on the other, consciousness. I have taken 'existence' to identify the psychic life as a whole when this is viewed from within, and my book is specifically about changing structures of existence. The conscious part of experience is always and only to be found as an aspect of the psyche—an important aspect, but not strictly necessary to its existence, and never inclusive of the whole of the psychic life. I see the psyche as an emergent within the evolutionary process and consciousness as an emergent within the development of the psyche. Chiefly I am interested in the emergence of new forms of psychic organization that involve consciousness in new roles and the correlative emergence of new types of consciousness. I do not see how this project can be carried out if one supposes that the consciousness achieved by the modern West is the given, universal character of human existence. A naturalist can be free of this starting point, and Whitehead offers naturalistic categories rich enough to describe much of the variety of subhuman and human forms of experience. I do not yet see how the continental approach can understand, in a pluralistic spirit, how consciousness emerged and developed in its diversity of forms.

Thus far in my response I have been defending my views of consciousness against Koch. But there are also features of his criticism with which I agree. Koch rightly criticizes me for writing too much as if the intrapsychic structure could be divorced from the experienced world. This is as inappropriate to Whitehead's understanding as it is to the continental view of consciousness. There would be differences, in that for Whitehead the world primarily experienced in some unconscious psychic processes would be the events in the brain, and in general the actual world from which an occasion cannot be separated in the world which has causal efficacy for the occasion more than the world of presentational immediacy, which is highlighted in idealism and phenomenology.

I also failed, as Koch notes, to express my view that God is a part of the actual world of every occasion and thus indissolubly bound up with it. I bracketed out this conviction for purposes of writing the book under discussion because I hoped to formulate an account of diverse structures of existence in a way that would not presuppose a theism that is irrelevant to some of them. My own view is that, whereas the experience of God is not thematically constitutive of all the Ways, traditions, or modes of existence that I treated, nonetheless God is the directivity apart from which there would have been no evolutionary-historical development.

I agree with Koch also that my effort to identify the essence of each structure of existence with the form of its first appearance is misleading. It exaggerates the abruptness of change and the degree of constancy in the periods between what I called threshold crossings. More seriously, it tends to make a past and given form of a movement normative for its further development. Today I would prefer to accept Koch's counterproposal that "the 'essence' of a thing is its history" or, as I have been more inclined to say, a historical movement has no 'essence.' I do not think this invalidates the effort to describe the great theshold crossings of the past and their distinctive results, but it does lead to a different relation today to these past forms. I appreciate Koch's perceptive highlighting of this problem with which I have begun to struggle only recently.

RESPONSE TO ALTIZER

I HAVE NEVER been able to respond directly to Altizer in an adequate way. What I learn from him enters deeply into my psyche and over the years bears fruit. I often find that he has understood me better than I have understood myself. He forces me to examine what I truly believe, what I affirm with conviction, in its distinction from beliefs that I continue to hold but which no longer move me. Consciously I am often testing my new ideas by their compatibility with the old. But Altizer notes the shift and sees its implications for fundamental changes. At the same time I fear I do not live and feel at the depths from which and to which Altizer calls. The only honest response I can make to his paper is introspective.

No one in our time has had a deeper sensitivity for the use of the word 'God' than Altizer. He rightly sees that for me, as for many others, intense concern, confusion, ambiguity, and falsehood have all focused on that word. Since the transcendent Christian God had been the close companion as well as Lord of my youth, my personal experience of his 'death' in university days was deeply painful and the wound may not yet be healed. I struggled with the empirical theology of Wieman, but at that time his fully immanent God did not fill the void within me. Hartshorne's vision, and through his, that of Whitehead appeared at first as a tantalizingly promising, if not quite convincing, answer to my need. I began to live into Whitehead's vision, which year by year became more my own. Within that encompassing way of thinking, God gradually became real to me again. But there has been an element of falseness in my words all the same; for I have often tried to affirm maximally, all to which I could possibly give credence, and thus I have often spoken beyond authentic conviction. I have written of God partly from my own experience of faith, but partly also from confidence in the authority of my mentors. So it was when I spoke "innocently" of God in *A Christian Natural Theology*.

The new climate of the late '60s, to which Altizer made a major contribution, pushed me to discriminate between what I myself fully believed, informed as it was by process philosophy, and what I was asserting at second hand. I have seen no need to repudiate the latter, but I have found that my personal confidence centers around God as the organ of novelty, what Whitehead once called the secular function of God. I developed more appreciation for Wieman's contribution, and this was expressed in *God and the World,* which was, as Altizer notes, a transitional work. I then involved myself more wholeheartedly in spelling out the effect of God in history in *The Structure of Christian Existence.* But in that book, as both Koch and Altizer note, I spoke little of God.

What, then, is my bedrock conviction about God in distinction from the many opinions I am prepared to defend? It is that the new does not come from the old, that the future is not the mere outgrowth of the past. But my conviction is more than that, for I cannot experience the new future except through the conceptuality that years of living into Whitehead's vision have fastened upon me. Hence I experience the new not only as new, but as a gift. I experience it as creative transformation that is both judgment and grace. I also experience it as leading to adventure. I live with a certain expectancy of the unpredictably redemptive in a context in which realistic projections point to disaster. In short, I believe in God.

I fear that this interpreted experience and experienced interpretation is 'liberal' in the sense offensive to Altizer; for though I am learning to appreciate the power and necessity of images, I still aim also to speak as univocally as I can. I think that my present position is in continuity with the Chicago School, although I find reading most of the earlier writing of this tradition somewhat flat and even irritating. This may be because Altizer is correct that this school never knew the transcendent God of Christianity and therefore did not appreciate the threat to human existence bound up with his death. My relation to that school is broken through the mediation of Hartshorne and Whitehead as well as through participation in the cultural and religious turmoil of the '60s. The latter threatened all sense of transcedence, while the process philosophers introduced a new way of experiencing it. From Whitehead I have learned that there is nothing transcendent that is not immanent, but also that there is nothing immanent that is not transcendent. Hence I cannot share Altizer's passion for absolute immanence or understand the mutual immanence of the divine and the human spirit as identity.

The call into the new future is fully concrete, and it is faithless to affirm that there is such a call without attending to its particularity for our world, for the church, for theology, and for myself. Hence I believe that theology must continuously not only transcend itself but also grasp for the way in which here and now it can and should transcend itself. This is not achieved by repeating the ideas of dipolar theism or applying White-head's system to new topics, although I am not averse to either of these. It is achieved only by openness to new ideas and images and willingness to be transformed by them, by taking the step at hand in confidence that when it is taken the direction of the next one will be clearer. At present I find myself drawn, on the one hand, back into a richer and more pluralistic appropriation of the Christian tradition and, on the other, to an internalization of Buddhist vision. I believe this to be true to the liberal spirit, but the result must be a transformation of liberalism.

I am unsure how to name the reality around which my conviction now centers. I cannot give up for myself the word 'God,' and sometimes I speak it with assurance. But in many circles, both outside the Christian ghetto and within, I speak more comfortably in other language. I can say what I want in language that betrays less explicitly its Christian origin. On the other hand, recently I have found myself speaking more of Christ and less of God or even Spirit. I do not know yet whether that is a passing phase or whether my imagination has received a new and lasting shape.

There is another side to my struggle with 'God.' For me God is bound up with what is to be hoped for as well as with the hope-producing powers of the new in the world. I am unsure what, if anything, I can anticipate other than personal and global extinction. But I cannot regard this question as unimportant. Hence I seize eagerly on every hopeful image whether this-worldly or otherworldly. At present the Buddhist notion of the emptiness that is perfect fullness provides me a persuasive access to Whitehead's hope-filled image of the Consequent Nature of God. I am also grasped by the concretization of the Teilhardian vision by Paolo Soleri. I believe that the encounter with Buddhism can help us to hope for a post-personal existence appropriate to this vision. A union through Buddhist mediation of a this-worldly Teilhardianism with Whitehead's Kingdom of Heaven now seems to me a possible form of hope. I hope that some such vision of hope can become truly convincing, both for my own sake and because I deeply fear the wider religious and social consequences of hopelessness.

RESPONSE TO NEVILLE

NEVILLE provides an excellent summary of my book *The Structure of Christian Existence*. He is generous in his appraisal and accurate in his criticism. The conclusion to which I came of the irreconcilable differences between Christianity and Buddhism is unsatisfactory to both. Further it is not Whiteheadian. Neville rightly sees that the Whiteheadian way of dealing with such differences is to convert them into contrasts capable of joint realization and contributory of new intensities. Hence I concede Neville his major point in criticism of my book and thank him for making it so clearly and fairly. Nevertheless, there are differences between the way I want to continue to pursue the task and the way Neville proposes, and it will be more interesting in what follows to stress these disagreements.

In the years since I published the book Neville reviews, I have been trying to get beyond the impasse to which it brought me. Some suggestions of how I now try to bridge the gap between Christian and Buddhist structures of existence can be found in *Christ in a Pluralistic Age*. I am continuing to work on this problem in current writings, and expressions of my interest are scattered through the responses in this volume. But though we agree in our dissatisfaction with the conclusion of the earlier book, we are seeking to overcome the problem in different ways. Neville's approach is primarily philosophical. Mine is more historical or eschatological. That is, Neville seeks unity through the mind's universal grasp of value and through a philosophical anthropology. I look for a movement toward unity through the actual encounter of two highly diverse structures of existence, each being modified by its specific appreciation for the other. Instead of directly seeking a universal structure that synthesizes all, I hope for a transformation of the Christian structure through Buddhism and a transformation of the Buddhist structure through Christianity.

Neville and I agree that there are common elements to human experi-

161

ence and also that there are differences. I have been chiefly impressed by the differences and with how parallel movements of equal sophistication have deepened these. I have concluded that the effort to describe human existence in diverse cultures as varied expressions of a common human nature or as varied responses to a common human situation ended up by imposing on all human existence a pattern derived from one form. Objectively common elements in the situation seem to me to have divergent meanings in diverse cultures.

Neville has read my book with sympathetic insight, but he is not persuaded. The commonality of the human situation and the parallel modes of response to be found in different cultures impress him more. And he believes that Plato's tripartite analysis of the soul can be adopted as a universal basis for understanding human diversity. Employing it, he has shown illuminating parallels without claiming that the problem of the multiple structures of existence is thereby resolved.

I, for my part, am instructed but not persuaded. For example, the analogies between Plato's spirit and the will, i.e., the deciding self of personal existence, are illuminating, but when the will is interpreted in terms of the Platonic spirit, I fear it is misunderstood. Right decision is similar to disciplined spirit, but it is also different. Further, the Buddhist account of the soul more adequately describes the Buddhist soul than does the Platonic one, and the use of Plato slants the normative decision in favor of the Western desire to perfect the several potentials of the soul against the Buddhist quest for the cessation of all cravings.

Even as I reaffirm my sense of the differences and of the importance of understanding each culture in its own terms, I realize the limitations of what I am saying. If the diversity is to be understood, it must be ordered by some common conceptuality. The question between Neville and myself is that of the level at which a common conceptuality is appropriately introduced. To advance discussion of this question I would suggest that each of us might attempt an account of Buddhist existence and then seek comments from Buddhists as to how adequately they could recognize themselves in these accounts.

There is no sharp opposition between us in our recognition of cultural relativism. Neville knows that as a Methodist from Missouri some possibilities are closed to him that are open to a Buddhist; and he recognizes that a new threshold crossing cannot be simply chosen and effected at will. But his emphasis is that he transcends this historical conditioning in his openness to truth, that he aims to be a part of the universal human community, and that we should jointly seek agreement on the best structures of existence for all. I fully agree. Perhaps he would agree with me that the strength of his urge toward universality is itself due to his Christian structure of existence, with its important Socratic components; for he knows that the vision of reality by which one lives affects the force of universal human tendencies. He senses that some relativistic visions of reality undercut the urge toward universal truth, and he fears that I give too much support to this kind of relativism.

We agree on the importance of our visions of reality in shaping the structures of our existence, and it is especially here that Neville wants to overcome relativism. I, on the other hand, stress the relativity of visions of reality as well as of structures of existence, and in doing so have proved confusing to many of my readers. In responding to Tracy I made an effort to clarify my combination of relativism and realism, and in concluding these comments I shall offer another image.

Imagine five people seated before a painting made up of millions of dots of many colors. To the naked eye the dominant pattern is red and the pattern of red dots makes for a picture a child might have painted of a house. Four of the five people are then provided with glasses. When they put them on, the simple sketch of a house remains, but behind it, within it, and around it there appear vastly subtler and richer designs. The significance of the house is quite changed. The glasses are then taken away.

Once the painting has been seen through the glasses the richer pattern is dimly discernible even without them. But efforts by any of the four to share the richer design with the one who has had no glasses fail. Further comparison of notes among them leads to bewildering results; for no two agree as to the design that was seen or the meaning of the house. One thinks that, despite the great divergence of their verbal accounts, all have really seen the same thing; for at least there is general agreement that the glasses have revealed depths of meaning initially invisible to the naked eye, and there are many analogies in the divergent reports. The second thinks that the others have been misled by their glasses but is sure that the painting really has the form and meaning she perceived. The third decides after the disputation that the richer designs were actually on the glasses themselves and should not be attributed to the picture which is correctly seen only by the one who never wore glasses. The fourth believes that the picture is so complex that all the designs are really there and that the meaning of the superficial picture can only be found when all the designs are separately and then conjointly perceived. Although the pattern she had seen vividly through the glasses dominates her vision, by careful listening she is able to attend to the dots that were decisive to others and fragmentarily to see these designs as well.

I identify my realistic relativism with the fourth person. Of course, realistic relativism is itself but one of many possible positions, and my adoption of this view is historically conditioned.

FURTHER REFLECTIONS
ON THE RELATIVITY OF BELIEF

THE TOPIC of relativity has been touched on in all the essays to this point, and in responding to Neville and Tracy I have dealt with it. Its effect on my thought is of sufficient importance to justify a more systematic treatment than has seemed appropriate in the individual responses. I have chosen to formulate my views in five theses.

First, there is no perspective from which to think except the utterly particular moment that is oneself here-now. Every aspect of this here-now is affected by every other aspect, so that no aspect, and therefore no belief, is free from the influence of biology, biography, and history in all its dimensions. Similarly, none of these influences is unaffected by rational, critical, and creative activity that occurs in the here-now.

Second, the awareness of this conditionedness is always partial. Sociologists of knowledge rarely reflect deeply on the sociology of the sociology of knowledge. Those who explain beliefs psychoanalytically rarely reflect deeply on the psychoanalytic explanation of their psychoanalytic explanations. Still more rarely do sociologists of knowledge take adequate account of the psychoanalytic explanation of the sociology of knowledge, or psychoanalysts sufficiently consider the sociological explanation of psychoanalytic activity. Even if we overcame these and many other specific limitations, our realization would remain partial; for any one of these reflexive explanatory pursuits can in principle be pursued *ad infinitum.*

Third, existential realization of our actual condition can only realize some aspects of it. This is illustrated in what may be the most profound form of such realization, Buddhist enlightenment. Enlightenment is the existential realization of the here-now as *pratitya-samutpada* (dependent co-origination, or pure relativity). The power and purity of this experience is such that I cannot doubt that what is realized is truly there to be realized. But it seems that what is realized is not equally every aspect of

165

the here-now. The aspect of the particularity of the creative novelties that are also elements in the here-now is neglected. An equally intense existential realization of this aspect of actuality would constitute a quite different 'enlightenment' from the Buddhist one. The here-now is too complex for any one existential realization to preempt the field.

Fourth, this analysis of the relativity of all things, including all belief, is itself relative, as is this judgment that it is relative, *ad infinitum.* If this is a 'vicious regress,' it is a vicious regress to which finitude condemns us. The charge that the relativist must assert relativity as an absolute is false. The relativist can recognize the relativity of relativism.

Fifth, this analysis of relativity inherent in every here-now presupposes that there have been, are, and will be other here-nows. This realistic belief is itself relative. The alternative is solipsism of the present moment, which absolutizes the one here-now as all that is. Against solipsism I am convinced of realism, but I recognize that that conviction is relative.

What, now, are the implications of this thoroughgoing relativism? Again I shall formulate my views in a series of propositions.

First, the relativity of a belief does not make it unimportant. Some beliefs are in fact trivial, and there is no reason to attend to them. But our ability to recognize this implies that we can distinguish these from important beliefs. The relativity of belief is compatible with great concern about beliefs.

Second, the relativity of a belief does not make it false. On the contrary, it is unlikely that we are capable of believing wholly false propositions. We have recently learned that the beliefs of the insane have their own truth. In any case, the important beliefs that have grasped and moved human beings all embody some positive relation to reality. The doctrine of universal relativity entails this, just as much as it challenges our supposition that some of our beliefs are absolutely true.

Third, all beliefs are reformable. Since there can be no unconditioned belief, there is no justification either for believing that we possess one or for seeking to obtain one. The quest for certainty or finality should be abandoned.

Fourth, the encounter with beliefs other than our own is an opportunity for reformation. Since beliefs are not true or false, but more or less adequate, clear, and free from distortion, the encounter between divergent beliefs should not be viewed in terms of either-or but as an occasion to achieve clearer, more adequate, and less distorted beliefs.

Fifth, the relativity of belief is compatible with decisiveness of action. The tension between cognitive uncertainty and the either-or of action has often been noted. Since non-action is a form of action, there is no escape. It is foolish to contrast this human condition with some other, supposedly conceivable, condition and to bemoan its absence. The recognition of the human condition should induce constant readiness to alter the course of action as beliefs are reformed. But there is no reason not to act decisively.

Sixth, the relativity of belief is compatible with strong convictions. Conviction is not certainty about the truth of particular propositions but the sense that a system of belief generally survives well in the encounters with alternatives. Such survival is not a matter of remaining intact and unaltered. It is instead to be constantly expanded, clarified, and corrected. The recognition that past survival does not ensure future survival is not debilitating once the quest for certainty is genuinely abandoned and once thought and action are accepted as adventure and risk. The greatest threat to strong conviction is the effort to hold a belief intact and unreformed in its encounter with other beliefs.

Some critics question whether relativism of this sort is compatible with following Whitehead's philosophy. I do not claim that Whitehead took exactly the position I have outlined, but I do believe that his philosophy supports this kind of relativism and that the spirit is fully congenial. Whitehead taught that whatever is actual is an instance of creativity, that is, of the many becoming one and being increased by one. This is a principle of universal relativity from which beliefs are in no wise exempted. In his book *Process and Reality* he taught that "the merest hint of dogmatic certainty as to the finality of statement is an exhibition of folly." He saw philosophies not as true or false but as more or less adequate expressions of more or less clearly grasped insights.

Of course, Whitehead's philosophy is relativized here along with everything else. But the kind of relativization involved is one that Whitehead shared. He viewed his own categorial scheme as reformable, and he set no limits as to where and how far such reformation might go. This kind of relativization is fully compatible with being a convinced Whiteheadian. Indeed, it is involved in being a convinced Whiteheadian. Thus far I have found through Whitehead a system of beliefs that generally survives well through encounters with alternatives. I recognize in principle that its past success for me does not guarantee future success, but I seek no such certainty. I will remain a convinced Whiteheadian unless and until I have encounters that require the adoption of a quite different perspective.

But is this Whiteheadian relativism compatible with Christian faith? That depends, of course, on how we understand Christian faith, but for me it seems not only compatible but required. Central to my Christian understanding is the radical finitude of every creature. For a finite creature to aim at the attainment of absolute knowledge or propositional certainty is to fail to realize its true condition. We are not God.

On the other hand, Christianity does offer existential assurance. It has often been argued that such assurance is possible only on the basis of propositional certainty and that, since human beings could not obtain this by thought, it is supernaturally given by God. But it has as often been rightly replied that, even if this supernatural scheme were true, there could be no propositional certainty about it. We could not be certain that the beliefs in question were given by God or that our apprehension was of just the correct propositions. The quest for certainty, which has undoubtedly been present in Christianity as in all human traditions, leads to absurdity. The refusal to accept our creatureliness cannot be the heart of Christian faith! Faith is trust, conviction, and faithfulness rather than cognitive certainty.

Further, the recognition of the relativity of belief does not entail the surrender of the belief that things are as they are independently of our beliefs. The relativity of my beliefs about another person's feelings entails that the beliefs are partial, unclear, and partly distorted. But to recognize this is to suppose that the other's feelings are as they are, independently of my beliefs about them. Similarly, the recognition of the relativity of my beliefs about God, including the belief that God exists, is fully compatible with the belief that God exists. My belief is that God's existence is also relative in the sense of relational, but this does not entail that God's beliefs, if we use that word, are inadequate, unclear, and distorted. These limitations are a function, not of universal relativity as such, but of the imperfect relativity that characterizes every creature. If God is equally related to everything and excludes nothing—if, in the Buddhist sense, God is empty—then God's relativity is absolute. The absolutely relative is the norm in terms of which creaturely relativity can be seen to introduce incompleteness, unclarity, and distortion.

Still it is true that this relativism relativizes also Christianity as a whole. Christianity as a whole is conditioned in particular ways that necessarily render it incomplete, unclear, and distorted. To commit myself unqualifiedly to Christianity would be inconsistent with a full recognition of the inadequacy, unclarity, and distortion of the beliefs through which I identify myself as a Christian. But to be a convinced Christian is not incompatible with this recognition. I am a convinced Christian because I have experienced the system of Christian beliefs as generally surviving well through encounters with alternatives. I am continuously engaged in testing their capacity for further reformation through these encounters. I will remain a convinced Christian unless and until I have encounters that force me to break with this process of continuously reforming Christianity and to adopt a fundamentally different approach.

In the Introduction to this volume Griffin speaks of my stress on relativity at another point, that of the understanding of Christianity. I have recently opposed the idea that Christianity has an essence. What it is in different times and places differs, and these differences are not necessarily superficial.

If Christianity had an essence, this would mean that there were some formal characteristic present in every community or individual, at all times and places, to which the term 'Christian' properly applies. That formal characteristic could be a mode of belief, a conscious relation to Jesus, a way of life, a style of interpersonal relations, or a vision of reality. My own contribution to the quest for the essence of Christianity was to describe a structure of existence definitive of Christianity both descriptively and normatively. I continue to believe that it is useful to think in terms of the distinctively Christian structure of existence, but I no longer believe it is desirable to conceive this, or any other formal characteristic, as the essence of Christianity.

My objection to the quest for an essence is twofold. First, any formulation of an essence tends to obscure the actual variety within the Christian movement. Even if features common to all forms of Christianity can be identified, they are not equally prominent in all these forms, and treating them as the essence distorts the actual weighting of importance in the several periods. Second, the identification of an essence encourages a conservative stance in the present. I found myself judging new ideas and proposals for creative change in terms of their appropriateness to what I regarded as the fixed essence of Christianity, that is, the structure of Christian existence. Conservatism and caution about change are fully appropriate, but they are also a one-sided stance into which we fall too easily. Openness to the new needs more encouragement than does the tendency to hold on to what is given. The quest for an essence is counterproductive.

Griffin's questioning reflects the deepest reason for the concern for an essence, i.e., that we need to be able to distinguish between change that is appropriate for Christianity and change that is corruption or perversion. If we do not meet this need through identifying an essence, we must do so in another way. This too applies to the historian, who must form a judgment as to both when a movement ceases a healthy development and is changed into something else and when, through all of its varied forms, it continues to be the same movement. There are, of course, no infallible rules. It will be some time before students will be able to decide whether Sokagakkai is truly a Buddhist sect or whether its spirit is alien to that of Buddhism so that it must be regarded as something quite distinct.

The issue here is not to decide those questions but to consider how decisions are to be made. The historian cannot decide in terms of a purely objective criterion of difference from and similarity to what has gone before or of the presence or absence of some predetermined essence. My own view is that Sokagakkai is not a true development of Buddhism. But it may be that the difference between Jodoshinshu, which I regard as a true development of Buddhism, and the Buddhism that antedated it was as great as the difference between Sokagakkai and established forms of Nichiren. The historian's decision must be made by a deeper penetration into what is going on in the turns and twists of events. The historian must attempt to discern whether the new movement is arrived at through a profound appropriation of the past in its interaction with other cultural elements and new ideas or whether its continuity with the antecedent movement is superficial.

When we face the existential question of how to respond as Christians to new situations, the issue is similar. There are no fixed guidelines. How, for example, is a Christian today to respond to the challenge of Buddhism? Are we to be open to what we can appropriate from Buddhism only within the limits that are set by our fixed commitment to an established essence of Christianity? Are we to enter the relation with Buddhism with no strong commitment to Christianity at all? Or are we to wrestle again with our own heritage to reformulate what we have received in the light of a context alien to that heritage, to find within it the possibility of a fuller openness to Buddhism? To me the third seems most Christian. But it leads to the possibility that what will emerge from the reappropriation of our tradition and the openness to Buddhism may be different in now unforeseeable ways from all past forms of Christianity. This is the way of creative transformation. I see creative transformation as the living Christ. I believe myself to be most faithfully Christian when I am most open to him.

RESPONSE TO DALY

READING Daly's essay is a consciousness-raising event. Since my own consciousness-raising with regard to sexism came late and slowly, I can only confess that she is right in much of her critique. My efforts to avoid sexist language began only in the spring of 1973, and the first book in which they are even imperfectly expressed is *Christ in a Pluralistic Age.* Further, I have progressively realized that my participation in sexist language and imagery has been also a participation in the sexist mythos. Daly has herself, both directly and indirectly, contributed to such understanding of this as I now have. This understanding is further heightened by her essay in this volume.

Like Daly, I have been more conscious of thinking in philosophical categories. I have been prone to treat the translation of conceptual meanings into symbols and images too lightly and even to see this too often as a way of making contact with traditional meanings. The 'death of God' theology and feminist theology have helped awaken me to the importance of images and to the realization that I, too, live in and through the images and the myths. I now recognize that my task as theologian is the task of shaping images, and I also recognize that my habits of mind are such that I am very much dependent on the stimulus of others if I am to share responsibly in that task. I picked up the image of 'androgyny' when its use by women persuaded me it would be helpful. Daly's essay opens my eyes to its inadequacy. I hope I remain open to continuing instruction.

As consciousness was raised to the white character of our theology, I judged that leadership in this process was with the black theologians and other ethnics. I played the role of observer and quiet self-questioner. I now think that was inadequate. As a white I should have avowed my disagreements when I felt them despite the guilt that made criticism of blacks so difficult. Daly recognizes that the task of creating the mythos of feminism belongs to women, but she encourages men to share their

171

reactions to what they see going on.

The deepest difference between us is that she is a woman and has chosen to identify herself as such and to devote herself to creative leadership in the development of that new mythos in which women can fully participate in be-ing, whereas I am a man who has become sensitive to the issues only as they have been forced on my attention by women. This difference is a factual given, and there is little that I can do besides recognize it. There is another issue, however, on which I do have something to say, even while I recognize that feminists will have to discuss it from a different perspective. This is the issue of the relation of feminism and Christianity. On this issue Daly has taken the stand that there is radical and insuperable incompatibility. I disagree.

The incompatibility to which Daly points is not a superficial one. It does not have to do with male dominance in the church or with the prevalence of sexist language, except insofar as these are symptoms of something much more fundamental. As I understand it, she holds that all Christian images of the divine are necessarily male-oriented, and that for women to relate themselves to male-oriented images of the divine is anti-feminist.

There is no doubt that she is *almost* correct. Almost all Christian images of the divine have in fact been male-oriented, and as a male I am in no position to challenge the judgment of women that to orient themselves to deity in this way is destructive. The only dispute is whether what has always been is necessary. This raises the issue as to what Christianity is; for if Christianity can be defined in terms of the forms it has embodied thus far, then the case that liberated women must leave it is a strong one. My view is that any such definition of Christianity is false, in spite of the fact that it is characteristic of most theology, including my own past efforts. If we were forced to define Christianity in terms of its past forms, it would certainly not be women alone who would have to leave. If Christianity were bound to the understanding of Jesus or the Bible that predated the rise of critical historical scholarship, then all those who are informed by such scholarship would have to leave. If it were bound to the supernaturalist understanding of the relation of God and the world that it adopted during the Newtonian age, then all those who reject the Newtonian world view would have to reject Christianity. Today, we are confronted by a profound tension between our appreciation of the other great traditions of humankind and our exclusivist Christian tradition. If Christianity is identified with what Christians have predominantly believed thus far about their exclusive relation to salvation, then those of us who recognize truths of ultimate importance in other religions must leave.

Against every definition of Christianity in terms of the forms it has embodied in the past, I urge that we recognize it to be a process. What Christianity is today at its growing edges is profoundly different from what Christianity was at its growing edges in the first, third, sixteenth, or nineteenth centuries. Undoubtedly there are certain forms that can be found in all these periods, but that does not mean that the essence of Christianity consists in those forms. Some forms present in the first and third centuries were lacking in the thirteenth, and others, shared also in the thirteenth, were gone in the sixteenth. What came to the fore in the sixteenth century was barely visible in the third and the thirteenth. There is no reason to suppose that those forms which survived intact through the nineteenth century will survive the twentieth. Nor is there reason to suppose that the displacement of received forms is faithlessness to the tradition. I would argue, on the contrary, that unwillingness to surrender what proves false or oppressive in a new context would be faithlessness.

Such comments provoke the question as to what constitutes the ongoing movement as 'Christian.' There is a widespread assumption that we can recognize identity in a movement only if some form characterizes it throughout. Against this I hold that there is another kind of unity, a dynamic unity, in which identity through time is based on a particular mode of relatedness to the past of the tradition rather than on preservation of its forms. This mode of relatedness is one of appreciative but critical transformation. Christianity will survive as long as living out of its history and its community is felt as grounding self-criticism and radical change appropriate to new situations and new understanding. Christianity dies when it attempts to defend what it has been. In respect to what Daly is showing us, this means that Christianity can live only if it accepts the justice of most of her criticisms and repents. It decays if it attempts to defend what it has been.

Repentance is not, of course, a mere matter of expressing regret. It requires profound reversals. At present I have only confused ideas as to what form those reversals should take. They will certainly involve drastic change of institutional structures, forms of worship, language about persons and about the divine, basic attitudes, and modes of existence. For the most part men will have to accept the leadership of women in discovering what changes work to transform Christianity from a male-oriented to an inclusive process. The needed changes will be very slow. Most of us men, and also many women, will be insensitive to the suffering of those who see more clearly what we are doing. A generation from now the problem will still be with us. I think I have few illusions as to the purity or virtue of the Christian movement. But I do believe that there are signs that Christianity *is* still a movement and, as long as that is so, I believe it is wiser to remain a part of it. I hope many prophetic women will do so.

My hope that enlightened women will not abandon the church is first, I confess, for the sake of the church. Often in the past the pace of needed change in the church has been slowed because its prophets have given up on it. This could happen again. But my concern is also for the women's movement. I do not doubt the value of creating new communities with new myths and rituals as a special phase of the women's movement. But the new myths must be rooted in the old at the same time that they are rejections of the old. It makes a great deal of difference what old myths are incorporated as our history, no matter how radically we oppose much of that history. I believe that in fact it is the Judeo-Christian history that has given birth to the current movement of liberation of women and that this is no accident. I believe the process of prophetic protest against the tradition is at the heart of the tradition itself. I believe that to cut off a new community from recognition of this continuity will lead to its impoverishment. I doubt the viability of leaping over the historical tradition to establish a more direct relation to a prehistorical matriarchal age.

Clearly Daly herself has just the relation to the tradition I am advocating. She is immersed in it and therefore can expose its sexism with unexcelled sensitivity. But in her understandable and justified anger against it and against its present expressions and defenders, she fails to appreciate the extent to which it witnesses against itself and thus supports her protest against it. This kind of appreciation requires that one see the movement which is Christianity in terms of its response to the real alternatives of changing historical epochs. What it is now called to do and to become is something radically new. It does not make sense to judge its beliefs about cosmology in earlier epochs by our present knowledge of science. Similarly I do not think it helps today to judge past Christians by our newly emerging understanding of women. The Christian view of women is now to be worked out, not by historical research but by the sort of radical criticism and constructive thinking in which Daly gives such remarkable leadership.

There are several respects in which I am optimistic that changes in the institution with which I am most closely associated will occur quickly, and I do not suppose my church to be unique. In the United Methodist denomination women are rapidly assuming equal roles with men in leadership in many local congregations. The denomination is now ordaining women with rapidly diminishing discrimination and in rapidly increasing numbers. The structure of the denomination is such that those who are ordained are assigned to churches, and in most cases prejudices against women ministers fade rapidly once the reality is established. Once there is a substantial minority of women ministers I expect that, as in the case of ethnic minorities, they will be given positions of denominational leadership disproportionate to their numbers. Once they achieve leadership, I expect them to lead in making other needed changes in the institution. My point is not that Methodists have anything to be proud of in their history. It is only that in matters of this sort change is both possible and probable.

But this is not the level at which Daly poses the real issue. The question is not whether women will be able to assume an equal role of leadership in the churches but whether women should continue to work in and through Christianity at all. Will they not in fact be serving a male deity, and, by their presence and leadership, be obscuring the deeper mythic-spiritual maleness of Christianity as such? Here her challenge is theological and fundamental, and to the best of my knowledge no Christian theologian has arrived at a satisfactory solution. Certainly I have not.

In *Christ in a Pluralistic Age* and *Process Theology: An Introductory Exposition* I have made some suggestions. When I wrote them I knew that they were no more than that. I now realize that even as suggestions or pointers they may be insensitive to real issues. I see two problems with respect to our Christian thought of deity. One is that all our language about deity is male and that, insofar as it is tied to Jesus, this is strictly inescapable. Even if Jesus (when compared with Mohammed, for example) is strikingly androgynous, Daly shows that this does not touch the depths of the problem. Christianity is bound up with the conviction that the divine has been historically manifest uniquely and decisively in a male. For the foreseeable future, to deny this will be to separate oneself from the mainstream of the Christian movement. But we can recognize the radically contingent character of this historical fact; that is, that it tells us nothing about the nature of the divine but only about the character of human society which precluded women from playing the kind of role that Jesus played. And we can cease to transfer the gender of Jesus to our way of thinking of the divine that is manifest in him.

Historically this transfer has ignored the androgynous character of Jesus himself. The images of deity, especially 'the Father,' which have dominated orthodox theology have been stereotypically masculine. Stereotypically feminine characteristics, which were embodied in Jesus, were not attributed to God the Father, and by assimilation of Jesus to God they were often denied to Jesus as well. One theological task is to show that deity is no more to be defined by stereotypically masculine characteristics than by stereotypically feminine ones, or rather that both sets are present in the divine. This point I tried to make in the Postscript to *Christ in a Pluralistic Age.* Whitehead's doctrine of the dipolarity of God in fact suggests masculine characteristics of the primordial nature and feminine characteristics of the consequent. For Whitehead, at least, religious concern attaches more to the latter than to the former. Also, in Whitehead, the consequent nature includes the primordial in a sense in which the primordial does not include the consequent. Hence, his doctrine of God could be called gynandry. When writing, however, I was not sensitive to this point.

It may be that, if the divine can be understood in terms of gynandry, the offense of the inescapable maleness of Jesus can be mitigated. Christianity is a fundamentally eschatological movement, that is, it moves toward that which retrospectively gives meaning to what occurs. It is the End that is fundamental rather than the proclaimer and promiser of the End. The End is also deity, and it is deity understood in terms of gynandry. Thus the androgynous proclaimer receives his importance from the gynandrous deity to which he points. Of course, he pointed toward that End in language that is masculine, the language of the Kingdom of God. But new gynandrous images can be developed to name this End.

Once again, these comments are at most suggestions that may share in a process of change. They presuppose existing stereotypical distinctions. Those distinctions are themselves in process of being transformed. Perhaps when that transformation has gone far enough, even the pairing of primordial and consequent natures with masculine and feminine will be irrelevant and my suggestion will be experienced as counter to the interests of women. But I prefer to risk the suggestion in hopes that it will help to liberate theology from its present Trinitarian images, so that it may become more able to share in the re-mythologizing needed for women's liberation.

RESPONSE TO TANAKA

IT IS A SOURCE of great joy to find my suggestion of a Whiteheadian Buddhist natural theology taken up with such seriousness and insight. I am more than ever persuaded by Tanaka's essay that Whitehead does offer an avenue through which Buddhists can themselves profit and Christians can understand and appropriate Buddhist insights. If Buddhists and Christians can express themselves through a common conceptuality, we can learn how our insights can supplement and enrich each other. We will also see more clearly when and how we differ.

In my introspective response to Altizer I explained how important to me is the function of God as providing novelty, or in Whitehead's technical terms, the 'initial aim' of each occasion at the realization of some intensity in itself and also in the relevant future. It is my judgment that this future-oriented aspect of human existence has been nourished and attended to in Christianity. It is my impression that Buddhism minimizes this aspect of experience. The element of aspiration toward the future is subsumed under craving, and it is accordingly suppressed or transcended. Buddhism instead takes its stance fully within the occasion of experience, freeing itself from concern both for the origin and for the destiny of the occasion as well as for the origin and destiny of the world. Thus while Christians attend to the origin of the occasion in God and its destiny as servant of the world, Buddhists attain the serenity of the now.

When Buddhism and Christianity are viewed in this way, they appear as mutually complementary rather than as opposed. Christians view the present moment in its relatedness to past and future. Buddhists learn to experience each present moment in its sheer immediacy. The results differ, both existentially and in the associated doctrines. But in principle we should be able to see that both perspectives are real and possible and that they both contribute to a grasp of the one inexhaustible truth.

Whitehead's philosophy will also be better understood in the process.

Tanaka states that "the more we understand Nishida, the more we under-stand Whitehead, and at the same time, the more we understand White-head, the more we understand Nishida" (above, 107). Tanaka's exposi-tion of Whitehead from a perspective shaped by Nishida illustrates the general point that Buddhists understand aspects of Whitehead's thought with an insight and penetration that has eluded Western Whiteheadians. Note, for example, the naturalness and clarity with which Tanaka shows how the experiencer is the superject of the experience (above, 104). Out of centuries of efforts to formulate rightly the relation of objectivity and subjectivity in the process of the many becoming one, Buddhists can help overcome the one-sidedness of most Whiteheadian accounts, sometimes toward subjectivity and sometimes toward objectivity (above, 108–110). Also one senses that whereas what Nishida means by Absolute Nothing-ness is implicit in Whitehead's cosmology, only a Buddhist can draw it out and show its potential importance.

The Christian, on the other hand, will lift to attention the implications of Whitehead's vision as to the graciousness of God in opening up the future for each occasion and preserving its achievement. These are em-phases that the focus of attention on pure immediacy excludes from Buddhism and from Tanaka's essay. Also, whereas Whitehead's philoso-phy accounts for the vision of the center as everywhere and the circumfer-ence nowhere, the Christian Whiteheadian seeks the circumference, in the sense of the orienting principle, in God.

My one point of criticism is to oppose the tendency to associate the Christian God with the Buddhist ultimate—in this case Absolute Noth-ingness. This is an almost universal tendency where common ground is sought between the two Ways, and it is not pressed by Tanaka. Yet I would like to see a much clearer recognition that Christianity and Bud-dhism have been oriented to different aspects of reality or to different ultimates.

I believe that what Nishida means by Absolute Nothingness correlates better in Western thought with Plato's Receptacle, and in Whitehead's conceptuality with the extensive continuum, than with God. That is not to say that it can be identified with either, but in Whitehead it is the extensive continuum which, lacking any standpoint of its own, both pro-vides all standpoints and establishes the relativity of all that actualizes those standpoints. Nishida sees in Absolute Nothingness a depth that Whitehead does not notice in the continuum, and he employs this con-cept to answer questions that are less clearly and forcefully pursued in Whitehead. But by the same token, Absolute Nothingness does not serve to answer the questions that lead Whitehead to speak of God. It will be better to recognize that what Whitehead calls God is not thematically treated in Nishida—or in Buddhism generally—than to try to assimilate God to established Buddhist notions of the ultimate. What Whitehead means by God arises for our conscious experience as we marvel at our freedom to transcend the past through participation in a novel order that, as possibility, is given to us from beyond that past. It arises as we perceive ourselves as part of a cosmic process of creative transformation. Nishida edges toward such a vision, but the notes of novelty and order do not grasp his imagination so as to lead to the theistic questions of whence and how. Whether the theistic question can be asked and answered without denial of essential Buddhist principles remains moot, but Whitehead's treatment provides grounds for hope that this can be done.

The Buddhist-Christian dialogue is still young. Exploration of the potentiality of Whitehead's philosophy—and Nishida's—to further that dialogue has barely begun. But the beginning is auspicious. From the Whiteheadian side it has already provided a way both for appreciating the Buddhist achievement and for grasping the meaning and the limitations of Whitehead more clearly. From the Christian side a vista opens up for the creative transformation of Christianity through inner appropriation of Buddhist contributions.

RESPONSE TO HARTSHORNE

HOW CAN I RESPOND to such a generous appraisal by my revered teacher? With thanks, of course, and also with a word of shame. How could it be that in the years I sat at Hartshorne's feet and read his books I was so oblivious to so many of his concerns? I did not understand the life-style he and Dorothy adopted, already decades ago, providing a model for our future. I did not even remember that he had written on population, pollution, and ecology until I was caught up in these concerns myself at the end of the '60s. In one sense, therefore, my little book is not much indebted to him. Yet in a deeper sense, I realized very late that the vision I gained from him was already fitted by him to the concerns to which I finally related it. My thanks are not only for his kind words but for that deeper gift by which he was for me the one person who was most truly my teacher.

RESPONSE TO REYNOLDS

REYNOLDS captures a mood and spirit appropriate to the ethics of process theism in a way that my own writing has not. He thinks from the dipolar understanding of God to the human situation, thus sketching a truly theological ethic. I have come closest to this kind of thinking in recent works addressed to a more general audience, and Reynolds is able to find passages in *Is It Too Late? A Theology of Ecology* that enter into the spirit of his thought. His comments on my treatment of ethics in *A Christian Natural Theology* are generous but reflect the difference in approach. Perhaps the most appropriate response to Reynolds' creative essay will be to reflect on the tensions between my experience of the relation between ethics and theology and his. The intention is confessional rather than apologetic or argumentative.

I find that when I think of ethics, I think of 'ought.' Reynolds rightly notes that my approach is therefore Kantian. He, too, affirms the need of "a way of taking account of our experience of moral obligation" (above, 126), but he comes to this from a dipolar theistic perspective. My experience was different. I had to find my way from deontological ethical thinking to process theology. The experience of ought was not a moment in a joyful and adventurous vision but a life-organizing principle in relation to which I sought my way as a Christian.

At the most formative period of my intellectual quest, the dominant philosophical mood emptied the 'ought' of all serious meaning through various forms of non-cognitivism. The resulting liberation from the law was an antinomianism which I could not accept. The formal treatment of obligation in *A Christian Natural Theology* was the result of my effort to establish ethics in its own autonomy, that is, in terms of ethical experience alone.

I experienced the undermining of the seriousness of moral obligation as the threat of existential nihilism, but I experienced the life of moral seriousness as restrictive and burdensome. Hence it was for me just as important to relativize ethics as to affirm its seriousness. Whereas I found in Whitehead only indirect assistance in the establishment of ethics, it has been through him that I have understood how to transcend it.

My experience of both affirming ethics and relativizing it has shaped my understanding of Christian faith. I see obligation as law and its transcendence as grace. I see grace as in no way lessening the force or reality of law but as nevertheless freeing the Christian from its bondage. And I find this pattern of ethical seriousness and its transcendence in those Christian figures of the past with whom I most easily identify and whose wisdom I most respect. Only gradually have I come to see that this pattern of law and grace is not necessarily the one normative form of Christianity, and that the faith into which we are now called has another dynamic and structure. Perhaps there will be no need in the future for the existential struggle with law to loom so large in the shaping of Christian life. This recognition has given me a new appreciation of Whitehead's vision. I incline less to use it scholastically as a means to affirm a Christian experience largely shaped apart from it, and more as itself embodying the Christian faith in a form appropriate to our time.

Coming to Reynolds' original essay from this perspective, I find myself ready to be guided into new ways of thinking of ethics. I am persuaded that the basic vision of reality within which one thinks and experiences is more crucial for how ethical issues arise and are dealt with than is the formal analysis of moral experience. Reynolds' formulation of the vision of process theology is both sound and able to communicate its ethical meaning. Of course, as he recognizes, there is much work to be done in filling out this sketch of a 'somatic ethics.'

In carrying out this further work, we will have to consider a number of distinctions. For example, there is the distinction between subjective rightness, on the one hand, and objective rightness. In *A Christian Natural Theology* I struggled with the question of subjective rightness, that is, to what my sense of obligation in fact inescapably attaches. The question seems to me final in its own right, but it is certainly true that a person may act in good conscience and nevertheless act in a way that is objectively evil. I think it is for this reason that Reynolds fears my ethical proposals may be "a vicious form of ethical relativism" (above, 128). Since beliefs about the nature of reality do vary so greatly, and since innocent ignorance will always be a part of human decision-making, I do not see how this kind of relativism can be avoided. Nor do I see why it is vicious. But I strongly agree that, more than this narrow deontological approach to ethics, we need to see the implications of our vision of reality for ethical questions. I also agree that the very place and role of the deontological questions are profoundly affected by visions of reality. Where, as in process theology, there is confidence that there is a divine perspective, we can assert it as transcending the relativity of all other perspectives and even, with Reynolds, consider how the world exists for it.

At another point Reynolds makes a distinction whose import has not yet become clear to me. He distinguishes a 'claim of goodness' from the 'claim of rightness.' Speaking now from the Whiteheadian perspective, I assume that God's immanence as it constitutes the initial phase of the subjective aim is a lure or call to the ideal actualization for that occasion. That ideal possibility is determined both by concern for the strength of beauty which that occasion is capable of realizing in itself and also by its potential contribution to the strength of beauty of subsequent occasions. This seems to me to be at once a 'claim of goodness' and a 'claim of rightness.' I myself introduced an additional objective element in 'the sense of obligation' which I see as the subjective form of certain imaginative propositional feelings. Reynolds seems to feel the need for something beyond both the initial aim and the sense of obligation, but I do not know what or why. Perhaps Reynolds hopes to ground in "the abstract constant character of God" (above, 126) some unchanging concrete moral principles. His interest in an ontological theory of natural law suggests this. If so, I think his project is questionable. I also doubt that he can find support either in Hartshorne's doctrine of the abstract pole of God or in Whitehead's doctrine of God's Primordial Nature.

My own problem is to think through the relation between the sense of obligation and the initial aim derived from God. I believe the former is ultimately derived from the latter; that is, there would be no sense of the normative at all if there were not, in addition to the causal efficacy of the past, also the lure of fresh possibility. Where such possibility and its source are not attended to, and where they are conceived in primarily non-ethical ways, the experience of the normative differs markedly from the traditional Western one. Where the Judeo-Christian tradition is unknown, and where it has lost conviction, the sense of obligation may be a minor and ineffective note in human existence. What is metaphysically given is God's call, and Christians need to re-image that call in ways that avoid the oppressive moralism of our past without abandoning the concern for responsibility for one another. Reynolds is particularly helpful here. His proposal to think of the call in terms of 'moral flourishing' strikes a happy balance.

These comments are directed to Reynolds in hopes of stimulating him in his further pursuit of the program that is suggestively sketched in this essay. Process theology needs to spawn a vision of how life is rightly lived.

This will certainly *not* focus on formal ethical considerations of alternative courses of behavior. Reynolds shows that he is sensitive to key aspects of process theology and has insight into how they can and should inform human life in its concreteness.

RESPONSE TO PANNENBERG

PANNENBERG'S CRITIQUE of my book *Christ in a Pluralistic Age* is just the sort of critique an author most covets. It is scholarly, fair, and brilliant. There are sufficient elements of commonality between us that it moves beyond global objections to specific, focused criticisms. Pannenberg understands both my own work and its philosophical background, so that I am not called on in response chiefly to explain my position. And in objecting to what I have done, he also makes clear the position from which he judges mine. Indeed, some features of his own thought emerge more sharply in this essay than elsewhere in his writings—for example, his conviction that philosophy, while important to theology, should emerge out of the historical-theological development, that such a philosophy must interpret history eschatologically, and that the concrete requirement of this eschatological vision for our time is the unification of the church. His perspective highlights the fact that in my approach a philosophically articulated natural theology has considerable autonomy, that eschatology, while important, does not control the theological program, and that the church, while necessary, is not theologically central to the meaning of Christ. In the following pages, I will comment on these contrasts along with related issues.

Pannenberg's opening pages treat in a fundamental way the issue of theological method. The question raised is that of proper starting point and procedure. Pannenberg begins with the history attested in Scripture. He does not exclude philosophical speculation, but he believes that this should be developed out of the history. He knows that when one approaches the history with dominant modern assumptions one will be blocked from finding what is there. Hence he engages in philosophical work to clear away distorting prejudices. But he believes that his positive philosophical assertions arise as requirements of the history itself.

My primary difficulty with this program is that I lack the scholarship to share in it. Indeed, Pannenberg is almost alone in the present theological world in his ability to engage in the reconstruction of a universal history growing out of Biblical history. I admire the program, but if I have a contribution to make, it must be of a different sort.

My justification for my different approach can take the form of a critical comment, not so much about Pannenberg's program as about his tendency to see it as the only legitimate theological program. His failure to convince the community of Bible scholars of the correctness of his approach to Scripture points to the power of contemporary conceptual presuppositions and of the presently established sense of importance for the way we uncover and recover our Christian roots. By lifting these features of our own *Zeitgeist* to consciousness, we can allow the Bible to question them, but we cannot divorce ourselves from them. As theologians we think in a circle in which the way we perceive our Christian history is deeply affected by all the forces that have made us what we are. While we recognize that among these forces our Christian history is of central importance, we cannot, and should not attempt to, empty ourselves of all the other contributions to our present understanding. The history of theology shows that different aspects of our total history become accessible to us as normative according to the cultural, intellectual context. We need to recognize this historical relativity, and by recognizing it, we can give some freedom to the historical events to judge the point of view from which they are perceived. But we deceive ourselves if we suppose this priority and objectivity of the events can be total.

Pannenberg and I both believe that the dominant modern viewpoint screens out much of what is most important in our heritage. Both of us find within the twentieth-century ferment possibilities for breaking out of this modernity. He seems to think that this breakthrough can restore the Biblical history to full primacy so that it can govern the formulation of a universal history and philosophy. I agree that what continues to urge us toward such universality is the continuation of the movement whose origin is in our Biblical history, but I believe that there is a givenness in our present, historically conditioned point of view that cannot and should not be denied relative authority as well.

My conclusion from this view of the interaction of present viewpoint and Christian history is that we need to clarify and develop our present viewpoint in the light of our history so as to render it more capable of appropriating what that history offers us. As Pannenberg says, I have leaned heavily on the philosophy of Whitehead for this purpose. I find that Whitehead goes beyond the limits of modernity impelled by a vision of importance that is deeply informed by Christian history. And I find that following him liberated me to learn much from Christian history that other contemporary points of view would have forced me to reject. I also find that his thought enables me to learn much from other Ways, such as Buddhism, as well. Of course, Whitehead should not be, and did not want to be, taken as a final authority, and it may be that in my enthusiasm for his accomplishments I have been too scholastic in my use of his thought. I am limited by my lack of the gifts requisite to producing my own philosophy, and I have not felt that such efforts as I have made to improve on Whitehead have been notably successful. As a result, I have found it necessary to adopt and adapt Whitehead's thought as a Christian natural theology. This puts me in a position, as Pannenberg notes, analogous to that of the Logos theologians of the early church, who adopted and adapted a conceptuality that was not primarily shaped by Biblical history for the purpose of articulating what they learned from that history.

At this point the deepest difference between us is manifest. Faithfulness to what was revealed once for all in Jesus Christ is for Pannenberg the essence of Christian faith. I, on the other hand, think of faithfulness as appropriate participation in the historical movement that owed its decisive impetus to Jesus but lives now in responsiveness to the living Christ within it. This movement is not bound to preserve any specifiable doctrine, even of Jesus, although its identity is constituted by the primacy of its memory of that history of which Jesus is the center, and its healthy continuance depends on constant re-encounter with Jesus and with the earliest witness to his meaning for the church. Incarnation is thus more central for me as a theological category, whereas Pannenberg prefers revelation. Both are grounded in the New Testament, but neither is thematically considered there.

Pannenberg's view clearly and properly leads to his conclusion that any concept or philosophy employed by the church must be creatively transformed by the church so as to serve its purposes—purposes that remain unchanged in the process of appropriating this instrument. My view leads me to believe that, in the encounter with Greek thought, not only Greek thought but also the church's message was, and should have been, creatively transformed. I do not see such transformation as abandonment, betrayal, perversion, or even compromise, although all of these could and did occur. Basically the church remained rooted in its Biblical heritage while successfully assimilating other traditions into its life; but in the process, the way it understood and appropriated its Biblical heritage was profoundly altered. There were even changes in the understanding of what we are saved from and what we are saved to and of how this salvation was effected by Jesus Christ. From a later perspective we can see that in these changes something of value in the Biblical heritage was lost. We can see that something of value in the Greek heritage was lost as well. But it is my conviction that what emerged in the achievement of synthesis was, with all its limitations and errors, a fundamentally faithful response of the Christian movement in that time and place. It was a greater synthesis, more faithful to Christ, precisely because the church did not denature the concepts and the philosophies of the Greeks in the process of appropriating them. Full subordination of these to the Biblical revelation might have prevented them from making their potential contribution to the ongoing Christian movement.

In positively appraising the achievement of the patristic age, I am not arguing that its conceptual and theological results are binding on all future Christians. They are an important part of our historical memory but not as central to the Christian movement as is the Biblical heritage. What I do hold is that today, as the church confronts the largely autonomous achievements of the sciences, and the fully autonomous achievements of non-Western Ways, we seek an analogous synthesis with them —one that not only transforms them but also respects their integrity, even while recognizing that this respect for their integrity must lead to our own creative transformation as well.

Stated in formal, methodological terms, our disagreement could be softened. But that it is real appears when we approach the crucial substantive difference between us. For Pannenberg what is revealed above all is the coming of the Kingdom of God. On this score I am disinclined to debate him exegetically, and I often find myself on his side in the reconstruction of New Testament events. But he rightly sees that I do not accord to this result of historical scholarship the force of once-for-all revelation definitive for all future theology. I see instead a long process in which a conviction that made sense in its original Jewish context has been, on the one hand, a powerful force in transforming eschatological ideas of other cultures, but, on the other hand, itself transformed. I do not regard these transformations of the Christian hope as necessarily betrayals or corruptions. Each case should be examined separately in the light of the total situation in which it occurs. Pannenberg himself accepts the transformation that moved the consummation from temporal imminence to the indefinite future. This seems to me a more fundamental change than Pannenberg appears to think, altering profoundly the meaning and importance of the secular world, of social and political institutions, and of other Ways. I think Pannenberg has also affirmed another transformation that gives a larger role to human activity in determining the coming of the Kingdom. I see still more radical transformations required as the Christian movement openly internalizes, by transforming, the scientific and Eastern visions, while respecting their autonomous integrity.

Pannenberg thinks that it is the excessive authority I accord Whitehead that interferes with faithfulness to the Biblical revelation of the coming of the Kingdom. Although it is hard to guess what I might think today if I had not come under Whitehead's influence, I doubt that I would be in a better position to share Pannenberg's vision. The everlastingness of the cosmos and the unlikelihood that the end of human history will involve an end of the created order are assumptions that I derived elsewhere before encountering Whitehead and which would be likely to survive disenchantment with his thought. My concern is to seek, within the context of such assumptions, images of hope that are appropriate to the Christian movement today. The very nature of Christianity as a movement requires images of hope, and the lack of convincing images is its deepest sickness today. I regard most highly Pannenberg's own creative contribution to providing a convincing image, but I am representative of a large segment of the contemporary church in being unable to appropriate it fully except through further transformations.

Pannenberg objects to my viewing the several images of hope I treat as "competitive." I think he misunderstands me here. When I juxtapose as competitive the 'Kingdom of Heaven' and the 'resurrection of the dead,' I mean specifically the images of Whitehead and of Pannenberg respectively. I believe that in fact, in recent theology, these have been competitive. Of course, there is nothing competitive between Pannenberg's view of the Kingdom of Heaven and his view of the resurrection of the dead. In my chapter on "The Unity of Hope," furthermore, it was my intention to display how we can get beyond this factual competition to a perception of these images as complementary. I am gratified that in note 21 Pannenberg agrees that the ideas of the bodiliness of the resurrection and its connection with the end of time that had troubled me in some of his earlier writings can be replaced by ideas that approximate notions acceptable to a Whiteheadian. These continuing transformations of images of hope as they interact with one another suggest that truly convincing images of hope can emerge for our time.

Pannenberg chides me for following the line of the early church's Christological development instead of focusing on the otherness of the historical Jesus to the Father. I fear that a reader of his critique might suppose that I have questioned the otherness of Jesus to God. I have tried to make clear that Jesus was in every sense a human being and that he shared the creaturely relationship to God with all human beings. But diverse forms of relationship to God are possible for human beings. My interest is in what is distinctive of Jesus' relation. What is distinctive is not that he distinguished himself categorically from the Father and denied his own goodness. Even I can do that. It is instead the mode of the divine presence in him. What is distinctive of this presence is not that it allows an element of overagainstness, but that it allows also and especially a peculiar intimacy and identification.

Pannenberg thinks I have not gotten beyond the dilemma of Monophysitism and Nestorianism. The crux of the problem is whether Jesus or God is the subject of the free choice whereby Jesus constituted his own selfhood as one with the presence of God within him (above, 141). It is precisely at this point that I believe substantialist notions prevent a solution that is open to a Whiteheadian.

For Whitehead we do not have first a subject who then decides. The subject comes into being in and through the decision. The decision is *causa sui,* but it is not *ex nihilo.* A human decision is conditioned both by one's personal past and by the creative opportunity offered by the immanence of God. The new, momentary self that is constituted through the choice is ordinarily constituted by its inheritance of its personal past. But there is no reason this must be so. The new self can also emerge jointly out of the personal past and out of the effective presence of God. In this case the self or 'I' is co-constituted by the personal past and by God's present efficacy. It is this structure which I attribute to important segments of Jesus' life, believing that this account is warranted by what we know of the historical Jesus and that it is a positive analogy to Chalcedon. This solution to the classical problematic is possible only when one abandons the idea of substantial subjects, an idea that underlies Pannenberg's formulation of the dilemma.

Pannenberg's criticisms point out tensions between my rhetoric and what he takes to be the limits imposed on what I can or should say if I do not further modify my commitment to Whitehead. In detail I believe that Whitehead's basic vision allows for richer renewal of historic Christian, and specifically Biblical, concepts than Pannenberg supposes. But what I have already said indicates that for me this is not the crux of the issue. We may need today, for many reasons, creatively to transform the Biblical as well as the traditional conceptions of divine creation and divine love. The same may be said for the doctrine of the Trinity which I addressed in the Postscript to *Christ in a Pluralistic Age* in connection with the problem of sexist language. This is for me unfinished business, and as I continue to reflect about it, I shall profit from Pannenberg's numerous criticisms. But it may be that today the considerations that should govern our use, or even our rejection, of such images as Father, Son, and

Holy Spirit should be quite different from those which have dominated the discussion thus far.

Pannenberg shows also that I have not treated several topics central to his own Christology. Certainly my silences are significant and a legitimate subject of criticism. I am conscious of the fragmentary character of my Christology and that my selections and emphases were guided by concerns different from his—especially my concern to show that the uniqueness and universality of Christ should and can be affirmed in a way that opens us radically to the achievements of other faiths, traditions, or Ways. But one omission is too important to pass over by simple acknowledgment of incompleteness. I have written at length about Christ and have mentioned the church only incidentally. This requires comment.

Pannenberg sees that I have been impressed by the individualism and personalism produced by Christianity, but that in my hope to go beyond these I neglect the church, which is the Christian institution of community. He chides me for exaggerating Christian individualism and even implies that I identify a specific, highly individualistic type of Protestant piety with the whole of Christian existence, which is not as individualistic. No doubt there is some truth in the charge that I have viewed the form of Christian existence I know best as more typical than it is, and that I have overemphasized the role of justification by faith in my treatment of Jesus and Paul. But I have based my view of the actual efficacy of Christ as leading to individualism more on Malraux, who is neither Protestant nor pietist, and who finds this individualism highly developed in Catholic cultures. The position to which I am led most closely approximates that of the Catholic Teilhard de Chardin. In terms of the development of my own thought, the context of the history of religions has played the largest role in accenting for me the attainment of individualistic personhood among Christians.

My defense here is important because, if the achievement and limitation in our heritage that I seek to transcend is, as Pannenberg suggests, a parochial one, then it can be solved, as he also suggests, by returning to the ecumenical church. However, I am convinced that this is too facile. Pannenberg does not mean that in fact today the existence of the church solves the problem posed by Christian individualism, but he believes that the reunion of the church is the prior and real task confronting us, and that in a reunited church the problem would be sufficiently dealt with. What further is to be anticipated, for him, belongs to the resurrection of the dead.

For my part, in the encounter with Buddhism I have come to a new appreciation of Christian individualism and personalism just because I meet a very different mode of existence whose serene openness and authority I find moving and even enviable. I am attracted to the possibility that a new mode of existence may be possible, a mode in which, without ceasing to be Christian, one can appropriate the Buddhist achievement too. A united Christian church might indeed be better able to conduct the dialogue with the East, but I find the dialogue too important to postpone.

Pannenberg chides me for supposing that a change of external form might precede an inner renewal of human social life (above, 145). I do believe that external form affects inner life as well as that inner life affects form. Hence the emergence of a unified church could indeed have a profound effect on our Christian existence. But by the same token a unified church will be more likely if there are profound changes in our inner life. The encounter with the East is an important stimulus to such change. But if this encounter is not thematically introduced into the process of institutionally expressing ecumenical Christianity, the principle of Christian unity may prove to be a principle of exclusion of the potential contribution of other Ways.

Like Pannenberg I reject the idea of a churchless Christianity. I, too, hope that the *church* will internalize the achievements of other traditions in its own life. But I cannot move from the idea of a church that is in this way increasingly inclusive to the expectation that it should replace what I hope will be other increasingly inclusive Ways, such as Buddhism. If Christianity and Buddhism eventually merge, this would not be by absorption of Buddhism into the Christian church but by transformation of both into something new. Hence the church does not play for me quite so final or decisive a role as for Pannenberg.

My most general criticism of Pannenberg's critique of my approach is not that mine is right and his wrong. His commitment to a pluralistic but united Christian church as a means of witnessing to the world is admirable. I object only that we also face the task of understanding Christ in a context where the Ways of the East are recognized as *prima facie* of equal importance and truth as our own, and that this task should be pursued at the same time that we seek church unity. We need to have a plurality of theological styles and approaches as well as to recognize the pluralism of Christian traditions in the context of a much more radical pluralism of traditional and modern Ways.

Bibliography of the Writings of John B. Cobb, Jr.

BOOKS AUTHORED
(Cited by abbreviation)

VP   *Varieties of Protestantism.* The Westminster Press, 1960.

LO   *Living Options in Protestant Theology: A Survey of Methods.* The Westminster Press, 1962.

CNT   *A Christian Natural Theology: Based on the Thought of Alfred North Whitehead.* The Westminster Press, 1965.

SCE   *The Structure of Christian Existence.* The Westminster Press, 1967. German tr., *Die christliche Existenz. Eine vergleichende Studie der Existenzstrukturen in verschiedenen Religionen.* Munich: Claudius Verlag, 1970.

GW   *God and the World.* The Westminster Press, 1969. German tr. (Ch. 6 omitted), *Christlicher Glaube nach dem Tode Gottes: Gegenwärtiges Weltverständnis im Licht der Theologie.* Munich: Claudius Verlag, 1971.

TE   *Is It Too Late? A Theology of Ecology.* Bruce Books, 1971. German tr., *Der Preis des Fortschritts: Umweltschutz als Problem der Sozialethik.* Munich: Claudius Verlag, 1972.

LCC   *Liberal Christianity at the Crossroads.* The Westminster Press, 1973.

CPA   *Christ in a Pluralistic Age.* The Westminster Press, 1975.

TPC   *Theology and Pastoral Counseling.* Fortress Press, 1977.

PT   *Process Theology: An Introductory Exposition* (with David Ray Griffin). The Westminster Press, 1976.

BOOKS EDITED
(Cited by abbreviation)

LH   *The Later Heidegger and Theology* (with James M. Robinson). New Frontiers in Theology, Vol. I. Harper & Row, Publishers, Inc., 1963. (Cobb's essay:

"Is the Later Heidegger Relevant for Theology?" 177–197.) German tr., *Der spätere Heidegger und die Theologie.* Munich: Zwingli Verlag, 1964.

NH   *The New Hermeneutic* (with James M. Robinson). New Frontiers in Theology, Vol. II. Harper & Row, Publishers, Inc., 1964. (Cobb's essay: "Faith and Culture," 219–231.) German tr., *Die Neue Hermeneutik.* Munich: Zwingli Verlag, 1965.

TH   *Theology as History* (with James M. Robinson). New Frontiers in Theology, Vol. III. Harper & Row, Publishers, Inc., 1967. (Cobb's essay: "Past, Present, and Future," 197–220.) German tr., *Theologie als Geschichte.* Munich: Zwingli Verlag, 1967.

TA   *The Theology of Altizer: Critique and Response.* The Westminster Press, 1971. Cobb wrote the Preface, 7–10, and parts I and II of the Introduction, 13–27.

MN   *Mind in Nature: Essays on the Interface of Science and Philosophy* (with David Ray Griffin). University Press of America, 1977. Cobb wrote the Preface, ii-iii; "Some Whiteheadian Comments on the Discussion," 32–35, 68–69; and "Concluding Editorial Comments," 147–148.

ARTICLES
(Cited by number)

1. "Theological Data and Method," *Journal of Religion,* 33 (July 1953), 212–223.

2. "The Possibility of a Universal Normative Ethic," *Ethics,* 65 (October 1954), 55–61.

3. "Protestant Theology and Church Life," *Religion in Life,* 25 (Winter 1955–56), 65–75.

4. "A Protestant Critique of Philosophy of Religion," *The Southern Philosopher,* 5/3 (October 1956), 1–4.

5. "Toward Clarity in Aesthetics," *Philosophy and Phenomenological Research,* 18 (December 1957), 169–189.

6. "Some Thoughts on the Meaning of Christ's Death," *Religion in Life,* 28 (Spring 1959), 212–222.

7. "A Theological Typology," *Journal of Religion,* 39 (July 1959), 183–195.

8. "The Philosophic Grounds of Moral Responsibility: A Comment on Matson and Niebuhr," *Journal of Philosophy,* 56 (July 2, 1959), 619–621.

9. "Nihilism, Existentialism, and Whitehead," *Religion in Life,* 30 (Autumn 1961), 521–533.

10. "An Ontological Approach to the 'Real Presence' in the Lord's Supper" (with Richard Overman), *Journal of the Inter-Seminary Movement of the Southwest,* 1 (1962), 33–47.

11. "The Post-Bultmannian Trend," *Journal of Bible and Religion*, 30 (January 1962), 3–11.

12. "Consultation on Hermeneutics" (with Robert Funk), *The Christian Century*, 79 (June 20, 1962), 783–784; also in *Drew Gateway*, 33 (Spring 1963), 123–126.

13. " 'Perfection Exists': A Critique of Charles Hartshorne," *Religion in Life*, 32 (Spring 1963), 294–304.

14. "On Being Post-Christian" (Response to Nels Ferré), *Christian Advocate*, June 6, 1963, 13–14.

15. "From Crisis Theology to the Post-Modern World," *Centennial Review*, 8 (Spring 1964), 209–220; also in *Toward a New Christianity: Readings in the Death of God Theology*, ed. by Thomas J. J. Altizer (Harcourt, Brace and World, Inc., 1967), 241–252; *The Meaning of the Death of God*, ed. by Bernard Murchland (Random House, Inc., 1967), 138–152; *Radical Theology: Phase Two*, ed. by C. W. Christian and Glenn R. Wittig (J. B. Lippincott Company, 1967), 191–205 (this pagination given in references); *Sources of Protestant Theology*, ed. by William A. Scott (Bruce Books, 1971); *Contemporary American Protestant Thought: 1900–1970*, ed. by William Robert Miller (The Bobbs-Merrill Company, Inc., 1973).

16. "Whitehead's Philosophy and a Christian Doctrine of Man," *Journal of Bible and Religion*, 32 (July 1964), 9–20.

17. "A New Trio Arises in Europe," *Christian Advocate*, July 2, 1964; also in *New Theology No. 2*, ed. by Martin E. Marty and Dean G. Peerman (The Macmillan Company, 1965), 257–263.

18. "Christian Natural Theology and Christian Existence," *The Christian Century*, 82 (March 3, 1965), 265–267; also in *Frontline Theology*, ed. by Dean G. Peerman (John Knox Press, 1967), 39–45 (this pagination given in references). German tr., "Natürliche Theologie und christliche Existenz," *Theologie in Umbruch: Der Beitrag Amerikas zur gegenwärtigen Theologie* (Munich: Claudius Verlag, 1968).

19. "Teilhard de Chardin: The Great Yes-Sayer," *Christian Advocate*, March 11, 1965, 7–8.

20. "Ontology, History, and Christian Faith," *Religion in Life*, 34 (Spring 1965), 270–287.

21. "Christianity and Myth," *Journal of Bible and Religion*, 33 (October 1965), 314–320.

22. "The Finality of Christ in a Whiteheadian Perspective," *The Finality of Christ*, ed. by Dow Kirkpatrick (Abingdon Press, 1966), 122–154.

23. "Can Natural Theology Be Christian?" (Response to Langdon Gilkey), *Theology Today*, 23 (April 1966), 140–142.

24. "The Objectivity of God," *Christian Advocate*, March 9, 1967, 7–8.

196   BIBLIOGRAPHY OF THE WRITINGS OF JOHN B. COBB, JR.

25. "Speaking About God," *Religion in Life*, 36 (Spring 1967), 28–39.

26. "The Intra-Psychic Structure of Christian Existence," *Journal of the American Academy of Religion*, 36 (December 1968), 327–339; also in *To Be a Man*, ed. by George Devine (Prentice-Hall, Inc., 1969), 24–40; largely identical with "The Nature of the Conversion Experience," *On Conversion: Four Views* (Report of the 1967 Theological Consultation of the Methodist Board of Missions), 3–15.

27. "The Author Responds" (to Claude Welch), *Journal of the American Academy of Religion*, 36 (December 1968), 342–344.

28. "The Possibility of Theism Today," *The Idea of God: Philosophical Perspectives*, ed. by Edward H. Madden, Robert Handy, and Marvin Farber (Charles C Thomas, 1968), 98–123. "Reply to Commentators," 134–138.

29. "Barth: An Appreciation from the Enemy Camp," *Christian Advocate*, March 20, 1969, 7–8.

30. "The Christian 'Dream,'" *The Church Woman*, 35 (March-April 1969), 13–15.

31. "Wolfhart Pannenberg's *Jesus—God and Man*," *Journal of Religion*, 49 (April 1969), 192–201.

32. "Position Paper," *ANNAL*, June 1969.

33. "Reaction to Henry Nelson Wieman's 'The Promise of a Naturalistic Theology,'" *Action/Reaction*, 2 (Winter 1969), 6–7.

34. "Freedom in Whitehead's Philosophy: A Response to Edward Pols," *Southern Journal of Philosophy*, 7 (Winter 1969), 409–413.

35. "What Is Alive and What Is Dead in Empirical Theology?" *The Future of Empirical Theology*, ed. by Bernard Meland (The University of Chicago Press, 1969), 89–101.

36. "A New United Methodist Creed," *Christian Advocate*, Jan. 8, 1970, 7–8.

37. "The Meaning of Salvation," *Mid-stream*, 9 (Spring 1970), 127–163. "Response" (to six respondents), 238–258.

38. "A Process Systematic Theology" (review of Daniel Day Williams' *The Spirit and the Forms of Love*), *Journal of Religion*, 50 (April 1970), 199–206.

39. "Justification by Faith," *Master Sermon Series* (August 1970), 473–482.

40. "Towards a Displacement of Historicism and Positivism," *Concilium*, 7 (September 1970), 33–41.

41. "The Population Explosion and the Rights of the Subhuman World," *IDOC-International: North American Edition* (Sept. 12, 1970), 40–62; abridged in *Dimensions of the Environmental Crisis*, ed. by John A. Day, F. F. Fost, and P. Rose (John Wiley & Sons, Inc., 1971), 19–32.

42. "The Descent Into Hell" (response to Altizer's book), *Christian Advocate*, Oct. 1, 1970, 7–8.

43. "Ecological Disaster and the Church," *The Christian Century*, 87 (Oct. 7,

1970), 1185–1187; also as "Out of the Ashes of Disaster," *Resource*, 12 (March, 1971), 20–23.

44. "A Whiteheadian Christology," *Process Philosophy and Christian Thought*, ed. by Delwin Brown, Ralph E. James, Jr., and Gene Reeves (The Bobbs-Merrill Company, Inc., 1971), 382–398.

45. "Christian Theism and the Ecological Crisis," *Religious Education*, 66 (Jan.-Feb. 1971), 3–8.

46. "The Prospect for Process Studies" (with Lewis Ford), *Process Studies*, 1 (Spring 1971), 3–8.

47. "Hope on a Dying Planet," *The Cresset*, May 1971 (no pagination).

48. "Alfred North Whitehead," *Twelve Makers of Modern Protestant Thought*, Revised, ed. by George L. Hunt (Association Press, 1971), 129–140.

49. "The 'Whitehead Without God' Debate: The Critique," *Process Studies*, 1 (Summer 1971), 91–100.

50. "Christian Mission and the Role of Worship," *The New World Outlook*, 62 (April 1972), 187–192.

51. "Spirit and Flesh: Dipolarity Versus Dialectic," *Philosophy of Religion and Theology: 1972* (AAR Working Papers), David Ray Griffin, Chairman (American Academy of Religion, 1972), 5–13.

52. "Man in Process," *Concilium*, 9 (May 1972), 31–47.

53. "What Is the Future?" *Hope and the Future of Man*, ed. by Ewert H. Cousins (Fortress Press, 1972), 1–14; also as "Was ist die Zukunft?" *Evangelische Theologie*, 32 (July-August 1972), 372–383.

54. "Opening Paper," *IDOC Seminar*, 47 (October 1972), 1–7.

55. "Regional Inclusion and the Extensive Continuum" (debate with Donald Sherburne), *Process Studies*, 2 (Winter 1972), 277–295.

56. "Natural Causality and Divine Action," *Idealistic Studies*, 3 (September 1973), 207–222.

57. "Ecology, Ethics and Theology," *Toward a Steady-State Economy*, ed. by Herman E. Daly (W. H. Freeman and Company, 1973), 307–320.

58. "A New Christian Existence," *Neues Testament und Christliche Existenz*, ed. by Hans Dieter Betz and Louise Schottroff (Tübingen: J. C. B. Mohr, 1973), 79–94.

59. "The Local Church and the Environmental Crisis," *The Christian Ministry*, 4 (September 1973), 3–7; also in *Foundations*, 17 (April-June 1974), 164–172.

60. "Mosha-Dharma and Prehensions: A Comparison of Nagarjuna and Whitehead" (with Ryusei Takeda), *Philosophy of Religion and Theology: 1973* (AAR Working Papers), David Ray Griffin, Chairman (American Academy of Religion, 1973), 179–192; also in abridged and revised form in *Process Studies*, 4 (Spring 1974), 26–36.

61. "To Pray or Not to Pray: A Confession," *Prayer in My Life,* intro. by Maxie Dunnam (Parthenon Press, 1974), 83–112.

62. "The Christian Concern for the Non-Human World," *Anticipation,* 16 (March 1974), 23–24.

63. "God's Love, Ecological Survival and the Responsiveness of Nature," *Anticipation,* 16 (March 1974), 32–34.

64. "Men and Animals," *The Christian Science Monitor,* May 6, 1974.

65. "The Christian, the Future, and Paolo Soleri," *The Christian Century,* 91 (Oct. 30, 1974), 1008–1011.

66. "Whatever Happened to Theology?" *Christianity and Crisis,* 35 (May 12, 1975), 117–118.

67. "Comment on Caroway's Critique," *Encounter,* 36 (Spring 1975), 112–114.

68. "For Another Transcendence, *Worldview,* 18 (June 1975), 36–37.

69. "Strengthening the Spirit," *Union Seminary Quarterly Review,* 30 (Winter-Summer 1975), 130–139.

70. "A Place to Go, a Place to Stand" (advance excerpt from *CPA*), *Kairos,* 1 (Autumn 1975), 5.

71. "Introduction: Conference on Mahayana Buddhism and Whitehead" (with Jay McDaniel), *Philosophy East and West,* 25 (October 1975), 393–405.

72. "Spiritual Discernment in a Whiteheadian Perspective," *Religious Experience and Process Theology,* ed. by Harry James Cargas and Bernard M. Lee (Paulist/Newman Press, 1976), 349–367.

73. "Theological Brief," *Christian Theology: A Case Method Approach,* ed. by Robert A. Evans and Thomas D. Parker (Harper & Row, Publishers, Inc., 1976), 66–69.

74. "Response to 'The Boston Affirmations,'" *Andover Newton Quarterly,* 16 (March 1976), 249–250.

75. "Can the Church Think Again?" *Occasional Papers* (United Methodist Board of Higher Education and Ministry), 1/12 (Aug. 9, 1976), 1–12; also in abridged form in *The Circuit Rider* (United Methodist Publishing House), 1/2 (November 1976), 18–21.

76. "Response to Ogden and Carpenter," *Process Studies,* 6 (Summer 1976), 123–129.

UNPUBLISHED PAPERS
(Cited by letter)

A. "Heidegger and Whitehead: A Comparison." 1961.

B. "The Christian Understanding of Sexuality." 1963.

C. "A Personal Christology." 1965.

D. "Affirming God in a Non-Theistic Age." 1967.

E. "Bible, Revelation, and Christian Doctrine." 1969.

F. "Reality and Experienced Reality" (response to Altizer). 1969.

BOOK REVIEWS

"The Basis of Christian Sociality," *Christian Eschatology and Social Thought*, by Ray C. Petry. *Interpretation*, 10 (October 1956), 462–463.

"Disturbing Complacency," *Essays in Christology for Karl Barth*, ed. by T. H. L. Parker. *Interpretation*, 11 (October 1957), 464–466.

"The Method of Analysis," *Faith and Knowledge*, by John Hick. *Interpretation*, 12 (October 1958), 456–458.

Aesthetics, ed. by E. Wilkinson. *Philosophy and Phenomenological Research*, 19 (December 1958), 263–264.

Art and the Human Enterprise, by Iredell Jenkins. *Philosophy and Phenomenological Research*, 20 (September 1959), 129–130.

"A Panorama of Theologies," *The Case for Orthodox Theology*, by Edward J. Carnell; *The Case for Theology in Liberal Perspective*, by L. Harold Dewolf; *The Case for a New Reformation Theology*, by William Hordern. *Interpretation*, 14 (January 1960), 94–96.

"The Problem of Authority," *Holy Writ or Holy Church*, by George H. Tavard. *Interpretation*, 14 (July 1960), 358–361.

A Protestant Speaks His Mind, by Ilion T. Jones. *The Pulpit*, 31 (August 1960), 252.

Spirit, Son, and Father, by Henry P. Van Dusen. *The Personalist*, 41 (Winter 1960), 107–108.

The Lure for Feeling, by Mary Wyman. *Religion in Life*, 30 (Winter 1960–61), 147–148.

The Language of Faith, by Samuel Laeuchli. *Christian Advocate*, July 19, 1962, 16.

Intellectual Foundation of Faith, by Henry Nelson Wieman. *Drew Gateway*, 32 (Winter 1962), 107–108.

Church Dogmatics IV/3, by Karl Barth. *Interpretation*, 16 (October 1962), 472–475.

On the Love of God, by John MacIntyre. *Journal of Religion*, 43 (April 1963), 154–155.

The Empirical Theology of Henry Nelson Wieman, ed. by Robert W. Bretall. *Religious Education*, 58 (July-August 1963), 405–406.

The Rationality of Faith, by Carl Michalson. *Christian Advocate*, Nov. 21, 1963, 19–20.

Jesus and Christian Origins, by Hugh Anderson. *Christian Advocate*, July 30, 1964, 14–15.

History, Sacred and Profane, by Alan Richardson. *Interpretation*, 19 (April 1965), 220–222.

Schleiermacher on Christ and Religion, by Richard R. Niebuhr. *Religious Education*, 60 (May-June 1965), 244–246.

Process and Divinity: The Hartshorne Festschrift, ed. by William Reese and Eugene Freeman. *Journal of Religion*, 45 (October 1965), 335–337.

A Handbook of Theological Terms, by Van Harvey. *Perkins School of Theology Journal*, 18 (Winter 1965), 39–40.

Zukunft und Verheissung, by Gerhard Sauter. *Erasmus*, 18/7–8 (1966), 206–207.

The Relevance of Science: Creation and Cosmogony, by C. F. von Weizsäcker. *Zygon*, 1 (March 1966), 111–113.

The Phenomenon of Life, by Hans Jonas. *Interpretation*, 21 (April 1967), 196–200.

History and Hermeneutics, by Carl E. Braaten. *Journal of Religion*, 47 (April 1967), 154–156.

No Other God, by Gabriel Vahanian. *Religion in Life*, 36 (Summer 1967), 295–296.

Worldly Theology, by Carl Michalson. *Christian Advocate*, Oct. 19, 1967, 15–17.

A Natural Theology for Our Time, by Charles Hartshorne. *Religious Education*, 62 (November-December 1967), 533.

Science, Man and Morals, by William H. Thorpe. *Journal of the American Academy of Religion*, 36 (March 1968), 68–72.

Memory and Hope, by Dietrich Ritschl. *Religious Education*, 63 (March-April 1968), 146–147.

Experience and God, by John E. Smith. *Religion in Life*, 37 (Winter 1968), 617–618.

Process Thought and Christian Faith, by Norman Pittenger. *Religious Education*, 64 (March-April 1969), 148–149.

Revelation as History, ed. by Wolfhart Pannenberg. *Christian Advocate*, May 29, 1969, 16–17.

A Rumor of Angels, by Peter L. Berger. *Theology Today*, 26 (July 1969), 221–222.

Systematic Theology: A Historicist Perspective, by Gordon D. Kaufman. *Journal of the American Academy of Religion*, 38 (June 1970), 219–221.

A Philosophy of the Future, by Ernst Bloch. *Theology Today*, 28 (July 1971), 249–252.

Experiential Religion, by Richard R. Niebuhr. *Interpretation*, 27 (January 1973), 100–101.

God the Problem, by Gordon D. Kaufman. *Review of Books and Religion*, 2 (Mid-February 1973), 7.

A House for Hope, by William A. Beardslee. *Religion in Life*, 42 (Spring 1973), 137–138.

The New Consciousness in Science and Religion, by Harold K. Schilling. *Religious Education*, 68 (November-December 1973), 752–756.

A Process Christology, by David Ray Griffin. *Religion in Life*, 43 (Winter 1974), 505–506.

The Becoming of the Church: A Process Theology of the Structures of Christian Experience, by Bernard M. Lee. *Process Studies*, 4 (Winter 1974), 303–304.

The Holy Spirit, by Norman Pittenger. *Religious Education*, 70 (May-June 1975), 342–343.

What Is Process Theology? by Robert B. Mellert *Religious Education*, 71 (January-February 1976), 101–102.

Thinking About God, by John Macquarrie. *Journal of Religion*, 56 (April 1976), 208–209.

Blessed Rage for Order, by David Tracy. *The Christian Century*, 93 (April 14, 1976), 369–371.